MEDEA AND OTHER PLAYS

EURIPIDES was born in Attica (the country whose main city was Athens) about 485 BCE. By the time of his death in 406 BCE he had written at least eighty plays, which were performed at the Great Dionysia, the Athenians' major drama festival. Seventeen of these survive complete. He was one of the three outstanding figures— with Aeschylus and Sophocles—who made fifth-century Athens pre-eminent in the history of world drama. While he lived his apparently reclusive life Euripides was less successful than the other two tragedians, winning the festival's prize only five times. But his vigorous, immediate, controversial, and flamboyantly theatrical plays soon became by far the most popular and frequently revived works in the ancient repertoire. The universality of the conflicts he explores, and the startling realism of his characterization, ensure that he has also been by far the most often adapted, staged, and filmed of the ancient dramatists from the Renaissance to the present day. The first three plays in this volume, which all date from the last twenty-five years of Euripides' life, offer extraordinary challenges to their audience. They pose disturbing questions about the power struggle between women and men (*Medea*, 431 BCE), transgressive and repressed sexuality (*Hippolytus*, 428 BCE), and the corrupting effect of the revenge ethic (*Electra*). The fourth play, *Helen* (412 BCE), with its melodramatic plot, blatant humour, and 'happy, ending, illustrates Euripides' desire to experiment and endlessly reinvent his genre. These four plays show that the dramatist whom Aristotle described as 'the most tragic' of them all was also the most playful, innovative, and versatile.

EDITH HALL is Leverhulme Professor of Greek Cultural History at the University of Durham and co-director of the Archive of Performances of Greek and Roman Drama at the University of Oxford. Her numerous publications on ancient Greek literature and society include *Inventing the Barbarian* (1989), and an edition of Aeschylus' *Persians* (1996).

JAMES MORWOOD is Fellow of Wadham College at Oxford University where he teaches Latin and Greek. His interest in drama goes beyond the classical world. He has written *The Life and Works of Richard Brinsley Sheridan* (1985) and co-edited *Sheridan Studies* (1995), a collection of essays on that playwright.

OXFORD WORLD'S CLASSICS

*For over 100 years Oxford World's Classics have brought
readers closer to the world's great literature. Now with over 700
titles—from the 4,000-year-old myths of Mesopotamia to the
twentieth century's greatest novels—the series makes available
lesser-known as well as celebrated writing.*

*The pocket-sized hardbacks of the early years contained
introductions by Virginia Woolf, T. S. Eliot, Graham Greene,
and other literary figures which enriched the experience of reading.
Today the series is recognized for its fine scholarship and
reliability in texts that span world literature, drama and poetry,
religion, philosophy and politics. Each edition includes perceptive
commentary and essential background information to meet the
changing needs of readers.*

OXFORD WORLD'S CLASSICS

EURIPIDES

Medea · Hippolytus
Electra · Helen

Translated and Edited by
JAMES MORWOOD

Introduction by
EDITH HALL

OXFORD
UNIVERSITY PRESS

OXFORD

UNIVERSITY PRESS

Great Clarendon Street, Oxford OX2 6DP

Oxford University Press is a department of the University of Oxford.
It furthers the University's objective of excellence in research, scholarship,
and education by publishing worldwide in

Oxford New York

Auckland Bangkok Buenos Aires Cape Town Chennai
Dar es Salaam Delhi Hong Kong Istanbul Karachi Kolkata
Kuala Lumpur Madrid Melbourne Mexico City Mumbai Nairobi
São Paulo Shanghai Taipei Tokyo Toronto

Oxford is a registered trade mark of Oxford University Press
in the UK and in certain other countries

Published in the United States
by Oxford University Press Inc., New York

Introduction and Bibliography © Edith Hall 1997
Translation and Notes © James Morwood 1997

The moral rights of the author have been asserted

Database right Oxford University Press (maker)

First published as an Oxford World's Classics paperback 1998

All rights reserved. No part of this publication may be reproduced,
stored in a retrieval system, or transmitted, in any form or by any means,
without the prior permission in writing of Oxford University Press,
or as expressly permitted by law, or under terms agreed with the appropriate
reprographics rights organizations. Enquiries concerning reproduction
outside the scope of the above should be sent to the Rights Department,
Oxford University Press, at the address above

You must not circulate this book in any other binding or cover
and you must impose this same condition on any acquirer

British Library Cataloguing in Publication Data

Data available

Library of Congress Cataloging in Publication Data
Euripides.
[Selections. English. 1998]
Medea and other plays / Euripides; translated and edited by
James Morwood; introduction by Edith Hall
(Oxford world's classics)
Includes bibliographical references (p.   ).
Contents: Medea—Hippolytus—Electra—Helen.
1. Europides—Translations into English. 2. Greek drama.
(Tragedy)—Translations into English. 3. Medea (Greek mythology)—Drama.
4. Hippolytus (Greek mythology)—Drama. 5. Helen of Troy.
(Greek mythology)—Drama. 6. Electra (Greek mythology)—Drama.
I. Moorwood, James. II. Title. III. Series: Oxford world's classics
(Oxford University Press).
PA3975.A2   1998b   882'.01—dc21   98–12866

ISBN–13: 978–0–19–282442–4
ISBN–10: 0–19–282442–2

12

Printed in Great Britain by
Clays Ltd, St Ives plc

CONTENTS

ACKNOWLEDGEMENTS

The translator would like to acknowledge his considerable debt to Professor Christopher Collard and Professor James Diggle. Any errors or misjudgements that remain are due to his own obstinacy or negligence.

ABBREVIATIONS

AJP	*American Journal of Philology*
BICS	*Bulletin of the Institute of Classical Studies*
CA	*Classical Antiquity*
CP	*Classical Philology*
CQ	*Classical Quarterly*
CR	*Classical Review*
G&R	*Greece & Rome*
GRBS	*Greek, Roman, and Byzantine Studies*
HSCP	*Harvard Studies in Classical Philology*
JHS	*Journal of Hellenic Studies*
PCPS	*Proceedings of the Cambridge Philological Society*
RSC	*Revista di Studi Classici*
SO	*Symbolae Osloensis*
TAPA	*Transactions and Proceedings of the American Philological Association*
YCS	*Yale Classical Studies*

s.d.	*stage direction*

INTRODUCTION

Edith Hall

Many of Euripides' most striking dramas have not even survived. The most scandalous, perhaps, was his *Aeolus*, notoriously portraying brother–sister incest leading to childbirth and suicide. The most bizarre may have been his *Cretans*, featuring Queen Pasiphaë's adulterous affair with a bull. But the most beautiful was held to be *Andromeda*, in which the Ethiopian princess, chained to a rock as a meal for a sea-monster, was rescued by the aerial epiphany of the winged hero Perseus.

According to the comic playwright Aristophanes, *Andromeda* was so delightful that it was the preferred holiday reading of Dionysus, the god of theatre himself (*Frogs* 53), and its fragments reveal an appealing concoction not unlike Euripides' *Helen*: it added the theatricality of exotic spectacle and song to emotive pathos and suspense, and distinctively 'novelistic' elements such as adventure, intrigue, a barbarian setting, and a romantic liaison. Yet Alexander the Great, no professional actor, is supposed to have been able to perform a whole episode of *Andromeda* off by heart, and did so at his last supper (Athenaeus, *Deipnosophists* 12.537d–e.); the single most significant reason for Euripides' astonishing ancient popularity was really the accessible and memorable poetry in which his characters expressed themselves. Princesses and paupers, demi-gods and warriors, practitioners of incest, bestiality, and murder: he made them all 'speak like human beings' (see Aristophanes, *Frogs* 1058).

The Greeks and Romans were passionate about Euripides. A character in a comedy announced that he would be prepared to hang himself for the sake of seeing this (dead) tragedian (Philemon fr. 118).[1] Aristotle's formalist discussion of tragedy complains about Euripides' use of the *deux ex machina*, his unintegrated choruses, and the 'unnecessary' villainy of some of his characters. Yet even

---

[1] R. Kassel and C. Austin (eds.), *Poetae Comici Graeci* (Berlin, 1983–95).

Aristotle conceded that Euripides was 'the most tragic of the poets', meaning that he was the best at eliciting pity and fear (*Poetics* 56ª25–7, 54ᵇ1, 61ᵇ21, 53ª30). Besides Euripides' impact on the literature of succeeding generations—especially Menander, Ennius, Virgil, Ovid, Seneca, and oratory—his plays are everywhere apparent in the *visual* culture of the Mediterranean. Homer apart, no author stimulated the arts more; the Romans painted Euripides' scenes on their walls and carved them on their sarcophagi; the Byzantines commissioned elaborate mosaics keeping his pagan myths alive in the visual imagination of Christendom.

The nineteenth-century scholar Benjamin Jowett said Euripides was 'no Greek in the better sense of the term',[2] for after his revivification in the Renaissance Euripides often suffered by comparison with the structural perfection, 'purity', and 'Hellenic' spirit perceived in his rival Sophocles. This is, however, to oversimplify the complex and largely unwritten story of Euripidean reception and performance. *Medea* has been much imitated and adapted (importantly by Corneille in 1635 and operatically by Cherubini); it inspired Pier Paolo Pasolini's enigmatic film *Medea* (1970), starring Maria Callas in her single cinematic role. *Hippolytus* has haunted the poetic imagination of the West, especially through Racine's influential adaptation *Phèdre*, a synthesis of Euripidean, Senecan, and Plutarchan material. *Electra*, on the other hand, although occasionally enjoyed before the nineteenth century, was condemned to neglect in both academe and performance by A. W. Schlegel's dislike for Euripidean innovation and pronouncement that *Electra* constituted 'perhaps the very worst of all his pieces'.[3] The Strauss *Elektra* is nearer to Sophocles, and some have argued that even Michael Cacoyannis's cinematic adaptation of Euripides' *Electra* (1961), filmed under Greek skies with Irene Papas as protagonist, is nearer to the elevated style of Sophocles. *Helen*, likewise, although rediscovered early this century, has rarely been performed.

Yet the twentieth century has smiled on Euripides more than any era since antiquity. One reason is his approach to myth, which has been characterized as subversive, experimental, playful, and eccentric in an identifiably modern way. Although he has occasionally been seen as a formalist or mannerist, the term 'irony' dominates

---

[2] See A. N. Michelini, *Euripides and the Tragic Tradition* (Madison, 1987), 11 n. 40.
[3] A. W. Schlegel, *A Course of Lectures on Dramatic Art and Literature* (2nd edn., trans. John Black, London, 1840), i. 174–6.

criticism. 'Irony' is taken to describe Euripides' polytonality—his ability to write in two simultaneous keys. This 'irony', however, is conceived in more than one way: sometimes it describes the hypocritical gap between the rhetorical postures Euripidean characters adopt and their true motives. Alternatively it defines the confrontation of archaic myths with the values of democratic Athens, a process which deglamorizes violence, casting heroic revenge narratives as sordid 'gangland killings'.[4]

Another reason for Euripides' modern popularity is that his supple and multi-faceted works easily adapt to the agendas of different interpreters. Euripides has been an existentialist, a psychoanalyst, a proto-Christian with a passionate hunger for 'righteousness', an idealist and humanist, a mystic, a rationalist, an irrationalist, and an absurdist nihilist. But perhaps the most tenacious Euripides has been the pacifist feminist.

'Radical' Euripides was born in the first decade of this century with Gilbert Murray as midwife. This famous liberal scholar, later Chairman of the League of Nations, initiated in Edwardian London a series of performances of Euripides in his own English translations. *Trojan Women* (1905) was interpreted by some as a retrospective indictment of the concentration camps in which the British had starved women and children during the Boer War: as a result of *Medea* (1907), the heroine's monologue on the plight of women (see below, 'Athenian Society') was recited at suffragette meetings. Murray's political interpretations of Euripides, developed in performance, found academic expression in *Euripides and his Age* (1913). This book has fundamentally conditioned all subsequent interpretation, whether by imitation or reaction. A decade later Euripides' radicalism had become apocalyptic: 'not Ibsen, not Voltaire, not Tolstoi ever forged a keener weapon in defence of womanhood, in defiance of superstition, in denunciation of war, than the *Medea*, the *Ion*, the *Trojan Women*'.[5]

EURIPIDES THE ATHENIAN

What would Euripides have made of his modern incarnations? The reliable external biographical information amounts to practically

---

[4] This phrase is borrowed from W. G. Arnott's excellent article, 'Double the Vision: A Reading of Euripides' *Electra*', *G&R* 28 (1981), 179–92.

[5] F. L. Lucas, *Euripides and his Influence* (London, 1924), 15.

nothing. No dependable account of Euripides' own views on politics, women, or war survives, unless we are arbitrarily to select speeches by characters in his plays as the cryptic 'voice of Euripides'. Aristophanes and the other contemporary Athenian comic poets, who wrote what is now known as 'Old Comedy', caricatured Euripides as a cuckolded greengrocer's son, but their portrait offers little more truth value than a scurrilous cartoon.

The problem is not any dearth of evidence but a dearth of factual veracity. The student of Euripides has access to a late antique 'Life' (*Vita*) and a fragmentary third-century biography by Satyrus. There are also the so-called 'Letters of Euripides', a collection of five dull epistles purporting to be addressed to individuals such as Archelaus (king of Macedon) and Sophocles, but actually written in the first or second century CE. Collectively these documents provide the first example in the European tradition of the portrait of an alienated artist seeking solace in solitude. This Euripides is a misogynist loner with facial blemishes who worked in a seaside cave on the island of Salamis, and retired to voluntary exile in Macedon as a result of his unpopularity. Unfortunately, however, this poignant portrait is demonstrably a fiction created out of simplistic inferences from Euripides' own works or from the jokes in Athenian comedy. Beyond what is briefly detailed below, the only aspect of the 'Euripides myth' almost certain to be true is that he possessed a large personal library (see Aristophanes, *Frogs* 943, 1049).

Euripides' lifespan was almost exactly commensurate with that of democratic Athens's greatness. He was born in about 485 BCE, and was therefore a small boy when the city was evacuated and his compatriots defeated the second Persian invasion in 480 BCE. He spent his youth and physical prime in the thriving atmosphere of the 460s and 450s, a period which saw the consolidation of Athens's empire and position as cultural centre of the Greek-speaking world. He wrote at least eighty plays, and possibly ninety-two. Nineteen have been transmitted from antiquity under his name. Of these, *Rhesus* is probably spurious, and *Cyclops* is a satyr play (a comic version of a heroic myth sporting a chorus of sex-starved satyrs). Euripides first competed in the drama competition in 455 BCE, was victorious in 441, won again in 428 with the group including *Hippolytus*, and posthumously (in ?405) with *Bacchae* and *Iphigenia at Aulis*.

But all the plays in this volume date from the two decades beginning with *Medea* in 431, the year which saw the outbreak of the Peloponnesian War fought between Athens and her rival Sparta over hegemony in the Aegean. The last play in the volume, *Helen*, dates from 412, the year after the worst Athenian disaster ever: the fleet and many thousands of men were lost at Syracuse in Sicily after an attempt to extend Athenian imperial influence. Thucydides, near-contemporary of Euripides and author of the *History of the Peloponnesian War*, saw the significance of the calamity (7.87): it was 'the greatest action of this war, and, in my view, the greatest action that we know of in Greek history. To its victors it was the most brilliant of successes, to the vanquished the most catastrophic of defeats.' Athens never fully recovered from this blow to her morale and her resources, and in 404 lost the war, her empire, and (briefly) her pride.

It is tempting to speculate on Euripides' own reaction to these unfolding events. There are heartbreaking dramatizations of the *effects* of war in *Trojan Women* (415) and *Iphigenia at Aulis* (?405). These, however, lend no substantial support to the widely held view that Euripides, after initially supporting Athenian expansionism, despaired and retreated from the contemporary scene as the promoters of war became more powerful. It may be that truth lies behind the biographical tradition that he spent his last two years at the Macedonian court of Pella; it may be that the very existence of the tradition reveals Euripides' anti-democratic sympathies. On the other hand, the lack of evidence for a political career, in contrast with Sophocles' attested appointments to high office, may suggest a neutral emotional detachment from public affairs. But Euripides was clearly engaged with the intellectual and ethical questions which the war had asked and which underlay the policy debates in the Athenian assembly. These appear in disguise in his tragedies: the conflict between Medea and Jason revolves around the identical confrontation of justice with expediency which informs Thucydides' first debate between the Corinthians and the Corcyreans.

One certainty is that Euripides, intellectually, was a child of his time. Every significant field studied by the professional intellectuals ('sophists') in contemporary Athens surfaces in his tragedies: ontology, epistemology, philosophy of language, moral and political theory, medicine, psychology, and cosmology. There is thus a kind of truth in Aulus Gellius' statement that Euripides studied Physics with Anaxagoras, rhetoric with Prodicus, and moral philosophy with Socrates (*Noctes Atticae* 15.20.4); in the first version of Aristophanes' *Clouds* (fr. 401)[6] it was even alleged that Socrates provided Euripides with the ideas for his clever tragedies! And Euripidean characters certainly adopt the new philosophical *methods*: they subtly argue from probability and relativism, and formulate their points as antilogy, proof, and refutation.

EURIPIDES IN PERFORMANCE

Most Euripidean tragedies were first performed at an annual festival in honour of Dionysus, the Greek god of wine, dancing, and theatrical illusion. The Great Dionysia was held in the spring, when sailing became feasible. It was opened by a religious procession in which a statue of Dionysus was installed in the theatre, along with sacrifices and libations. Yet the Dionysia was also a political event. It affirmed the Athenian citizenry's collective identity as a democratic body with imperial supremacy: front seats were reserved for distinguished citizens, and only Athenians could perform the prestigious benefaction of sponsorship (*chorēgia*). The spectators included representatives from Athens's allied states. They displayed their tribute in the theatre, where they also witnessed a display by the city's war orphans. The plays were expected to befit this audience: insulting Athens at the Dionysia seems to have been a prosecutable offence (Aristophanes, *Acharnians* 501–6). It is not certain whether women attended the drama competitions, although most scholars assume that, if women were present at all, it was in small numbers, perhaps including only important priestesses.

The tragedies were performed over three successive days in groups by three poets: each poet offered three tragedies plus one satyr play. In 431 BCE, for example, Euripides took third place with three tragedies (*Medea*, *Philoctetes*, and *Dictys*), followed by a satyr play called *Theristai*, 'Reapers': the other two competitors were Euphorion (Aeschylus' son), who won first prize, and Sophocles, the runner-up. The plays were judged by a panel of democratically selected citizens, and care was taken to avoid juror corruption, but the audience's noisy applause and heckling influenced the outcome (Plato, *Republic* 6.492b5–c1).

The plays were performed in the theatre of Dionysus on the south slope of the Athenian acropolis. Individual actors probably per-

---

[6] Kassel and Austin, *Poetae Comici Graeci*.

formed their speeches and songs most of the time on the stage (*skēnē*), while the chorus of twelve sang and danced to forgotten steps and gestures in the dancing arena (*orchēstra*). All the performers were male, and all were masked. For performance conventions we have to rely on the characters' words, since the Greeks did not use stage directions. The last two decades have produced important work on the visual dimension and its contribution to the meaning of tragedy: scholarship has focused on physical contact, and on entrances and exits. The evidence for the material resources of the theatre as early as the fifth century is slight, although the poets had access to a machine which permitted the airborne epiphanies *ex machina*. There was also the *ekkyklema*, a contraption allowing bodies to be wheeled out of the doors of the house forming the 'backdrop' to most surviving tragedies. Vase-paintings offer a stylized reflection of the costumes, masks, and scenery, and some are directly inspired by individual tragedies.

MEDEA

At a superficial level *Medea* is the simplest of all Euripides' tragedies: its action consists of little more than its implacable protagonist's revenge on her treacherous husband by murdering his new bride and his sons. Nor was its status as a masterpiece immediately apparent: its group came last in the tragic competition in 431 BCE. Perhaps the play seemed stiff and old-fashioned, for it includes no solo singing in purely lyric metres (see below, 'Music, Chorus, Song'), and is visually austere until the final, overwhelming, epiphany of Medea, aloft in the sky-borne chariot. Euripides chose, moreover, to make a play which could be played by only two actors: there is no complex scene with a 'triangular' requirement for three speaking actors, unlike all the other plays in this volume. This simplicity serves to throw the dominating figure of Medea into grander relief, by stressing that in her serial bipolar encounters with men— Creon, Jason, Aegeus, Jason, the tutor, the messenger, and Jason again—she repeatedly extracts by sheer rhetorical power or by psychological manipulation whatever result she requires.

Medea may have failed to please because it ends with the barbarian murderess flying off to take up the offer of a safe haven in Athens that she had earlier extorted from Aegeus. Nor may the audience have enjoyed watching one of their kings expatiate on the

subject of his infertility: the Athenian tragedians tend to take care
to portray mythical Athenians with dignity. Moreover, the international situation in 431 meant that Athens was in no mood to see
any refugee from Corinth, even in myth, demanding favours or asy-
lum.

The play must have been ethically shocking. Medea stands alone
amongst tragic felons in committing her offence with impunity. In
extant Greek tragedy no other kin-killers reach the end of their
plays unpunished. Euripides slightly ameliorates this scandal by
suggesting that Medea, as granddaughter of the Sun, is not quite
mortal and thus not entirely accountable to ordinary theological
rules. Indeed, we never fully understand whether she is mortal or
divine, a wronged and sympathetic wife or an agent of divine justice, for Euripides has confusingly also given her and Jason some of
the most 'human' dialogue in ancient Greek. The play at one level
is but 'a bourgeois quarrel between an obtusely selfish man and an
over-passionate woman'.[7] The vengeful, competitive, and sexually
honest Medea, in escaping unpunished, was any Athenian husband's worst nightmare realized.

Medea had been previously implicated in murder on the
Euripidean stage, in his *Peliades* of 455 BCE. But the shocking effect
of the actual infanticide was exacerbated because Euripides almost
certainly invented it. His Medea is also the first known child-killing
mother in Greek myth to perform the deed in cold blood; the others
(Ino, Agave, Procne) seem always to have been given the 'excuse'
of temporary madness. This permits Euripides to introduce the
extraordinary soliloquy where Medea has difficulty steeling herself
to the slaughter (1019–80). But it also leaves the most disturbing
crime in extant Greek tragedy premeditated, its culpability undi-
minished even by mental disturbance.[8] Alone amongst the plays in
this volume *Medea* exemplifies the distinctively Euripidean use of
children. There is no evidence for children in Aeschylus, and
Sophoclean children (e.g. Antigone and Ismene at the end of *Oedipus
the King*) seem to have been non-speaking characters. But Euripides
fully exploits the opportunities for pathos the children present: we
see them long before Medea, and their death cries represent one of
the most heart-breaking moments in Western theatre.

[7] D. W. Lucas (trans.), *The Medea of Euripides* (London, 1949), 3.

[8] On the child-killing, see P. E. Easterling, 'The Infanticide in Euripides' *Medea*',
YCS 25 (1977), 177–91.

The emotional motor of Euripides' *Medea* renders it one of the more apparently 'timeless' of ancient tragedies: the despair, humiliation, and vindictiveness of a woman abandoned by her man in favour of a younger model speak loud across the centuries. Yet there are features specific to Athens in the second half of the fifth century, in particular the question of Medea's acceptability as an alien to her new city state. At Athens the possession of citizenship was tied to the descent group, and guarded with paranoid anxiety. In 451/450 BCE the statesman Pericles had initiated a law excluding from citizen privileges all but those who could prove that both their parents were members of Athenian citizen families. In 431 BCE Jason's plight may have elicited understanding if not actual sympathy from its male audience: Medea stresses that a barbarian wife could cause embarrassment (591–2). One way of looking at Jason is as a man trying to make a life in a xenophobic new city, while burdened with a wife who was not only not local but not even Greek. From an Athenian perspective Medea's ethnicity must have cast doubts even on the legitimacy of the union's unfortunate offspring.[9] Medea's difference from the women of Corinth must have been emphasized, moreover, by her clothing and appearance: Euripides was almost certainly the first poet to turn her from a Corinthian into a barbarian.

But the unenthusiastic original reception of this play cannot be wholly dissociated from Medea's betrayal of 'femininity'. She fundamentally repudiates the gender role assigned to her as a woman in fifth-century Greece. From her very first monologue (which also marks her first exit from the 'feminine' sphere of the house), and its extraordinary focus on the 'masculine' notions of 'cleverness' and citizenship, we know this is no ordinary woman. She combines in one psyche the 'feminine' qualities of compassion and maternal love with the 'masculine' heroic values of honour, status, and revenge.[10] Yet by the end of the play the inadequacy of the existing sociolinguistic distinctions between public and private, friend and foe, and especially between woman and man, has been unmasked through the characters' failure to communicate except in the most dislocated of linguistic modes. If Euripides' characters did indeed speak 'like human beings', then human beings undergoing marital breakdown have not changed much, after all.

[9] See further Edith Hall, *Inventing the Barbarian* (Oxford, 1989), 172–81.
[10] Helene Foley, 'Medea's Divided Self', *CA* 8 (1989), 61–85.

Euripides' *Medea* did not find success in the dramatic competition; nor did his first attempt at a dramatization of the story of Phaedra and Hippolytus, which has survived only in fragments. Phaedra in the first *Hippolytus* loved shamelessly and lied blatantly, staying alive to bear false witness against her stepson. It is therefore tempting to see Euripides as deliberately changing strategy in the surviving revised *Hippolytus* of 428 BCE, the most 'Sophoclean' of all his plays. This time all the characters are trying to do their best within their individual moral frame of reference, and acting within an unusually perfect literary structure emphasizing the parallels between the two deviant characters who die in it. The play has even been interpreted as an eloquent manifesto of the humanist principle that virtue has its own reward in the face of apparently arbitrary suffering and death: this message is supposed to have spoken loudly to the Athenians in 428 BCE, when they were scarcely beginning to recover from the ravages of an unusually terrible plague.

Judaeo-Christian and Greek traditions include several examples of the wife who becomes sexually obsessed with a younger man, and whose rejection leads to persecutory behaviour. The Old Testament offers the passion of Potiphar's wife for the young Joseph: the *Iliad* tells how Bellerophon was pursued by his host's wife (6.156–90). Euripides himself dramatized Bellerophon's story in yet another lost tragedy, *Stheneboea*, spectacularly featuring the hero astride the winged horse Pegasus. It was probably produced in the 420s, not long either before or after *Hippolytus*.

But Greek culture distrusted stepmothers in particular. In a society where childbirth was extremely hazardous, and widowers remarried, there were proportionately more families in which a new wife was introduced to stepchildren often no younger than herself. The Athenian legal speeches attest to the domestic conflicts to which this could lead. But it could also cause sexual confusion, and the canonical Greek articulation of the illicit love of a married woman for a single man, the famous love of Phaedra for Hippolytus, is compounded by the quasi-incestuous connotations of the step-parent–stepchild bond.

The legend the play dramatizes may have functioned as a ritual narrative helping to prepare brides psychologically for marriage, expressing with the extremism characteristic of myth the polar notions of sexual aggression and repudiation of sexuality. It certainly constitutes the most powerful enacted articulation of the ancient Greek perception that eros is 'the most dangerous of all relations' and poses 'a serious threat to the boundaries of the autonomous self by putting it in another's power under the magnetic pull of desire'.[11] Both Phaedra and Hippolytus deviate from socially endorsed models serving to delimit the power of eros, and both are outsiders who owe their deviance partly to genetic inheritance. She, as the play stresses, is a Cretan princess, daughter of the lustful Pasiphaë who bore the Minotaur, and granddaughter of Aërope who adulterously slept with her own husband's brother: Cretan women in tragedy are unusually susceptible to transgressive erotic impulses (and indeed both Aërope and Pasiphaë appeared in lost Euripidean plays). Hippolytus, on the other hand, inherits his rejection of sexual maturity, repudiation of marriage, and extreme antipathy to the opposite sex from his mother's origin as queen of the Amazons, the matrilineal race of warrior women who spurned 'normal' conjugal relations and roamed the virginal wild.

The plot emphasizes above all the power of language to reveal and silence to conceal. Phaedra's passion would have damaged none but herself had it remained unknown. If she had not been pressurized by the nurse into confession, if the nurse had not told Hippolytus, if Hippolytus had not articulated his misogyny, if Phaedra had not inscribed her stepson's death warrant into her suicide note, and if Theseus had not cursed Hippolytus, then instead of tragic words and tragic action there would have been only a mutely tragic situation: a frustrated wife, a preoccupied husband, a maladjusted youth.

A feminist reading can hardly fail to see the drama as a charter text for patriarchy, a 'male-bonding' play: the *Hippolytus* has been seen as empowering men and reaffirming their authority by privileging the relationship between them and by displacing the female: Phaedra was forced into the loneliest of deaths, in order to try and salvage her reputation. Structuralist readings emphasize the dualities embodied in the goddesses, and the symbolic likenesses and antinomies in the natural world which they represent. Yet the most distinctive feature of *Hippolytus* is the stark dualism with which the

[11] F. I. Zeitlin, 'The Power of Aphrodite: Eros and the Boundaries of the Self in Euripides' *Hippolytus*', in *Playing the Other: Gender and Society in Classical Greek Literature* (Chicago, 1996), 219–84, at 223.

action delineates human responsibility and divine determination for the catastrophe.

Euripides makes us serially watch each one of the four equally important main characters (they have similar numbers of lines) make a decision or take an action which will bring disaster closer. But he has also made us learn from Aphrodite that she is responsible for everything that will ensue. *Hippolytus* thus juxtaposes two alternative views of the causation of human action, much as Sophocles' *Oedipus the King*, produced around the same time, probes the relationship between Oedipus' precipitation of his downfall by his personality and actions and the predetermination of Apollo.

Greek thought was inherently dialectical: Greek myth includes blind seers, benevolent personified Curses, and a virgin goddess who presides over maidens' passages out of virginity into marriage. It could also cope with humans choosing actions which gods have preordained. Theseus is ultimately left alive and alone, doubly bereaved, knowing both that he has himself contributed to the catastrophe and that it was part of Aphrodite's grand design. Euripides' mortals help to define Athenian morality by deviating from its ideals. Yet there is no possibility of deviation from the tragic paths they choose but which are simultaneously decreed for them by Euripides' vindictive gods.

ELECTRA

Euripides' *Electra* made a less obvious impact than *Medea* or *Hippolytus* on later antiquity, although its domestic tone and rustic setting were formative in the development of New Comedy. Yet one ancient anecdote reveals that *Electra*'s profound tragic force was recognized. When Athens lost the Peloponnesian War in 404 BCE, the story goes that a Theban leader proposed that the city be razed to the ground. But Athens was saved by a man who performed to the allied generals the chorus's entrance song from Euripides' *Electra* (beginning at 167). Electra's pitiable plight seemed similar to that of conquered Athens; as a result, the generals are supposed to have decided against destroying such an illustrious city (Plutarch, *Life of Lysander* 15).

Amongst extant Greek tragedies the only story dramatized by all three playwrights relates Electra's and Orestes' conspiracy to murder their mother and usurping uncle Aegisthus. Consequently much

scholarly ink has been expended on comparing this play with
Aeschylus' *Choephoroe* (458 BCE) and Sophocles' *Electra*, and in particular on the relative chronology of the Sophoclean and Euripidean
versions. It is fascinating how differently two individuals can read a
myth: in Sophocles the matricides' triumphalism is undercut only
implicitly, if at all. But there is no way to prove the date of either
Electra, or which was the earlier. More instructive is Euripides' parody of the Aeschylean recognition scene. When Euripides' Electra
objects that her foot cannot be the same size as a man's, even if he
is her brother (534–7), it is not only an unusual 'intertextual' com-
ment on the Aeschylean prototype (227–8): it is undoubtedly meant
to be *funny*.

Consequently the precise emotional register of Euripides' *Electra*
has defied specification. The play's detractors have complained that
all the preparations for the crimes are marked by 'levity'. At the
other extreme, it has been regarded as a bleak example of
psychosocial realism anticipating Chekhov, a masterpiece, whose
'power of sympathy and analysis' was 'unrivalled in ancient
drama'.[12] The translator of this volume has noted elsewhere the
complex *shifts* of register, especially the pattern by which the choral
songs move from pictures of charm and allure, to darkness and
destruction, a pattern in keeping with the 'questioning mode' and
'irrecoverably dark world' of the tragedy.[13] Indeed, most admirers
have seen its moral position as unambivalent: its humour simply
sharpens its exposure of the barbarism inherent in unthinking reciprocal violence.

Does Euripides' Clytemnestra deserve to die at all? The play's ethical tension results from the absence of an answer. The Greek mind
was more able than ours simultaneously to contain contradictory
dimensions of a situation: the action is presented as both outrageous
and delivering a kind of justice. Clytemnestra was a murderess: it
was just that she had died. But matricide was (equally?) an outrage:
her killing by Orestes and Electra was dreadful. As Castor finally
announces, the fate Clytemnestra suffered was right, but the children did not act rightly (1244). However comic some of its scenes,
the play ends on the bleakest of notes: Orestes begs Electra to sing
him a dirge as if at his grave (1325–6), a request so jarring in the

---

[12] G. M. A. Grube, *The Drama of Euripides* (London, 1941), 314.
[13] James Morwood, 'The Pattern of the Euripides *Electra*', *AJP* 102 (1981),
326–70.

context of the 'happy ending' that it shocks even the god in the machine. It is difficult for a modern reader not to conceptualize the incipient pursuit of Orestes by the Erinyes as symbolizing our notion of internal torture by conscience, by a personal sense of 'guilt'. Perhaps this notion is not so modern: Cicero argued that 'the blood of a mother . . . has a great power; it is a mighty bond, of awful sanction. If any stain be conceived from it, not only can it not be washed out, but it penetrates through to the mind to such an extent that raving madness and insanity results. . . . These are the constant, secret, Furies which . . . exact punishment on behalf of their parents both by day and by night' (*Pro Sexto Roscio Amerino* 24.66).

Euripides' Electra incorporates extremes. She participates in the action more than in Sophocles, jointly wielding the matricidal sword (1225). But her commitment to a 'masculine' vengeance code conflicts with her immoderate assertions of the patriarchal view that women are secondary to men. It is shameful, she announces to Aegisthus' corpse, for a woman to be in charge of a household: but it is Electra, not Orestes, who is 'in charge' of the tragic action of the play (931–3). She thus implicitly subverts the gender hierarchy she explicitly endorses. It is left to Clytemnestra to articulate the inequity of marriage: why, she asks, should women be criticized for acquiring a new partner when male adultery is never censured (1036–40)?

Euripides put his inimitably demotic stamp on Electra's story by having Aegisthus marry her off to a peasant. Aegisthus' goal was to prevent her from bearing to an illustrious father a son who might one day punish him. The mythical motif of the cruel parent persecuting a daughter through fear of a possible grandchild has parallels, yet it is instructive to see how Euripides discovered in this motif the brilliant ruse of the invented grandchild which fundamentally colours his tragedy. The fictional baby lures Clytemnestra to her death, focuses attention on Electra's pitifully childless status, and extraordinarily complicates the distribution of audience sympathy. It is difficult to appreciate the heroic justice of reciprocal bloodletting when the victim thinks she has just become a grandmother.

HELEN

At the close of *Electra* Castor explains *ex machina* that Helen 'has come from the house of Proteus from Egypt—she did not go to

Troy'. The explanation for Helen's illusory presence at Troy was an artificial image sent by Zeus to cause strife and death among men (1280–3). This mythical exculpation of Helen had originally been invented by the lyric poet Stesichorus, and had been rationalized by Herodotus in his account of Egyptian antiquities (2.118–20). In his *Helen* of 412 BCE Euripides elaborated on these sources by constructing an entire play around Helen's sojourn in Egypt.

Helen has caused even more problems of generic categorization than *Electra*. Of all Greek tragedies, including the not dissimilar *Iphigenia in Tauris*, it is by far the lightest and funniest. It certainly conforms least with commonplace preconceptions of 'the tragic' ultimately derived from Aristotle. Nobody dies (except some Egyptian sailors the audience has not met), the ending is happy, and there are many laughs along the way to Helen's escape from the libidinous pharaoh Theoclymenus. Criticism has consequently often centred on definitions: is *Helen* light-hearted 'self-parody', 'melodrama', 'tragicomedy', 'romantic comedy', or just plain 'comedy'?

A year after *Helen* and *Andromeda*, Aristophanes treated these new tragedies to extended parody in his comedy *Women at the Thesmorphoria*. He was struck by *Helen*'s 'escape' plot, the comic 'door-knocking' scene with the female porter, and the geographical context of Egypt, which seems never to have been the setting for a tragedy previously. But it had formed the backdrop to both comedies and satyr plays: Euripides himself produced a satyric *Busiris*, featuring a mythical king of Egypt who subjected all foreigners to human sacrifice. Thus Theoclymenus seems to have walked in almost straight from the satyric stage. There are other features reminiscent of satyr drama, especially the motif of Menelaus' shipwreck and the coastal setting. It may, therefore, be that *Helen*'s genre-transgressive quality has more to do with satyric than comic drama: an appropriate definition of *Helen* could be the critic Demetrius' description of satyr drama—'tragedy at play' (*On Style* 169).

Whatever challenge it presents to generic classification, *Helen*'s complex tissue of plots and sub-plots has long attracted admirers; it has been supposed to mark the birth of fiction as the first novel in Greek literature. An influential reading has drawn on Northrop Frye's study of the lighter plays of Shakespeare to demonstrate that a distinctive feature of *Helen* is its collision of two worlds: a 'real' world of pain and trouble and an 'ideal' world of serenity and simplicity, a duality negotiated in the manner of true 'romance' by a calumniated heroine whose virtue restores her and her beloved to happiness ever after in their kingdom.[14]

The play's brilliance lies in its juxtaposition of this romantic dimension with considerable intellectual bravura. Euripides uses the folkloric notion of a human simulacrum to explore the epistemological issue of the impossibility of true belief: and therefore not only the language but the very plot of *Helen* express the tension between what is and what only seems to be. Sophists contemporary with Euripides such as Gorgias had questioned whether there is a fully knowable real world, and whether language was adequate to describe it: *Helen* repeatedly explores the gap between reality and repute, speech and truth. Gorgias had written a rhetorical exercise consisting of a defence of the mythical Helen in which he argued that a speech can 'mould the mind in the way it wishes', is able to 'please and persuade a large crowd because written with skill, not moulded with truth', and that philosophical speeches, in particular, show that 'quick-wittedness makes the opinion which is based on belief changeable'.[15]

Fittingly for a play so emphatically dealing with the impossibility of cognitive certitude, the visual element of *Helen* is unusually important. The heroine perceives that her beauty—her superficial 'appearance'—has been her undoing, and wishes that it could be washed off her face like the paint off a beautiful statue (262–3); this raises the issue of 'metatheatricality', for 'Helen' herself is but a male actor wearing a sculpted mask painted with beautiful colours. By drawing attention to this false 'face', the actor draws attention to one of the illusory conventions of the theatrical performance in which he is participating. Much additional play is made of illusion and of doubleness. The entrance of Menelaus mirrors the previous appearance of Teucer; the Egyptian twins have a pair of equally spectacular entrances (Theonoe with incense and religious procession at 865–72, Theoclymenus with hunting dogs and nets 1165–70), and the play concludes with a theophany of twins. Costume possesses significance; besides the comic effect of seeing Menelaus wrapped in salvaged materials from a shipwreck (422), Helen herself completely changes her appearance (probably both

[14] Northrop Frye, *A Natural Perspective: The Development of Shakespearean Comedy and Romance* (New York, 1965); Charles Segal, 'The Two Worlds of Euripides' *Helen*', in *Interpreting Greek Tragedy* (Ithaca, NY, 1986), 222–67.

[15] Gorgias, *Encomium of Helen*, trans. D. M. MacDowell (Bristol, 1982), 13.

robes and mask) in order to 'appear' as a widow (1186–8), when paradoxically she has just regained the status of 'wife' in the true sense again.

Helen also confronts ontological paradoxes, especially the problematic notions of subjectivity, the self, and identity: who is the 'true' Helen? If 'Helen of Troy' did not cause the Trojan War, then why is she the subject of a work of literature? The trope of mistaken identity serves to emphasize further both the theme of recognition (*anagnōrisis*), and its ironic duality in this play: Menelaus' recognition of his wife involves recognizing that he fought a protracted and bloody war for the sake of an illusion. Here lies a clue to the relation between this superficially frothy, whimsical romp and its immediate historical context. Against the 'real' backdrop of the Sicilian carnage, Euripides' spectators cannot have failed to draw some connection between their own bereavements and the play's implication that all the losses of the Trojan War had been incurred for no reason at all.

ATHENIAN SOCIETY

Euripides' plays were first performed in Athens at a festival celebrating Athenian group identity, and consequently reveal an 'Athenocentrism' manifested in praise for the beauty of Athens's environment, the grace of its citizens, its cultural distinction (*Medea* 824–45), and the fairness of the Athenian court of the Areopagus, where Castor says that votes are always cast with meticulous impartiality (*Electra* 1258–63).

Yet the social fabric of the city which Euripides inhabited was heterogeneous. In 431 BCE an estimated 300,000 human beings lived in the city state of Attica. But at least 25,000 were resident non-Athenians ('metics'), including businessmen and professionals; a third were slaves, the majority of whom came from beyond Hellenic lands—from the Balkans, the Black Sea, Asia, or Africa. This ethnic pluralism perhaps finds expression in the 'multi-ethnic' casts of tragedy: the present volume alone introduces Egyptians in *Helen*, Black Sea barbarians in *Medea*, and an Amazon's son in *Hippolytus*.

Slavery was fundamental to Athenian economy and society, and tragedy reminds us of this unfortunate portion of the population (e.g. *Electra* 632–3). In *Acharnians* Aristophanes commented on the intelligence Euripides imputed to his slaves (400–1), and his plays include slaves with important roles as well as mute attendants: *Medea* is opened by a household servant, and in *Hippolytus* and *Electra* the nurse and the tutor respectively are crucial to the plot. The institution of slavery is itself much discussed: a character in a lost play affirmed that a noble slave is not dishonoured by the title, because 'many slaves are superior to the free' (fr. 511).[16] There are two such 'honourable slaves' in *Helen*: Menelaus' loyal manservant (see 726–31), and the Egyptian prepared to die for Theonoe (1639–41).

The ethical dilemmas and emotional traumas in Euripides are never wholly inseparable from the decidedly unheroic pressures of finance and economics. It is not just that the metaphorical fields often owe much to financial practice (blood spilt in revenge is 'owed' like a loan (*Electra* 858)), but money or lack of it motivates both action and rhetoric. Many characters express anxiety about maintaining the means to live, especially in exile; Electra's husband complains that he is economically embarrassed (37–8). Medea's first monologue clarifies the socio-economic imperatives underlying her own and other women's predicament: 'Of everything that is alive and has a mind, we women are the most wretched creatures. First of all, we have to buy a husband with a vast outlay of money—we have to take a master for our body. . . . divorce brings shame on a woman's reputation and we cannot refuse a husband his rights. . . . I would rather stand three times in the battle line than bear one child' (*Medea* 230–51). She trenchantly exposes the jeopardy in which marriage placed women: besides the insulting dowry system, women were subject to legalized rape in marriage, a hypocritical double standard in divorce, and agonizing mortal danger in childbirth.

This kind of speech outraged the Christian writer Origen, who criticized Euripides for inappropriately making women express argumentative opinions (*Contra Celsum* 7.36.34–6); in *Frogs* Euripides claimed to have made tragedy 'more democratic' by keeping his women—young ones and old ones—talking alongside their masters (948–50). It is indeed a remarkable feature of Euripidean tragedy that most of his best thinkers and talkers are women: Medea is a superior rhetorician to any man in her play; Phaedra's philosophical consideration of her dilemma (373–430) makes Hippolytus' misogynist ravings seem positively facile; the debate scene in *Electra*

---

[16] All references to fragments of Euripides are cited from A. Nauck, *Tragicorum Graecorum Fragmenta*, 2nd edn. with supplement by B. Snell (Hildesheim, 1964).

is between two women, and in *Helen* the heroine is nearly as intellectually superior to her husband as Theonoe is to her credulous thug of a brother.

Women are of course prominent in tragedy generally: patriarchal cultures often use symbolic females to help them imagine abstractions and think about their social order. It is also relevant that women performed the laments at funerals, that Dionysus' cult involved maenadism and transvestism, and that women were perceived as more emotionally expressive and susceptible to eros and possession. They were also regarded as lacking moral autonomy: Athenian men were obsessed with what happened in their households behind their backs, and all the transgressive women in tragedy are temporarily or permanently husbandless. The plays are products of an age where huge sexual, financial, and affective tensions surrounded the transfer of women between the households that made up the city state. But there was certainly a feeling in antiquity that Euripides' focus on women was sharper than that of either Aeschylus or Sophocles; until recently critics were debating whether Euripides was a misogynist or a feminist. But the only certainties are that he repeatedly chose to create strong female characters, and that as a dramatist he had a relativist rhetorical capacity for putting both sides of the argument in the sex war.

The position of women in the real world of Athens has itself long been a contentious issue, especially the degree of confinement to which citizen women were subject. But it is clear that most men would have preferred their wives and daughters to stay indoors, to be little discussed in public, to practise thrift, to possess unimpeachable sexual fidelity, and serially to produce healthy sons. Women could not vote or participate in the assembly; nor could they speak for themselves in the courts of law or normally conduct financial transactions except through the agency of their male 'guardian' (*kyrios*)—father, husband, or nearest male relative. But women did, of course, negotiate with the existing power structures (we hear hints in the orators of the need for men to seek their womenfolk's approval), and were prominent in the central arena of public life constituted by official religion. This illuminates the dignified priestess in Euripides' *Ion* (the 'Pythia' of Apollo at Delphi), and Theonoe in his *Helen*. In a lost play the wise woman Melanippe defended women against practitioners of misogynist rhetoric like

Hippolytus (*Hippolytus* 616–68),[17] one of her strategies was to list
the Panhellenic cults which women administered (fr. 499).

Men's criticism of women is worthless twanging of a bowstring and evil
talk. Women are better than men, as I will show. . . . Consider their role in
religion, for that, in my opinion, comes first. We women play the most
important part, because women prophesy the will of Zeus in the oracles of
Phoebus. And at the holy site of Dodona near the sacred oak, females con-
vey the will of Zeus to inquirers from Greece. As for the sacred rituals for
the Fates and the Nameless Ones, all these would not be holy if performed
by men, but prosper in women's hands. In this way women have a right-
ful share in the service of the gods. Why is it, then, that women must have
a bad reputation?[18]

EURIPIDES AND RELIGION

Melanippe's words are a fitting introduction to the category of
dramatis personae constituted by the gods. What is to be deduced
about Euripides' religion from his on-stage divinities in these plays
(Aphrodite, Artemis, the Dioscuri), and the Apollo, Death, Thetis,
Madness, Hermes, Athena, Poseidon, and Dionysus who physically
appear in others? One function of Euripides' gods from the machine,
especially in *Electra* and *Helen*, is certainly to act as a metatheatri-
cal 'alienation' device drawing attention to the author's power over
the narrative. But does this mean that he was an atheist?

Allegations that Euripides was a religious radical began in his lifetime. Aristophanes' caricature includes the charge that Euripides'
tragedies had persuaded people 'that the gods do not exist' (*Women
at the Thesmophoria* 450–1), and portrays him praying to the Air
('Ether') and 'Intelligence' (*Frogs* 890–2). By later antiquity it was
believed that it was at Euripides' house that Protagoras, the great
relativist and agnostic thinker, read out his famous treatise on the
gods, beginning 'Man is the measure of all things' (fr. 80 B 1; Diog.
Laert. 9.8.5).[19]

---

[17] Practising generalized invective against women seems to have been a favoured
pastime: an example of the behaviour of Theophrastus' 'tactless man' is not that he
inveighs against womankind, but that he does it *at weddings* (12.6)!

[18] Translation taken from M. R. Lefkowitz and M. B. Fant, *Women's Life in Greece
and Rome: A Source Book in Translation* (2nd edn., London, 1992), 14.

[19] H. Diels and W. Kranz (eds.), *Die Fragmente der Vorsokratiker* (6th edn.; Dublin,
1951–2).

Some characters in Euripides undoubtedly articulate views which must have sounded modern and 'scientific' to his audience. They depart from traditional theology by attributing the workings of the universe either to physical causes or to the power of the human mind. In *Trojan Women* Hecuba wonders whether Zeus should be addressed as 'Necessity of nature or the mind of man' (884–6). In one lost play a character asserted that 'the mind that is in each of us is god'; in another the first principle of the cosmos was Air, which 'sends forth the summer's light, and makes the winter marked with cloud, makes life and death'; in a third Air was explicitly equated with Zeus (frr. 1018, 330.3–5, 941).

Consequently there has always been a critical tendency to see Euripides as seeking to overturn or challenge traditional religion, especially belief in the arbitrary, partisan, and often malevolent anthropomorphic Olympian gods of the Homeric epics. It has been argued that in figures such as Aphrodite and Artemis in *Hippolytus* he included the most Homeric of all Greek tragic gods precisely to undermine them. Thus his theatrical divinities are a literary throwback to the old anthropomorphism, constituting a consciously reductive enactment of the commonly accepted personalities of the Olympians. Alternatively, Euripides is interpreted as a humanist who denies any but human motivation to human action and whose works operate on a similar principle to Thucydides' rationalist and atheological determination that it is human nature, *to anthrōpinon* (3.82.2), which drives and conditions history. Critics have even seen Theonoe as a proselyte advocating a new Euripidean doctrine: her striking statement that Justice has a great shrine in her heart (*Helen* 1002–3, see also *Trojan Women* 886) offers, allegedly, a completely new religion of peace and justice, which Euripides is urging should replace the old Olympian cults.

Yet it is mistaken to confuse Euripidean characters' more innovative theological opinions with his own (unknown) personal views. Moreover, many of the expressions of scepticism are more complicated than they seem. One rhetorical function of scepticism is to *affirm* the belief being doubted simply by raising it to consciousness. Helen, for example, may explicitly doubt her own divine paternity (16–22), but her scepticism brings her ambiguous status in relation to gods and mortals to the forefront of the audience's minds. This helps them to appreciate the play's underlying argument, which emphatically reaffirms that her father is Zeus.[20]

The overall impact of Euripidean tragedy does nothing to disrupt the three fundamental tenets of Athenian religion as practised by its citizens: that gods exist, that they pay attention (welcome or unwelcome) to the affairs of mortals, and that some kind of reciprocal allegiance between gods and humans was in operation, most visibly instantiated in sacrifice. The tragic performances were framed by the rituals of the Dionysia, and ritual fundamentally informs tragedy's imagery, plots, and songs: a study of wedding and funeral motifs, for example, has shown how they become conflated into sinister variations of the figure of the 'bride of death'.[21] The plays themselves frame accounts of ritual: in *Helen* a propitiatory bull sacrifice to Poseidon and the Nereids secures a safe homeward voyage (1554–87); in *Electra* another bull sacrifice is minutely described— the bowls, baskets, and barley grain; the skinning of the animal and inspection of its innards (800–26).

There is a tension between the critical presentation of divinity and the practice of ritual, especially sacrifice, which often plays a positive role; in *Electra*, set against the background of the festival of Hera at Argos, the regular religion of the polis offers a paradigm of ritual regularity against which the irregular deeds of the royal family can be measured.[22] In cult, moreover, Hera presides over married women's lives, and her festival is thus an 'ironically' apt setting for a play about two women with distinctly dysfunctional marriages.

Euripidean plots are also repeatedly driven by violations of the great taboos and imperatives constituting popular Greek ethics, the boundaries defining unacceptable behaviour which Sophocles' Antigone calls the 'unwritten and unshakeable laws of the gods' (*Antigone* 454–5), and which Euripidean characters are more likely to call 'the laws common to the Greeks' (e.g. *Heraclidae* 1010).

---

[20] T. C. W. Stinton (' "Si credere dignum est": Some Expressions of Disbelief in Euripides and Others', *PCPS* 22 (1976), 60–89) discusses the complicated impact of apparently sceptical remarks in both *Helen* and *Electra* (74–82).

[21] In *Medea*, for example, Medea turns her husband's bride into a bride of death with a lethal wedding present: Rush Rehm, *Marriage to Death: The Conflation of Wedding and Funeral Rituals in Greek Tragedy* (Princeton, 1994), 103–4.

[22] H. P. Foley, *Ritual Irony: Poetry and Sacrifice in Euripides* (Ithaca, NY, 1985), 21; F. I. Zeitlin, 'The Argive Festival of Hera and Euripides' *Electra*', *TAPA* 101 (1970), 645–89.

These regulated human relationships at every level. In the family they proscribed incest, kin-killing, and failure to bury the dead: kin-killing and kin-burial are features of both *Medea* and *Electra*. At the level of relationships between members of different households and cities, these 'common laws' ascribed to Zeus the protection of three vulnerable groups: suppliants, recipients of oaths, and parties engaged in the compact of reciprocal trust required by the guest–host relationship.

Supplication is a formal entreaty, accompanied by ritualized touching of knees, chin, or hand, which puts the recipient under a religious obligation to accede the suppliant's requests. Supplication in Euripides characterizes numerous crucial scenes. Medea uses supplication to get her way with both Creon and Aegeus (324, 709); Phaedra's nurse manipulates both her mistress and Hippolytus by supplication (326–55, 607); Helen supplicates Theonoe (894–6). Oaths are also frequent: in *Medea* Jason's most important offence is perhaps his violation of uxorial oaths, and in *Hippolytus* the hero cannot act in his own self-protection because he piously refuses to break the oath of silence he has sworn to Phaedra's nurse. The regulation of hospitality is also apparent in these plays: in *Electra* the peasant demonstrates the correct way of receiving guests, while in *Helen* Theoclymenus demonstrates the opposite by slaughtering visitors to Egypt.

The history of religion, moreover, seems to have fascinated Euripides, who includes in his tragedies numerous 'aetiological' explanations of the origin of cults. Medea is to carry her children's bodies to the Corinthian precinct of Hera, and 'institute a holy festival and sacred rites' (1378–82); *Hippolytus* explains the origin of a temple of Aphrodite at Athens (30–3), and of the Troezenian rites of unwed maidens, who 'will cut their hair in tribute' to Hippolytus throughout eternity, singing maidens' songs to immortalize Phaedra's love (1425–30).

MUSIC, CHORUS, SONG

We have lost the melodies to which the lyrics of tragedy were sung to the accompaniment of pipes (*auloi*). But it is possible partially to decipher what John Gould has called 'strategies of poetic sensibility'[23]

[23] J. Gould, 'Dramatic Character and "Human Intelligibility" in Greek Tragedy', *PCPS* 24 (1978), 43–67, esp. 54–8.

within the formal, conventional media open to the tragedian: besides the choral passages, which were danced and sung, the tragedian had several modes of delivery to choose from for his individual actors. In addition to set-piece speeches and line-by-line spoken dialogue (*stichomythia*), they included solo song, duet, sung interchange with the chorus, and an intermediate mode of delivery, probably chanting to pipe accompaniment, signalled by the anapaestic rhythm (∪ ∪ –).

In this edition the sung and chanted sections have been laid out in shorter lines so that the reader can appreciate the shifts between speech and musical passages. This matters because it mattered in antiquity. The musicologist Aristoxenus said that speech begins to sound like song *when we are emotional* (*Elements of Harmony* 1.9–10). It certainly affects our appreciation of Electra's state of mind, for example, that Euripides chose to make her *sing* her grief in her first scene (*Electra* 112–212); it matters that the nurse extracts from Phaedra the information which will precipitate two deaths in *spoken* dialogue exchanged line by line (*stichomythia*), heightening the pace and tension.

The chorus can also speak, and even function as an 'umpire' between warring parties in a debate (*Medea* 576–8). Sometimes it has to be sworn to collusive silence (*Hippolytus* 710–12). Sometimes its songs 'fill in' time while actors change roles, or 'telescope' time while events happen offstage (e.g. *Helen* 1451–511). Often the chorus sings forms of lyric song derived from the world of collective ritual. A choral song may be a simple hymn of praise, like the hymn to Artemis at her statue in *Hippolytus* (61–2). The ode which Medea's dying sons interrupt is a sung prayer to Earth, the Sun, and Helios (1251–92). In *Helen* the chorus's role includes a subtle and allusive lament (*thrēnos*) for the suffering caused by the Trojan War (1107–64), and a hymn to the divine Mother (1301–68).

Yet many choral odes are philosophical in orientation, and meditate in general terms on the issues which have been explored in the concrete situation of the play's previous episode. Thus the chorus of *Medea* reflects on the sorrow inherent in sexual passion and homelessness (627–62), and on the troubled condition of parenthood (1081–115). Such contemplative songs allude to parallels in myths quite unrelated to the actions the chorus is witnessing: in *Hippolytus* the chorus is reminded that sex has brought death in the past, with Heracles and Semele (545–62) cited as examples. But the mythical narrative may function, rather, to supply details of the past in the same family, as the 'golden-lamb' ode in *Electra* recounts the earlier troubles of the house of Atreus (698–746).

In Aristophanes' *Frogs*, a prominent feature of Euripidean tragedy is the spoken 'programmatic' prologue (of the kind which opens every one of the plays in this volume), which is characterized as predictable in both metrical form and in 'scene-setting' function. But this is unfair: the prologue typically establishes expectations, themes, and images which will subsequently become central to the drama. Euripides, moreover, varied the impact by his choice of speaker: he keeps Medea at an emotional distance from the audience by opening her play with her anxious nurse, casts an entirely different theological light on the actions of *Hippolytus* by choosing the vindictive goddess Aphrodite as prologist, and lets his winsome Helen walk straight into his audience's hearts by granting her a semi-comic autobiography at the beginning of the play which bears her name.

The Roman rhetorician Quintilian (10.1.67) judged Euripides of more use than Sophocles to the trainee orator, and the modern reader will undoubtedly be struck by the peculiarly formal debates in some of these plays: Medea versus Jason, Theseus versus Hippolytus, Electra versus Clytemnestra. The debate (*agōn*) is one of the features which Athenian tragedy assimilated from the oral performances which characterized two other great institutions of the democracy: the law courts and the assembly. To meet the increasing need for polished public speaking and its assessment under the widened franchise, the study of the science of persuasion, or the art of rhetoric, developed rapidly around the middle of the fifth century; this is reflected in tragedy's increased use of formal rhetorical figures, tropes, 'common topics' such as pragmatism and expediency, and hypothetical arguments from probability. One form of exercise available to the trainee orator was the 'double argument'—the construction or study of twin speeches for and against a particular proposition, or for the defence and prosecution in a hypothetical trial. As a character in Euripides' lost *Antiope* averred, 'If one were clever at speaking, one could have a competition between two arguments in every single case' (fr. 189). In assessing Euripidean rhetoric it must be remembered that his audience had become accustomed to startling displays by litigants in lawsuits (Aristophanes, *Wasps* 562–86); by the 420s political oratory sometimes descended into competitive exhibitionism in which the medium had superseded the message (Thucydides 3.38).

Euripides' gift for narrative is perhaps clearest in his 'messenger speeches', vivid mini-epics of exciting action, whether it is the gruesome deaths of Medea's first victims, inflicted by toxic flaming robes (1136–230), the attack by the bellowing bull from the sea which caused Hippolytus' chariot crash (1173–254), or the fake funeral which turns into an international maritime incident in *Helen* (1526–618). All Euripides' poetry is marked by exquisite simile and metaphor, often traced thematically through a play (in *Medea* maritime imagery, in *Electra* athletics): his 'picturesque' style was much admired in antiquity ('Longinus', *On Sublimity* 15.1–4).

Euripides showed infinite versatility of register, and was capable of selecting rare poetic words for special effect (Aristotle, *Poetics* 58^{b}19–24). Yet he still revolutionized the diction of tragedy by making his characters speak in his distinctively 'human way': Aristotle affirms that it was not until Euripides wrote roles using language drawn from everyday conversation that tragedy discovered natural dialogue (*Rhetoric* 3.2.5). This ordinary quality to his characters' language attracted emulation by able poets even within his lifetime, yet in Aristophanes' *Frogs* Dionysus dismisses them as insignificant 'chatterers' in comparison (89–95). Euripides was really doing something extremely difficult in making his unforgettable characters speak 'like human beings'. Thus the author of an encomium to Euripides in the *Palatine Anthology* justifiably discourages the aspiring imitator (7.50):

> Poet, do not attempt to go down Euripides' road;
> It is hard for men to tread.
> It seems easy, but the man who tries to walk it
> Finds it rougher than if it were set with cruel stakes.
> If you even try to scratch the surface of Medea, daughter of Aeetes,
> You shall die forgotten. Leave Euripides' crowns alone.[24]

[24] Warmest thanks are due to both Lindsay Hall and James Morwood for their perceptive comments on a previous draft.

NOTE ON THE TRANSLATION

This is a prose translation. However, lyrical and choric passages—intended for sung or chanted performance—have been laid out on shorter lines. These will inevitably have the appearance of free verse, but the translator's aim has simply been to denote the distinction between the spoken and sung or chanted areas of the play.

The translations are from James Diggle's Oxford Classical Text. Readers will need to consult that text to discover which passages he believes to be spurious or corrupt. I have translated the plays in their entirety.

Asterisks (*) signify that there is a note on the words or passages so marked.

I have used the Latinized spellings of the Greek names except in *Helen* (see the opening note on that play).

Line numbers refer to the Greek text.

SELECT BIBLIOGRAPHY

This selective bibliography supplements those works detailed in the footnotes to the Introduction.

GENERAL BOOKS ON GREEK TRAGEDY

Pat Easterling (ed.), *The Cambridge Companion to Greek Tragedy* (Cambridge, 1987); Simon Goldhill, *Reading Greek Tragedy* (Cambridge, 1986); Rush Rehm, *Greek Tragic Theatre* (London, 1992); Charles Segal, *Interpreting Greek Tragedy: Myth, Poetry, Text* (Ithaca, NY, 1986); Oliver Taplin, *Greek Tragedy in Action* (London, 1978); John J. Winkler and F. I. Zietlin (eds.), *Nothing to do with Dionysos? Athenian Drama in its Social Context* (Princeton, 1990).

GENERAL BOOKS ON EURIPIDES

P. Burian (ed.), *New Directions in Euripidean Criticism* (Durham, NC, 1985); Christopher Collard, *Euripides* (Greece & Rome New Surveys in the Classics 24; Oxford, 1981); D. J. Conacher, *Euripidean Drama* (Toronto, 1967); *Euripide* (Entretiens sur l'antiquité classique, 6; Fondation Hardt, Geneva, 1960); H. P. Foley, *Ritual Irony: Poetry and Sacrifice in Euripides* (Ithaca, 1985); G. M. Grube, *The Drama of Euripides* (2nd edn., London, 1962); M. Halleran, *Stagecraft in Euripides* (London, 1985); E. Segal (ed.), *Euripides: A Collection of Critical Essays* (Englewood Cliffs, 1968); P. Vellacott, *Ironic Drama: A Study of Euripides' Method and Meaning* (Cambridge, 1976); C. H. Whitman, *Euripides and the Full Circle of Myth* (Cambridge, Mass., 1974).

EURIPIDES' LIFE AND BIOGRAPHIES

Hans-Ulrich Gösswein, *Die Briefe des Euripides* (Meisenheim am Glan, 1975); J. Gregory, *Euripides and the Instruction of the Athenians* (Ann Arbor, 1991); P. T. Stevens, 'Euripides and the Athenians', *JHS* 76 (1956), 87–94; M. R. Lefkowitz, *The Lives of the Greek Poets* (London, 1981), 88–104, 163–9; R. E. Wycherley, 'Aristophanes and Euripides', *G&R* 15 (1946), 98–107.

OPINIONS AND INTERPRETATIONS

R. B. Appleton, *Euripides the Idealist* (London, 1927); E. Delebecque, *Euripide et la guerre du Péloponnèse* (Paris, 1951); V. di Benedetto, *Euripide: teatro e societa* (Turin, 1971); Robert Eisner, 'Euripides' Use of Myth', *Arethusa*, 12 (1979), 153–74; E. R. Dodds, 'Euripides the Irrationalist', *CR* 43 (1929), 97–104; H. Reich, 'Euripides, der Mystiker', in *Festschrift zu C. F. Lehmann-Haupts sechzigsten Geburtstage* (Vienna, 1921), 89–93; K. Reinhardt, 'Die Sinneskrise bei Euripides', *Eranos*, 26 (1957), 279–317; W. Sale, *Existentialism and Euripides* (Victoria, 1977); A. W. Verrall, *Euripides the Rationalist* (Cambridge, 1895).

RECEPTION OF EURIPIDES

Stuart Gillespie, *The Poets on the Classics* (London, 1988), 90–4; K. Mackinnon, *Greek Tragedy into Film* (London, 1986); Martin Mueller, *Children of Oedipus and Other Essays on the Imitation of Greek Tragedy 1550–1800* (Toronto, 1980), 46–63; James C. Clauss and Sarah Iles Johnston (eds.) *Medea: Essays on Medea in Myth, Literature, Philosophy, and Art* (Princeton, 1997).

VISUAL ARTS

Vase-paintings illustrating scenes from Euripides are collected in A. D. Trendall and T. B. L. Webster, *Illustrations of Greek Drama* (London, 1971), 72–105, and supplemented in the articles under the names of each important character (e.g. 'Medea') in the multi-volume ongoing *Lexicon Iconographicum Mythologiae Classicae* (Zurich, 1984–?). See also Oliver Taplin, 'The Pictorial Record', in Easterling, *Cambridge Companion*; Kurt Weitzmann, 'Euripides Scenes in Byzantine Art', *Hesperia*, 18 (1949), 159–210.

PRODUCTION AND PERFORMANCE CONTEXT

Giovanni Comotti, *Music in Greek and Roman Culture* (Eng. trans., Baltimore, 1989), 32–41; E. Csapo and W. J. Slater, *The Context of Ancient Drama* (Ann Arbor, 1995), 79–101; John Gould, 'Tragedy in Performance', in B. Knox and P. E. Easterling (eds.), *The Cambridge History of Classical Literature*, i (Cambridge, 1985), 258–81; S. Goldhill, 'The Great Dionysia and Civic Ideology', in J. Winkler and F. I. Zeitlin (eds.), *Nothing to do with Dionysos?*

Athenian Drama in its Social Context (Princeton, 1990), 97–129; Nicolaos C. Hourmouziades, *Production and Imagination in Euripides: Form and Function of the Scenic Space* (Athens, 1965); Maarit Kaimio, *Physical Contact in Greek Tragedy* (Helsinki, 1988); A. Pickard-Cambridge, *The Dramatic Festivals of Athens*, 3rd edn., rev. by J. Gould and D. M. Lewis (Oxford, 1988); Erika Simon, *The Ancient Theater* (London, 1982); Oliver Taplin, 'Did Greek Dramatists Write Stage Instructions?', *PCPS* 23 (1977), 121–32.

On satyr drama, see Pat Easterling, 'A Show for Dionysos', in Easterling, *Cambridge Companion*; Richard Seaford (ed.), *Euripides' Cyclops* (Oxford, 1984), 1–45.

SOCIAL AND HISTORICAL CONTEXT

J. K. Davies, *Democracy and Classical Greece* (Glasgow, 1978), 63–128, and 'Athenian Citizenship: The Descent Group and the Alternatives', *Classical Journal*, 73 (1977–8), 105–21; Anton Powell, *Athens and Sparta: Constructing Greek Political and Social History from 478 BC* (London, 1988).

The introduction to J. Blok and H. Mason (eds.), *Sexual Asymmetry: Studies in Ancient Society* (Amsterdam, 1987), 1–57; D. Cohen, *Law, Sexuality, and Society: The Enforcement of Morals in Classical Athens* (Cambridge, 1991); John Gould, 'Law, Custom, and Myth: Aspects of the Social Position of Women in Classical Athens', *JHS* 100 (1980), 38–59; Virginia Hunter, *Policing Athens* (Princeton, 1994), 9–42; R. Just, *Women in Athenian Law and Life* (London/New York, 1989).

SPECIFIC ASPECTS

Rachel Aélion, *Euripide. Héritier d'Eschyle* (2 vols.; Paris, 1983); W. G. Arnott, 'Euripides and the Unexpected', *G&R* 20 (1973), 49–63; Richard Hamilton, 'Prologue, Prophecy and Plot in Four Plays of Euripides', *AJP* 99 (1978), 277–302, and 'Euripidean Priests', *HSCP* 89 (1985), 53–73; Bernd Seidensticker, 'Tragic Dialectic in Euripidean Tragedy', in M. S. Silk (ed.), *Tragedy and the Tragic: Greek Theatre and Beyond* (Oxford, 1996), 377–96; Sophie Trenkner, *The Greek Novella in the Classical Period* (Cambridge, 1958), 31–78; R. P. Winnington-Ingram, 'Euripides: *poiētēs sophos*', *Arethusa*, 2 (1969), 127–42.

For the lost plays of Euripides, see C. Collard, M. J. Cropp, and K. H. Lee (eds.), *Euripides: Selected Fragmentary Plays*, i (Warminster, 1995), 53–78; T. B. L. Webster, *The Tragedies of Euripides* (London, 1967).

On slaves, see K. Synodinou, *On the Concept of Slavery in Euripides* (Eng. trans.; Ioannina, 1977); E. Hall, 'The Sociology of Athenian Tragedy', in Easterling, *Cambridge Companion*; D. P. Stanley-Porter, 'Mute Actors in the Tragedies of Euripides', *BICS* 20 (1973), 68–93. On children, see G. Sifakis, 'Children in Greek Tragedy', *BICS* 26 (1979), 67–80. For women, see H. Foley, 'The Conception of Women in Athenian Drama', in H. P. Foley (ed.), *Reflections of Women in Antiquity* (London, 1981), 127–67; Ruth Herder, *Die Frauenrolle bei Euripides* (Stuttgart, 1993); Nicole Loraux, *Tragic Ways of Killing a Woman* (Eng. trans., Cambridge, Mass., 1987); Richard Seaford, 'The Structural Problems of Marriage in Euripides', in A. Powell (ed.), *Euripides, Women and Sexuality* (London, 1990), 151–76; Nancy Sorkin Rabinowitz, *Anxiety Veiled: Euripides and the Traffic in Women* (Ithaca, NY, 1993), 155.

For religion, see M. R. Lefkowitz, 'Was Euripides an Atheist?', *Studi italiani di filologia classica*, 5 (1987), 149–65; J. D. Mikalson, *Honor thy Gods: Popular Religion in Greek Tragedy* (Chapel Hill, NY, 1981); Harvey Yunis, *A New Creed: Fundamental Religious Beliefs in the Athenian Polis and Euripidean Drama* (Hypomnemata 91; Göttingen, 1988). On supplication scenes, see J. Gould, 'Hiketeia', *JHS* 93 (1973), 74–103.

On the philosophical and intellectual background, see J. H. Finley, 'Euripides and Thucydides', in *Three Essays on Thucydides* (Cambridge, Mass., 1967); S. Goldhill, *Reading Greek Tragedy* (Cambridge, 1986), 222–43; G. B. Kerferd, *The Sophistic Movement* (Cambridge, 1981); W. Nestle, *Untersuchungen über die philosophischen Quellen des Euripides* (*Philologus* suppl. 8.4 (1901), 557–655), and *Euripides: Der Dichter der griechischen Aufklärung* (Stuttgart, 1901); F. Solmsen, *Intellectual Experiments of the Greek Enlightenment* (Princeton, 1975).

On rhetoric, see V. Bers, 'Tragedy and Rhetoric', in I. Worthington (ed.), *Greek Rhetoric in Action* (London, 1994), 176–95; Richard Buxton, *Persuasion in Greek Tragedy* (Cambridge, 1982); C. Collard, 'Formal Debates in Euripidean Drama', *G&R* 22 (1975) in M. Lloyd, *The Agon in Euripides* (Oxford, 1992); D. J. Conacher, 'Rhetoric and Relevance in Euripidean Drama', *AJP* 102

(1981), 3–25; E. Hall, 'Lawcourt Dramas: The Power of Performance in Greek Forensic Oratory', *BICS* 40 (1995), 39–58.

On speech, style, and imagery, see Shirley Barlow, *The Imagery of Euripides* (London, 1971); I. J. F. de Jong, *Narrative in Drama: The Art of the Euripidean Messenger-Speech* (Leiden, 1991); P. T. Stevens, *Colloquial Expressions in Euripides* (Wiesbaden, 1976); Ernst Schwinge, *Die Verwendung der Stichomythie in den Dramen des Euripides* (Heidelberg, 1968).

INDIVIDUAL PLAYS

Medea

Commentaries: D. L. Page (ed.), *Euripides' Medea* (Oxford, 1938).

Studies: E. Bongie, 'Heroic Elements in the *Medea* of Euripides', *TAPA* 107 (1977), 27–56; Anne Burnett, 'Medea and the Tragedy of Revenge', *CP* 68 (1973), 1–24; T. V. Buttrey, 'Accident and Design in Euripides' *Medea*', *AJP* 79 (1958), 1–17; R. Friedrich, 'Medea *apolis*: On Euripides' Dramatization of the Crisis of the Polis', in Alan H. Sommerstein, S. Halliwell, J. Henderson, and B. Zimmermann (eds.), *Tragedy, Comedy and the Polis* (Bari, 1993), 219–39; David Kovacs, 'On Medea's Great Monologue', *CQ* 36 (1986), 343–52, and 'Zeus in Euripides' *Medea*', *AJP* 114 (1993), 45–70; R. B. Palmer, 'An Apology for Jason: A Study of Euripides' *Medea*', *CJ* 53 (1957), 49–55; Pietro Pucci, *The Violence of Pity in Euripides' Medea* (Ithaca, NY, 1980); K. J. Reckford, 'Medea's First Exit', *TAPA* 99 (1968), 329–59; Seth L. Schein, '*Philia* in Euripides' *Medea*', in M. Griffith and D. J. Mastronarde (eds.), *Cabinet of the Muses: Essays on Classical and Comparative Literature in Honor of Thomas G. Rosenmeyer* (Atlanta, Ga., 1990), 57–73; Margaret Williamson, 'A Woman's Place in Euripides' *Medea*', in A. Powell (ed.), *Euripides, Women and Sexuality* (London, 1990), 16–31.

Hippolytus

Commentaries: W. S. Barrett (ed.), *Euripides' Hippolytus* (Oxford, 1964); Michael R. Halleran, *Hippolytus* (Warminster, 1995).

Studies: George E. Dimock, 'Euripides' *Hippolytus* or Virtue Rewarded', *YCS* 25 (1977), 239–58; Barbara Goff, *The Noose of Words* (Cambridge, 1990); M. Halleran, '*Gamos* and Destruction in

Euripides' *Hippolytus*', *TAPA* 121 (1991), 109–21; Bernard Knox, 'The *Hippolytus* of Euripides', *Word and Action* (Baltimore, 1979), 205–30 (first published in 1952), and '*Hippolytus*: A Study in Causation', *Euripide* (Entretiens sur l'antiquité classique, 6; Fondation Hardt, Geneva, 1960), 171–91; David Kovacs, 'Shame, Pleasure, and Honor in Phaedra's Great Speech', *AJP* 101 (1980), 287–303; C. Luschnig, *Time Holds the Mirror: A Study of Knowledge in Euripides' Hippolytus* (*Mnemosyne* suppl. 102, Leiden, 1988); K. J. Reckford, 'Phaethon, Hippolytus, Aphrodite', *TAPA* 103 (1972), 405–32, and 'Phaedra and Pasiphaë: The Pull Backward', *TAPA* 104 (1974), 307–28; C. P. Segal, 'Shame and Purity in Euripides' *Hippolytus*', *Hermes* 98 (1970), 278–9, and 'The Tragedy of the *Hippolytus*: The Waters of Ocean and the Untouched Meadow', *HSCP* 70 (1965), 117–69; Wesley D. Smith, 'Staging in the Central Scene of the *Hippolytus*', *TAPA* 91 (1960), 62–77; F. Solmsen, 'Bad Shame and Related Problems in Phaedra's Speech', *Hermes* 101 (1973), 420–5.

Electra

Commentaries: J. D. Denniston (ed.), *Euripides' Electra* (Oxford, 1939); M. J. Cropp (ed.), *Euripides' Electra* (Warminster, 1988).

Studies: G. W. Bond, 'Euripides' Parody of Aeschylus', *Hermathena*, 118 (1974), 1–14; George Gellie, 'Tragedy and Euripides' *Electra*', *BICS* 28 (1981), 1–12; J. W. Halporn, 'The Skeptical Electra', *HSCP* 87 (1983), 101–18; N. Hammond, 'Spectacle and Parody in Euripides' Electra', *GRBS* 25 (1984), 373–87; D. Konstan, 'Philia in Euripides' Electra', *Philologus*, 129 (1985), 176–85; M. Kubo, 'The Norm of Myth: Euripides' Electra', *HSCP* 71 (1966), 15–31; M. Lloyd, 'Realism and Character in Euripides' Electra', *Phoenix*, 40 (1986), 1–19; K. Matthiessen, *Elektra, Taurische Iphigenie und Helena* (Hypomnemata, 4; Göttingen, 1964); M. J. O'Brien, 'Orestes and the Gorgon: Euripides' Electra', *AJP* 85 (1964), 13–39; Vincent J. Rosivach, 'The "Golden Lamb" Ode in Euripides' *Electra*', *CP* 73 (1978), 189–99; F. Solmsen, *Electra and Orestes: Three Recognition Scenes in Greek Tragedy* (Amsterdam, 1967); T. A. Tarkow, 'The Scar of Orestes: Observations on a Euripidean Innovation', *Rheinisches Museum*, 74 (1981), 143–53; G. B. Walsh, 'The First Stasimon of Euripides' Electra', *YCS* 25 (1977), 277–89.

Helen

Commentaries: A. M. Dale (ed.), *Euripides' Helen* (Oxford, 1967). Richard Kannicht (ed.), *Euripides. Helena* (Heidelberg, 1969).

Studies: Karin Alt, 'Zur Anagnorisis in der Helena', *Hermes*, 90 (1962), 6–24; Norman Austin, *Helen of Troy and her Shameless Phantom* (Ithaca, NY, 1994); A. Pippin Burnett, *Catastrophe Survived: Euripides' Plays of Mixed Reversal* (Oxford, 1971) and (as A. Pippin), 'Euripides' *Helen*: A Comedy of Ideas', *CP* 55 (1960), 151–63; D. Galeotti Papi, 'Victors and Sufferers in Euripides' Helen', *AJP* 108 (1987), 27–40; Helen Foley, '*Anodos* Dramas: Euripides' *Alcestis* and *Helen*', in R. Hexter and D. Selden (eds.), *Innovations of Antiquity* (London, 1992), 133–60; John Griffith, 'Some Thoughts on the *Helen* of Euripides', *JHS* 73 (1953), 36–41; E. Hall, 'The Archer Scene in Aristophanes' *Thesmophoriazusae*', *Philologus*, 133 (1989), 38–54; Bernard Knox, 'Euripidean Comedy', in *Word and Action* (s.v. *Hippolytus*), 250–74; D. Sansone, 'Theonoe and Theoclymenus', *SO* 60 (1985), 17–36; Friedrich Solmsen, '*Onoma* and *pragma* in Euripides' *Helen*', *CR* 48 (1934), 119–21; D. F. Sutton, 'Satyric Qualities in Euripides' *Iphigeneia in Tauris* and *Helen*', *RSC* 20 (1972), 312–30; C. W. Willink, 'Reunion Duo in Euripides' *Helen*', *CQ* 39 (1989), 45–69; C. Wolff, 'On Euripides' *Helen*', *HSCP* 77 (1973), 61–84.

A CHRONOLOGY OF EURIPIDES'
WORK AND TIMES

Dates of productions of extant plays (adapted from C. Collard, *Euripides* (Oxford, 1981), 2)

Dates in the history of Athens

		462 Radical democracy established in Athens
455	first production	
		448 Building of Parthenon begun
441	first prize (play unknown)	
438	*Alcestis*—second prize	
431	*Medea*—third prize	431 Outbreak of Peloponnesian War between Athens and Sparta
430–428	*Heraclidae*	430 Outbreak of plague in Athens
428	*Hippolytus* (revised from earlier production)—first prize	
?425	*Andromache*	
before 423	*Hecuba*	
?423	*Supplices*	
?before415	*Hercules Furens*	
before 415	*Electra*	
		416 Slaughter by the Athenians of the men of the island of Melos and the enslavement of its women and children
415	*Troades*—second prize	415 Disastrous Athenian exped- -413 ition to Sicily
before 412	*Iphigenia at Tauris*	
?before 412	*Ion*	
412	*Helen*	
?412	*Cyclops* (satyr play)	
411–408,		411 Oligarchic revolution in Athens
?409	*Phoenissae*—second prize	
408	*Orestes*	
after 406	*Iphigenia at Aulis* and *Bacchae*—first prize	
		404 Defeat of Athens by Sparta in the Peloponnesian War

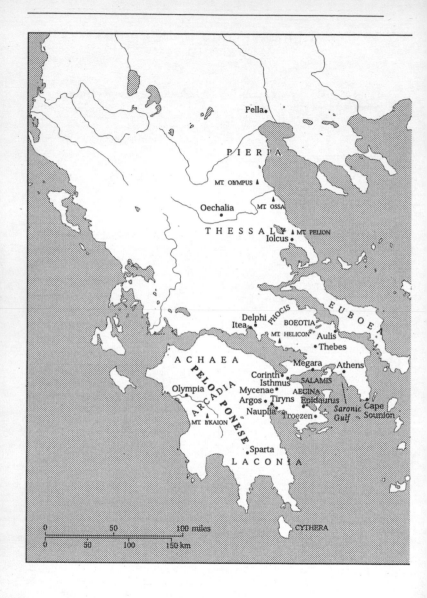

Map of the Greek World

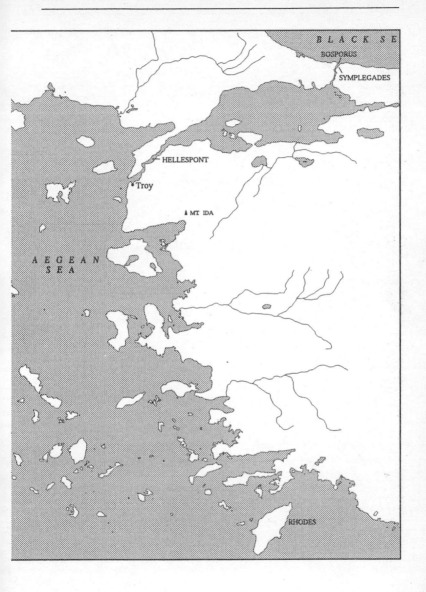

Euripides

Medea
and Other Plays

MEDEA

Characters

NURSE of Medea
TUTOR to Medea's children
MEDEA'S TWO CHILDREN
MEDEA
CREON, king of Corinth
JASON
AEGEUS, king of Athens
MESSENGER

CHORUS OF CORINTHIAN WOMEN

The action takes place outside MEDEA'S *house in Corinth. The* NURSE *comes out of the house.*

NURSE. How I wish that the Argo had not flown through the dark Clashing Rocks on its sea-journey to the Colchians' land—that the pine had never fallen, hewn amid the glens of Mount Pelion, and furnished oars for the hands of those heroic men who went to win the golden fleece for Pelias.* Then my mistress Medea would never have sailed to the towers of the land of Iolkos, her heart unhinged in her love for Jason, she would not have persuaded the daughters of Pelias to kill their father* and would not now be living with ₁₀ her husband and children* in this land of Corinth, gladdening the citizens to whose country she has come in her exile, a woman totally in accord with Jason himself. And this is the greatest security of all—when a wife is not in disharmony with her husband.

But now hatred has corroded everything and dearest love grows sick. Jason has betrayed his own children* and my mistress and beds down in a royal match.* He has married the daughter of Creon who rules this land. Unhappy Medea, ₂₀ thus dishonoured, cries out, 'His oaths!', invokes that weightiest pledge of his right hand, and calls the gods to witness how he has repaid her. She lies there eating nothing,

surrendering her body to her sorrows, pining away in tears
unceasingly since she saw that her husband had wronged
her. She will not look up, will not lift her face from the
ground, but listens to her friends as they give advice no more
than if she were a rock or a wave of the sea—save that   30
sometimes she turns away her pale, pale neck and bemoans
to herself her dear father and her country and the home
which she betrayed to come here with the man who now
holds her in dishonour. Schooled by misfortune, the poor
woman has learnt what it is to be parted from one's fatherland.

   But she hates her children* and feels no joy in seeing
them. I am afraid that she may be planning something we
do not expect. Her temperament is dangerous and will not
tolerate bad treatment. I know her, and I fear that she may
go silently into the house where her bed is laid and drive a   40
sharpened sword into their heart, or even that she may kill
the princess and the bridegroom and then meet some greater
disaster. For she is fearsome. No one who joins in conflict
with her will celebrate an easy victory.

   But here come the children. They've stopped running their
races.* They take no thought for their mother's sorrows. A
youngster's mind makes no habit of grieving.

         The TUTOR *enters with* MEDEA's *two children.**

TUTOR. Ancient servant of my mistress's house, why are you   50
   standing on your own like this at the gates, bewailing your
   sorrows to yourself? How comes it that Medea is willing to
   be left alone without you?
NURSE. Old attendant of the children of Jason, good slaves are
   sympathetic when their owners' fortunes fall out badly—
   their hearts too are affected. I have come to such a pitch of
   distress that a longing swept over me to come here and
   speak of my mistress's woes to the earth and sky.*
TUTOR. Has not the wretched woman yet ceased from her
   laments?
NURSE. You are in blissful ignorance. Her sorrows are at their   60
   outset, not yet halfway run.
TUTOR. Poor fool—if one may speak of one's mistress like that.
   She knows nothing of her more recent sorrows.

NURSE. What is it, old man? Don't refuse me an answer.

TUTOR. Nothing—I am sorry I said even that just now.

NURSE. I entreat you by your chin,* do not keep this from your fellow-slave. I'll cloak this matter in silence if I must.

TUTOR. When I came to the place where the old men sit playing draughts,* by the sacred waters of Peirene,* I eavesdropped and heard someone saying that Creon, the ruler of this country, is intending to drive these children with their mother from the land of Corinth. I do not know if this information is true. I hope it isn't. 70

NURSE. And will Jason allow his children to suffer this fate—despite his quarrel with their mother?

TUTOR. Old ties take second place to new ones, and that man is no friend to this house.

NURSE. It is all over with us then if, before we have seen out our first disaster, we must now shoulder this new one too.

TUTOR. But you must keep silence—not a word: it is not the right time for our mistress to know this. 80

NURSE. O children, do you hear how your father is behaving towards you? Curse him—but no, he is my master. Yet he stands plainly convicted of being a traitor to his friends.

TUTOR. But is anyone different? Are you only now realizing that everyone loves himself more than his neighbour, some justifiably, others simply to improve their situation—seeing that their father no longer loves these children because of his new marriage?*

NURSE. Go inside the house, children—all will be well. As far as possible keep these boys on their own and don't bring them near their mother in her depression. For I saw her eye just now glinting at them like a bull's* as if she meant to do something to them. And she will not give up her rage—I know it clearly—before she swoops down on someone. But may she choose her enemies for some mischief, not her friends. 90

MEDEA [*chants off-stage*]. Oh,
    how unhappy I am, how wretched my sufferings—
    Oh, woe is me, I wish I could die!

NURSE [*chants*].
    That's what I meant, dear children. Your mother

stirs her heart, stirs her rage.
Hurry quickly into the house   100
and do not approach near her sight,
but be on your guard
against her wild character, the hateful temper
of her wilful mind.
Go now, go quick as you can inside.
It is plain that soon she will make
the cloud of her laments which now begins to gather
flash forth as her passion grows.
Her heart is full of spirit, not easily to be soothed—
stung by these injuries, whatever will she do?   110
MEDEA [*chants*]. Aiai.
I have suffered in my wretchedness, suffered woes
which call for great laments. O accursed children
of a hateful mother, may you die
with your father, may the whole house fall in ruin.*
NURSE [*chants*]. Alas, I say. O, the cruel woman!
What share do you think your boys have
in their father's wrong-doing? Why hate them? Alas, chil-
    dren;
how I grieve for you in my fear that some suffering may
    await you.
Our royal masters have dangerous spirits* and, perhaps
    because
they are subject to little control while their power is great,   120
their moods veer violently.
To accustom oneself to live on equal terms with others
is preferable. For my part, as long as my old age is secure
I shall be happy if it is far from greatness.
For first, I say, the name of Moderation*
has a better ring than that of Greatness, and in experience
it proves by far the best for men—
while Excess brings no profit to mortals
and, when the god has grown angry with the house,
it pays the penalty of greater ruin.   130

        The CHORUS OF CORINTHIAN WOMEN *enters.**

CHORUS [*chants*]. I heard the voice, I heard the cry
  of the wretched woman from Colchis. Is she

not yet calm? Tell me, old woman.
For I heard her laments
inside her house through its double door.
And I do not rejoice, woman,
at the griefs of the house,
since it has come to be dear to me.

NURSE [*chants*]. There is no house. All that is over now.
A royal marriage keeps my master elsewhere,   140
while in her bedroom my mistress wastes away her life,
and her heart finds no comfort, none,
in the words of any of her friends.

MEDEA [*chants*]. Aiai!
Come, Zeus' bolt of lightning, and pierce my head!
What do I gain still by living?
Alas, alas! May I find rest in death,
leaving this hateful life.

CHORUS [*chants*]. O Zeus and Earth and Light,* did you hear
what a cry the wretched girl
sings out?   150
What love is this you have conceived, rash woman,
for the dread resting place?
Will you hurry on death's finality?
Do not pray for that.
If your husband is solemnizing his new marriage,
do not be cut with anger at him for that.
Zeus will be your advocate here.*
Do not wear yourself down so much in these laments for
    the partner of your bed.

MEDEA [*chants*]. O great Themis and Lady Artemis,*   160
do you see what I suffer, though I bound
my accursed husband with great oaths?
May I one day see him and his bride
pounded to nothing, house and all,
since they have dared to wrong me unprovoked.
O father, o city, how shamefully I left you,
I, the killer of my brother.*

NURSE [*chants*].
Do you hear what she says, how she cries out upon
Themis, goddess of prayers, and Zeus,
acknowledged the protector of oaths among mortals?   170

Certainly it will be by no trivial action
that my mistress will lay her anger to rest.
CHORUS [*chants*].
  I wish that she could come to see us
  and listen to the tone of our words
  as we offer them.*
  Perhaps she might then free her heart
  from its mood of dangerous passion.
  I hope that my wish to help
  will never fail my friends.
  Go and bring her here   180
  from the house. Say that we here are her friends.
  Hurry before she harms those inside.
  This her grief has a terrible momentum.
NURSE [*chants*]. I shall do so. But in my fear I doubt
  if I can persuade my mistress.
  Still, I shall grant you this difficult favour.
  Yet she darts on her servants
  the wild glance of a lioness with young*
  whenever any of them goes near to say something.
  You would not be wrong if you denounced our ancestors
  as fools and ignoramuses—   190
  they discovered songs for festivities, banquets and feasts
  to charm the ears and enhance our lives.
  But no one has discovered how music and songs
  with rich accompaniment of strings can put an end
  to men's hateful sorrows—which lead to deaths
  and dreadful misfortunes that overturn the house.
  And yet it would be a gain if men
  could cure these things with music.   200
  Why do they pointlessly tune their sounds
  to add a gloss of sumptuousness to the feast?*
  The abundance of the food which is there
  gives of itself delight to men.   [*The* NURSE *goes into the house.*
CHORUS [*chants*]. I heard the mournful sound of her laments,
  as she shouts out shrilly her painful sorrows,
  damning that traitor to her bed, her evil husband.
  Victim of injustice, she calls upon the gods,
  upon Themis, daughter of Zeus, goddess of oaths,
  who brought her to Greece across the sea   210

through the gloomy waters to the Hellespont,
the salty strait that locks the boundless Black Sea.

Enter MEDEA *from the house.*

MEDEA. Women of Corinth, I have come out of the house fearing
that you may find some fault with me. I know that many people are proud, some of them away from men's eyes, others
publicly so. But others win a bad reputation for idleness from
their quiet tenor of life. Men do not judge justly with their eyes
when, before they know for sure the true nature of a person's   220
heart, they hate on sight, though they have suffered no griev-
ance. A foreigner especially must fall in with the city's ways,
and I do not praise a citizen who in his obstinacy proves a
thorn in his fellows' flesh through ignorant perversity.*

But in my case, this thing which has struck me so unex-
pectedly, has broken my heart. I am lost, I have forfeited all
joy in living, my friends,* and I want to die. For well I know
that the man who was my everything has proved the vilest
of all—my husband.

Of everything that is alive and has a mind, we women are   230
the most wretched creatures. First of all, we have to buy a
husband with a vast outlay of money—we have to take a
master for our body. The latter is still more painful than the
former. And here lies the most critical issue—whether we
take a good husband or a bad. For divorce brings shame on
a woman's reputation and we cannot refuse a husband his
rights. We come to new ways of behaviour, to new customs—and, since we have learnt nothing of such matters at
home, we need prophetic powers to tell us specifically what   240
sort of husband we shall have to deal with. And if we manage this well and our husband lives with us and bears the
yoke of marriage lightly, then life is enviable. But if not,
death would be welcome.

As for a man, when he has had enough of life at home,
he can stop his heart's sickness by going out—to see one of
his friends or contemporaries. But we are forced to look to
one soul alone. Men say of us that we live a life free from
danger at home while they fight wars. How wrong they are!   250
I would rather stand three times in the battle line than bear
one child.*

However, the same reasoning does not apply to you and to me. You have this city, your father's house, a fulfilled life and the company of your friends, while I, a desolate woman without a city, shamefully injured by my husband who carried me as plunder from a foreign land, have no haven from this disaster, no mother, no brother, no relative at all.* So I shall ask you to grant me this favour and no more. If I can find some means, some scheme to take a just revenge for these evils on my husband and the man who gave his daughter to him and that daughter whom he married, I ask you to keep silence.* In all other respects a woman is full of fear and proves a coward at the sight of iron in the fight, but when she is wronged in her marriage bed, no creature has a mind more murderous.* 260

CHORUS. I shall do what you ask, since you will be right to exact vengeance from your husband,* Medea. I do not wonder that you grieve over what has happened.

Look, I see Creon now, king of this land, coming to tell you his new plans. 270

Enter CREON.

CREON. Medea, scowling there so enraged with your husband, I proclaim that you must go into exile from this land and take your children with you. No delay. There is no appeal against this command of mine, and I shall not go back home again before I cast you outside the borders of this land.*

MEDEA. Aiai! How wretched I am, ruined, utterly ruined. My enemies are sailing against me at top speed and there is no easy haven for me to land at and escape ruin.* My sufferings are bitter, but even so I shall ask you for what reason you are sending me from your land, Creon. 280

CREON. I am afraid of you—I mustn't beat about the bush— afraid that you may do my child an incurable hurt. There are many things I can point to which contribute to this. You are a clever woman,* skilled in many evil wiles. You are distressed at the breakdown of your marriage and the loss of your groom.* I hear that you are threatening—so they tell me—to take some action against the husband and his bride and me, who gave my daughter to him. And so I shall take precautions against these things before we fall victim to

them. It is better, woman, that I should be hated by you now 290
than weaken and repent too late.

MEDEA. Alas, alas. Not now for the first time but often, Creon,
my reputation has harmed me and done me great damage.
Any man who is sensible should not have his children
taught to be clever beyond the norm. For besides the indolence they get a name for, they also foment bitter animosity
from the citizens. If you present stupid people with a wisdom
that is new, you will strike them as useless and idiotic.*
Then again, if you are considered superior to those who 300
think they are subtly clever, you will be thought offensive in
the city. I myself do not escape this ill feeling. I am clever,
and so to some I am a butt for their odium, to others I seem
wrapped up in myself, to others quite the opposite, and then
again to others I appear anti-social—but I am not excessively
clever. And so you fear me. What harsh evil are you afraid
you may suffer at my hands? But it is not my way—have no
fear of me, Creon—to offend a royal family. After all, how
have you wronged me? You gave your daughter to the man 310
to whom your heart directed you. It is my husband that I
hate. In my opinion you were sensible to do what you did.
And now I do not grudge it you that your fortunes smile. Let
the marriage proceed—and good luck go with you all. But
allow me to live in this land. Wronged I may be, but I am
mastered by a stronger power and shall hold my peace.

CREON. Your words are soft to hear, but terror makes me
shrink—you may be plotting something evil in your heart.
And so I trust you that much less than before. A woman
who is quick-tempered—a man too for that matter—is eas- 320
ier to guard against than one who is clever and keeps quiet.
Leave my land with all possible speed. Stop this talk. My
decision is irrevocable and no craft of yours will enable you,
my enemy, to remain among us.

MEDEA. No, I beseech* you by your knees* and your newly
married daughter.

CREON. You are wasting your words. You will never persuade
me.

MEDEA. But will you drive me out and show no respect for my
prayers?

CREON. Yes, for I love my family rather more than I love you.

MEDEA. O fatherland, how intensely I recall you now!

CREON. I understand: my children apart, I love my country far
above all else.*

MEDEA. Alas, alas, how utterly disastrous is the effect of love   330
on men.

CREON. In my view, that depends on the circumstances.

MEDEA. Zeus, do not let the man guilty of these evils escape
your vigilance.

CREON. Off with you, you foolish woman, and trouble me no
more.

MEDEA. I suffer troubles—no troubles do I lack.

CREON. You will soon be pushed out forcibly by my attendants'
hands.

MEDEA. Not that, I beg you, but I beseech you, Creon . . .

CREON. It looks as if you're going to make a nuisance of yourself, woman.

MEDEA. I shall go into exile.* It's not this that I am supplicat-
ing you to grant me.

CREON. Why then are you being so aggressive and not simply
letting go of my hand?*

MEDEA. Allow me to stay this one day and to think out how I   340
can best go into exile and find a haven for my children, since
their father does not trouble himself to make any plans for
them. But pity them. You too are a father, you have children. You are likely to be sympathetic to mine. I take no
thought for my situation should we be exiled, but I weep for
them, the victims of ill fortune.

CREON. I am far from tyrannical by temperament and by showing mercy I have often come to grief. And now too I can see   350
that I am making a mistake, woman, but nevertheless you
will have what you ask for. But I tell you this, if the sun
god's light tomorrow shall behold you and your children
within the boundaries of this land, you shall die. This is my
final word—I mean what I say. But now, if you must
remain, stay for a single day, since you won't be able to do
any of the terrible things which frighten me.

[*Exit* CREON.

CHORUS [*chants*].
            Alas, alas, you pitiable woman.

wretched in your sufferings.
Wherever can you turn?
Where can you find a host to welcome you,
what home, what country 360
to shield you from disaster?
For the god has brought you, Medea,
to an overwhelming sea of woes.*

MEDEA. It has all ended in disaster—who can deny it? But it has not come to that—do not think that yet! There are still struggles for the newly-weds and no small troubles for the man who made the match. Do you think that I would ever have fawned on this man were there no profit in it or were it not part of my scheming? No, I wouldn't even have spo- 370 ken to him or touched him with my hands. But he has plummeted to such depths of stupidity* that, though it was possible for him to thwart my plots by throwing me out of the land, he has granted me this one day to stay here—a day in which I shall make three of my enemies corpses, the father, the daughter, and my husband.* Out of the many possible ways I have to kill them, I do not know what will be my first choice, my friends—should I set fire to the bridal house or go silently into the room where their bridal bed is 380 laid and drive a sharpened sword through their hearts? But there is one thing that is against me. If I am caught as I enter the room to carry out my plot, I shall be killed and give my enemies the last laugh. It is best to take the direct route—here I am the supreme expert—and kill them with poison.*

Well then, suppose them dead. What city will take me in? What host will give me refuge in a land secure from attack, in a home where I can be safe, and will protect Medea? There's no one. And so I'll stay here a little time longer to see if some secure place of refuge comes to light for me, and 390 I shall tread my path to this murder in scheming silence. But if misfortune is to drive me out, my plots frustrated, I shall myself take a sword, even if I am going to die, and I shall kill them—I shall proceed to an act of ruthless daring. For never, I swear by the mistress whom I revere above all gods and have chosen as my co-worker, Hecate,* who dwells in

a recess of my hearth, never shall any one of them grieve
my heart and smile to see it. Bitter and grim shall I make
their marriage for them, bitter the match and my exile from   400
this land.

But come. Spare nothing of your expertise, Medea, as you
plot and scheme. Go forward to your deed of terror. Now
comes the trial of your courage. You see what you are suffering? You must not bring laughter on yourself through
Jason's marriage into the house of that traitor Sisyphus,*
you the daughter of a good father and grandchild of the
Sun.* You have the skill—and what is more we are women,
supremely helpless when there's good to be done, supreme
in clever craftsmanship of all bad deeds.*

CHORUS [*sings*]. The waters of the holy rivers flow upstream*   410
and Justice and the universe are turned upside down.
It is men who plan trickery,
and trust in the gods no longer stands firm.
But what they say of a woman's life will change—
I shall be celebrated.
Honour is coming to the female sex.
Women will be free from the bitter tongue of slander.   420

And the Muses of yesteryear's poets will cease to sing
of my faithlessness. For Phoebus, lord of poetry,
did not grant to woman's spirit
the inspiration of lyre-song.*
Otherwise I would have rung out my answer,
singing against the male sex. The long expanse of time
has much to tell of our side, yes,
but much to tell of men as well.   430

You sailed from your father's house
with frenzy in your heart, passing through
the sea's twin rocks. You live in a foreign land,
you have lost your marriage bed, you have no husband,
poor woman, and are being driven from the land,
an exile without honour.

The spell of reverence for oaths is no more, no longer
does reverence abide in great Hellas—it has flown   440

up to the skies. You, wretched Medea, have no father's
  house
to seek as a refuge from your toils.
Another royal lady has displaced you as wife
and now rules in the house.

Enter JASON.

JASON. I have noticed many times before, not only now,* how
  harsh passions lead to impossible deeds. After all, if you had
  borne the decisions of people who are stronger than you
  with a good grace, it would have been possible for you to
  stay in this land and in this house. As it is, because you   450
  pointlessly insisted on having your say, you will be banished. This doesn't matter to me. As far as I personally am
  concerned, you can go on for ever saying that Jason is an
  utter scoundrel. But, as for what you have said against the
  royal family, you should consider it all gain that you are
  being punished simply with exile. For my part, when their
  majesties' passions were roused, I always did my best to
  calm them and I wanted you to stay. But you would not
  moderate your foolish behaviour, and always spoke badly of
  them. And so you will be banished from the land. But nevertheless, even after this, I have not abandoned my friends
  and have come here because I am thinking about your   460
  future, my lady, and how you and the children can avoid
  being banished without any money—or in want of anything
  at all. Exile brings many evils in its train. The fact is that,
  even if you hate me, I could never feel badly towards you.
MEDEA. Vilest of traitors—yes, I can at least call you that, the
  most cutting insult against a man who is no man—so you
  have come to us have you, bitterest of enemies to us, to the
  gods, to me and the whole human race? It is not boldness or
  courage when one hurts one's friends, then looks them in   470
  the face, but the greatest of all human sicknesses, shame-
  lessness. But you have done well to come, since I shall
  relieve my feelings by denouncing you and you will grieve
  to hear me.
  I shall begin to speak at the beginning. I saved you, as all
  those Greeks who embarked together on that same ship, the
  Argo, know, when you were sent to master the fire-breathing

bulls with the yoke and to sow the field of death.* I killed the
dragon which, ever unsleeping, guarded the all-golden fleece, 480
encircling it with many folding coils, and held up for you the
beacon of safety. I betrayed my father and my house and
came with you—more passionate than wise—to Iolkos under
Mount Pelion, and I killed Pelias* at the hands of his own
children—the most grievous of all ways to die—and destroyed
their whole house. And though, vilest of men, you reaped
these benefits from me, you betrayed me, and made a new
marriage—and this though we have children, since if you 490
had still been without a child, it would have been pardonable
for you to desire this match. No more is there any trusting to
oaths, and I am at a loss to understand whether you think
that the gods you swore by then no longer rule or that men
now live by new standards of what is right—for well you
know that you have not kept your oaths to me. Alas for this
right hand which you often held, alas for these knees—
touched by an evil man in an empty gesture—how we have
missed our hopes.

Come now, I shall converse with you as if you were a
friend. Yet what benefit can I think I shall receive at your 500
hands?—but converse I shall nevertheless, for questions will
show up your vileness still further. Where can I turn now?
To my father's house? But I betrayed it, and my fatherland
too, when I followed you here. Or to the wretched daughters of Pelias? How warmly they would welcome me in their
house—I killed their father! For this is the situation: I have
earned the hatred of those dear to me at my home, and have
made enemies of those whom I should not have harmed by
doing you a favour. In recompense for all this, in the eyes of
many women of Greece you have made me happy indeed. 510
What a wonderful husband, what a trustworthy one, I,
wretched woman, have in you—if I am to be flung out of
the land into exile, bereft of friends, my children and myself
all, all alone—a fine reproach to the newly married man,
that his children and I who saved you should wander round
abegging.

O Zeus, why have you given men clear ways to recognize
what gold is counterfeit, but on the body put no stamp* by
which one should distinguish a bad man?

CHORUS. Passions are fierce and hard to cure when those close 520
   to each other join in strife.
JASON. I must, it seems, be no poor speaker, but escape the
   wearisome storm of your words, lady, like the trusty helmsman of a ship using the topmost edges of his sail.* Since you
   lay too great a stress on gratitude, I consider that it was
   Aphrodite* alone of gods and men who made safe my voyaging. You are a clever woman—but it would be invidious
   to spell out how Love forced you with his inescapable arrows 530
   to save me. But I shan't go into that in too much detail. You
   helped me and I'm pleased with the result. However by
   saving me you took more than you gave, as I shall tell you.
   First of all, you live in the land of Greece instead of a barbarian country, you understand the workings of justice and
   know what it is to live by rule of law and not at the whim
   of the mighty.* All Greeks saw that you were clever and you 540
   won a reputation. If you were living at the furthest limits of
   the earth, no one would have heard of you. I for my part
   would not want to have gold in my house or to sing a song
   more beautifully than Orpheus* if my good fortune did not
   become far-famed.
      That is what I have to say to you about my labours. After
   all, it was you who provoked this war of words. As for your
   reproaches against me over my royal marriage, I shall show
   you first of all that I am sensible to make this match, as well
   as demonstrating good sense and in addition proving a powerful friend to you and my children. [MEDEA *makes a gesture* 550
   of impatience.] No, keep quiet. When I moved here from the
   land of Iolkos, dragging with me many hopeless troubles,
   what happier godsend could I have found than to marry the
   king's daughter, poor exile that I was. It was not—and this
   is what really gets under your skin—that I hated sleeping
   with you,* or that I was overwhelmed with desire for my
   new bride, or that I was eager to outdo our family by having a larger one. I have enough children already and I find
   no fault with them. My object was—and this is the most
   important thing—that we should live well and not be in 560
   want, for I know that everyone steers well clear of a friend
   in need—and that I should bring up our children in a manner worthy of my house, and by producing brothers to my

children by you, I should place them all on a level footing, unite them into one family and be prosperous. Why should you want more children? And it is in my interests to benefit those alive now by those that are to be born.* Surely I have not planned this out badly? You would agree with me if the matter of sex were not provoking you. But you women have sunk so low that, when your sex life is going well, you think that you have everything, but then, if something goes wrong with regard to your bed, you consider the best and happiest circumstances utterly repugnant. The human race should produce children from some other source and a female sex should not exist. Then mankind would be free from every evil.* 570

CHORUS. Jason, what you have said is superficially convincing. But none the less, even if I shall speak against what you think, you seem to me to be acting unjustly by betraying your wife.

MEDEA. Truth to tell, I often view matters differently from many people. In my opinion an unjust man who is a clever speaker incurs the greatest retribution, since if he is confident that his tongue can gloss over injustice cleverly, he has the audacity to stop at nothing. And so he is not so very clever. This is the case with you too. Do not then make a show of generous behaviour towards me with your skilful speaking, for one word will lay you flat. If you had not been a bad man you should have talked me round before making this marriage— not done it without your loved ones' knowledge. 580

JASON. Yes, I would have had your full backing for this plan, I think, if I'd spoken of the marriage to you—since even now you cannot bring yourself to soften your heart's great rage. 590

MEDEA. It wasn't that which stopped you, but your marriage with a barbarian was proving a source of no glory for you as you faced old age.

JASON. Rest assured of this then—it was not for the sake of the woman that I made the royal marriage in which I live now. As I have said already, I wanted to keep you safe and produce royal offspring to be brothers and sisters to our children and thus defend our house.

MEDEA. I hope I never have a wealthy life which brings me sorrow or the kind of happiness which galls my heart.

JASON. You must change your wish, you know, and then you 600
will seem more sensible. You must never see what is to your
benefit as distressing to you or think that fortune is against
you when it smiles on you.

MEDEA. Go on insulting me. You have your escape route while
I shall go in desolate exile from this land.

JASON. You yourself made this choice. You have no one else to
blame.

MEDEA. What did I do to deserve it? Was it I who married and
betrayed you?

JASON. You uttered unholy curses against the royal family.

MEDEA. Yes, and I am a curse to your house too.

JASON. Enough—I shall not discuss these matters with you
any further. But, if you wish to receive any assistance from 610
my resources for the children or yourself in your exile, tell
me—for I am ready to give with unstinting hand, and to
send tokens of introduction* to guest-friends of mine who
will treat you well. And you will be foolish to refuse this
offer, woman. If you lay aside your rage, you will do better
for yourself.

MEDEA. We shall make no use of your guest-friends or accept
any favours from you—do not try to give us anything. A bad
man's gifts can bring no good.*

JASON. Well then, I call the gods to witness that I am willing 620
to give every help to you and the children. But you recoil
from what is good for you and in your obstinacy you drive
away your friends. This will simply add to your sufferings.

MEDEA. Off with you. As you linger here away from home,
desire of the girl you have just married overwhelms you. Go
on with your marriage. For perhaps—with god's help it will
be said—this will prove the kind of match which will bring
you tears.

[*JASON goes out.*

CHORUS [*sings*].
When love comes too violently to men,*
it gives them
no glory for moral virtue.
But if Cypris come in moderation, 630
no other goddess is so delightful.

Never, o mistress, may you anoint with desire
your golden bow's inescapable arrow and shoot it at me.

May temperance befriend me,
the gods' most lovely gift,
and may dread Cypris never madden my heart
with adulterous love   640
and attack me with quarrelsome anger
and insatiate feuding. May she give honour to unions free
    from war
and prove a sharp judge* of women's marriages.

O my fatherland, o my home,
may I never be without my city,
trudging on life's difficult path
of helplessness—
the most pitiful of sorrows.
Before that may I have done with this light of life
laid low by death, by death.   650
Of all miseries none is worse
than to lose one's native land.

We have seen this for ourselves. Not as a story
heard from others do I tell it but at first hand.
For, Medea, no city and none of your friends
will pity you as you suffer
the most terrible of sufferings.
If a man cannot unlock a pure heart   660
and respect his friends,
may he perish without reward.
He will never be a friend of mine.

Enter AEGEUS.*

AEGEUS. Medea, greetings. 'Greetings,' I say, because no one
    knows a better way than this to start a conversation with
    friends.

MEDEA. And greetings to you too, Aegeus, son of wise Pandion.
    From where have you come to reach this land of Corinth?

AEGEUS. I'm on my way back from the ancient oracle of
    Phoebus.*

MEDEA. Why did you set out to the navel of the earth* where
    the god sings his prophecies?

AEGEUS. I wanted to know how I could beget offspring.*

MEDEA. By the gods, have you led the whole of your life up till 670
now without children?

AEGEUS. I am childless by the stroke of some divine power.

MEDEA. Have you a wife or are you unmarried?

AEGEUS. I am not unmarried. I am paired with a wife.

MEDEA. What then did Phoebus say to you about children?

AEGEUS. His words were too clever for a mere man to interpret.

MEDEA. Is it right that I should know the god's response?

AEGEUS. Certainly—for a clever brain is certainly needed.

MEDEA. What was his oracle then? Tell me, if it is right for me
to hear.

AEGEUS. Not to unloose the wineskin's hanging foot . . .

MEDEA. Before you do what, or arrive at what land? 680

AEGEUS. Before I come again to the hearth of my fathers.*

MEDEA. What do you want that you have sailed to this country?

AEGEUS. There is a man called Pittheus, the king of the land of
Trozen.*

MEDEA. Yes, as they say, the son of Pelops, a most reverent man.

AEGEUS. I want to impart the oracle of the god to him.

MEDEA. Yes, for he is a clever man and experienced in such
matters.

AEGEUS. And he is the dearest to me of all my allies.

MEDEA. I wish you well and hope you meet with all that you
desire.

AEGEUS. But why are your eyes so dull and this your skin so
wasted?

MEDEA. Aegeus, I have the worst of all husbands. 690

AEGEUS. What are you saying? Tell me clearly what makes you
sad.

MEDEA. Jason wrongs me though I did him no harm.

AEGEUS. What has he done? Tell me more clearly.

MEDEA. He has a woman who supplants me* as mistress of his
house.

AEGEUS. Surely he has not been so brazen as to act in so
shameful a way?

MEDEA. Be assured of it—and we, his former friends, are now
dishonoured.

AEGEUS. Was he in love or couldn't he bear his relationship
with you?

MEDEA. Very much in love—he has proved a traitor to his dear ones.

AEGEUS. So let him go if, as you say, he is a bad man.

MEDEA. He conceived a passion to marry into the royal house. 700

AEGEUS. Who gave her to him? Tell me the whole story.

MEDEA. Creon, who rules over this land of Corinth.

AEGEUS. It is understandable that you are hurt.

MEDEA. It is all over with me. But it is not just that he is leaving me. I am being driven out of the country.

AEGEUS. By whom? Now you are telling me of yet another, fresh disaster.

MEDEA. Creon is driving me into exile from the land of Corinth.

AEGEUS. And does Jason consent? I do not approve of this either.

MEDEA. He says he doesn't, yet he is willing to endure it. But I beg you by this your beard and your knees*—now I am 710 your suppliant—pity, pity me in my wretchedness and do not look on as I go into desolate exile, but receive me in your country at the hearth of your palace. So may your desire for children with the gods' help find fulfilment and may you come to death a happy man. You do not know what a godsend you have found here in me. I shall put an end to your childlessness—through me you will beget children. I know the medicines for this.

AEGEUS. For many reasons, lady, I am eager to grant you this 720 favour, first because of the gods, then of the children whose birth you promise me—for in this matter I am totally at a loss. This is how I see things. If you come to my country, I shall try to protect you as I am in right bound to. However, this much I must state plainly in advance, lady: I shall not be willing to take you from this land. You must leave this country on your own initiative. But if you come to my palace yourself, you will stay there safe from harm and I shall not hand you over to anyone. I want to be without 730 blame in the eyes of my guests and my hosts alike.*

MEDEA. Excellent. But if I could have some pledge of this, I should be completely happy with your part in the affair.

AEGEUS. Don't you trust me? If it's not that, what makes you unhappy?

MEDEA. I trust you. But Creon and the house of Pelias hate me. If you are bound to me by oaths, you would not hand me

over to them if they tried to take me from the land. But if
our compact is simply one of words, not ratified with oaths
to the gods, you may perhaps listen to their overtures and
become their friend. My situation is weak while they have   740
all the wealth of a royal house.

AEGEUS. You have shown a great deal of caution about the
future in what you say. But if you think it a good idea, I do
not refuse to do this. It is indeed safer for me* to have some
pretext to offer your enemies, and your own situation will
be the more assured. Name your gods.

MEDEA. Swear by the land of the Earth and the Father of my
father, the Sun,* and each and every god in addition.

AEGEUS. To do or refuse to do what? Tell me.

MEDEA. Never to cast me out of your land yourself nor, if any   750
of my enemies wishes to take me, to hand me over willingly
as long as you live.

AEGEUS. I swear by the Earth and the Sun's bright light and all
the gods to abide by the words I hear you utter.

MEDEA. Enough. What are you to suffer if you do not abide by
this oath?

AEGEUS. Such fates as befall impious mortals.

MEDEA. Go on your way and good luck go with you. All is well
and I shall come to your city as quickly as possible—when
I have done what I intend to do and got what I want.

CHORUS [*chants*].
　　May Hermes, son of Maia, the god of travel,
　　bring you home and may you achieve the purpose   760
　　you are so eager to gain,
　　for in my judgement, Aegeus,
　　you have appeared a noble man.   [AEGEUS *goes out.*]

MEDEA. O Zeus and Justice, daughter of Zeus, and light of the
Sun,* now, my friends, I shall win a glorious victory over
my enemies. Now I am on the way. Now I can hope that my
enemies will pay a just price. For this man—in that dilemma
where we were foundering most—has appeared as a haven
to save my plans. To him I shall fasten my stern cable* by   770
going to Athens, city of Pallas.

　　Now I shall tell you all my plans. Don't expect to receive
my words with pleasure.* I shall send one of my servants to

Jason to ask him to come to see me. When he arrives I shall
speak soft words to him, saying that I too think these things
are good, that it is well that he has made this royal marriage
and betrayed me, that all is for the best, all has been well
thought out. I approve of the marriage he has made to the
princess by betraying me. And I shall ask him to let my chil-   780
dren stay. Not that I would leave my children in a hostile
country for my enemies to insult. No, my purpose is to kill
the king's daughter with trickery. For I shall send them
holding gifts in their hands, and bringing them to the bride
to win repeal from exile from this land—a delicate robe and
a golden garland. And if she takes these adornments and
puts them on her flesh, she will die horribly—as will anyone
who touches the girl, with such drugs shall I anoint the
gifts.

But that is enough of that. I cry out when I think what   790
kind of deed I must do afterwards. For I shall kill the children, my own ones.* Nobody is going to take them away
from me. My heart steeled to the unholiest of deeds, I shall
wreak havoc on the whole house of Jason and leave the land
in flight from the charge of murder, the bloody murder of
my beloved children.

Laughter from my enemies is not to be endured, my
friends. Come what may come! What do I have to gain by
living? I have no fatherland, no house, no refuge from
calamity. It was then that I made my mistake—when I left   800
my father's house, persuaded by the words of a Greek man
who with god's help will pay me the penalty. He will never
see his sons born of me alive again and he will have no son
by his newly wed bride, since that wretched creature must
die a wretched death from my drugs.

Let no one think of me as weak and submissive, a
cipher—but as a woman of a very different kind, dangerous
to my enemies and good to my friends.* Such people's lives   810
win the greatest renown.

CHORUS. Since you have shared these words with us and I
    wish both to help you and to support men's laws, I forbid
    you to do this.*

MEDEA. There is no other way. I can pardon you for saying this
    for you do not suffer cruelly as I do.

CHORUS. But will you bring yourself to kill the fruit of your
   womb, lady?
MEDEA. Yes, for this would be the best way to hurt my husband.
CHORUS. But you would become the most miserable of women.
MEDEA. On with it! Until the deed is done, all words are wasted.
   [to *the* NURSE] But now, go and bring Jason here. I employ 820
   you in all matters of trust. But say nothing of what I have
   determined on if you care about your mistress and are a true
   woman.

> [*The* NURSE *goes out.*

CHORUS [*sings*]. Descendants of Erechtheus, happy for so long,*
   children of the blessed gods,
   sprung from a holy and unconquered land,
   feeding your fill of most glorious knowledge, ever moving
   with easy grace under the brightest of skies,   830
   where they say that once the nine Muses,
   the sacred maidens of Pieria, gave birth to golden-haired
      Harmony—

and dwelling by the waters of the fair-flowing Cephisus,
which, as the story goes, Aphrodite drew
and breathed upon the land the gentle and sweet breath
of her breezes. And always, as she casts   840
fragrant garlands of roses on her hair,
the Loves escort her, the companions of Knowledge
and inspirers of all the arts.

How then shall the city
of sacred rivers or the land
which gives safe conduct to friends
receive you, the child-murderer,
the unholy one, and give you a home?   850
Think what it is to stab your children,
think what kind of killing you undertake.
Do not, we beg you by your knees
unreservedly, in every way,
do not kill your children.

Where will you find so bold a spirit
or such dreadful courage
for your heart and hand

as you bring them against your children?
And how, when you cast your eyes upon them,   860
will you hold fast to their fate of death
and not weep? When your boys
fall in supplication, you will not be able
to wet your hand in their blood
with unflinching heart.

Enter JASON.

JASON. I have come as you told me to. For the fact is that,
though you are my enemy, you will not fail to win this. I
shall listen to you. What new thing is it that you want from
me, lady?

MEDEA. Jason,* I beg you to pardon what I said before. It is
only reasonable that you should bear with my passionate   870
moods, since we have exchanged many acts of loving kindness. I have debated the matter with myself and have
reproached myself: 'What lunacy makes me so stubborn,
why do I bear ill will to those whose counsels are good, why
do I make myself hateful to the rulers of this land and to my
husband who is pursuing the course that is most advantageous to us in marrying a princess and producing brothers
for my children? Shall I not be rid of my anger? What is
wrong with me when the gods are providing well for me?   880
Do I not have children? Am I not aware that we are going
into exile from this land and need friends badly?'

I thought over these things and saw that I was being very
foolish and that my rage was needless. And so now I
applaud you. You seem to me to show good sense in making this marriage in addition to ours—and I seem idiotic. I
ought to be sharing in these plans and helping to bring them
to fulfilment, standing beside the marriage bed and taking
pleasure in waiting upon your bride.

But we are what we are—I won't call us evil—we   890
women. And so you should not be like us in our weaknesses
nor match folly with folly. I ask for your good will and admit
that I viewed the business wrongly before but now have
come to see it with better judgement. O children, children,
come here, leave the house. [*The* CHILDREN *enter with the
TUTOR.] Come out here and embrace your father and talk to

him with me. Be like your mother and as you greet him be
reconciled from your previous hatred towards one who loves
you. We have made peace—anger has given way. Take his
right hand.—Ah me! One of my hidden troubles comes to   900
my mind.—Children, will you live a long life and stretch
forth your loving arms at your father's grave? How quick I
am to weep, unhappy woman, and how full of fear! At last
I have brought our quarrel with your father to an end and
these my soft eyes fill with tears.*

CHORUS. A pale tear starts from my eyes too. There is trouble
enough now. Pray god it goes no further.

JASON. I approve of what you say, woman, and I find no fault
with your former attitude either. It is fair enough that one
of your sex, a woman, should fly into a passion with a hus-   910
band who traffics in contraband love.* But your heart now
follows a better course. You have taken your time, but you
have now come to a wiser view. This is the behaviour of a
sensible woman. And, as for you, my children, your father
has not been thoughtless but has furnished great hope of
safety if the gods so wish. I think that you will yet live to
prove the chief citizens of this land of Corinth with your
brothers-to-be. Only grow up. Your father and any of the
gods who is kindly will bring about the rest. I pray to see   920
you thriving as you reach the fullness of youth, triumphant
over my enemies.

But you, Medea, why do you bedew your eyes with pale
tears and turn away your ashen face? Aren't you glad to
hear what I have just said?*

MEDEA. It's nothing. I'm thinking about these children.

JASON. Have no fear then. I shall make all well for them.

MEDEA. I shall do as you say. I do not mistrust your words. But
a woman is a delicate creature, ever prone to tears.

JASON. Yes, but why do you cry so very much for these children?

MEDEA. I gave them birth, and when you prayed that they   930
should live, pity swept over me as I wondered whether your
prayer would be granted.

But as to the matters you have come here to discuss
with me, some of them we have dealt with, and now I shall
mention others. Since the royal family has decided to send me

from the land—and it is best for me, as I now well understand,
not to give annoyance to you and the lords of this country by
living here, for I appear to be an enemy to their house—I shall
leave the land as an exile, but you must beg Creon that our   940
children should not go into exile from this country so that
they can receive their education at your hands.

JASON. I do not know whether I am likely to persuade him, but
I must try.

MEDEA. At least bid your wife to entreat her father that the
children should not go into exile from this land.

JASON. Certainly, and, if she is like the rest of her sex, I think
I shall persuade her.*

MEDEA. I too shall give you assistance in this task. I shall send
the children to her bearing gifts which I know are the most
beautiful in the world by far, a delicate robe and a golden
garland. Let one of the servants bring the adornments here   950
as quickly as possible. She will win not one but countless
blessings—in you she has gained the best of men as her husband and she has received the adornments which once the
Sun, the father of my father, gave to his children. Take these
bridal gifts into your hands,* children, carry and bring them
to the royal bride, that happy woman. These are no con-
temptible gifts that she will receive.

JASON. Why, foolish woman, are you emptying your own
hands of these things? Do you really think that a royal   960
palace is in need of robes or of gold? Keep them, do not give
them away. If my wife values me at all, I am confident that
she will put me before mere possessions.

MEDEA. No! No! They say that gifts persuade even the gods.
Gold has more power with men than an infinity of words.
Hers is the fortune, hers the life god now exalts, she is young
and a princess. To save my children from exile I would give
up not only gold but my life.

Now, children, go into that rich house and supplicate
your father's new wife, my mistress, begging her that you   970
may not be exiled, and give her these adornments. For it is
vital that she takes these gifts into her hands. Go with all
speed. I pray that you succeed and return with good tidings
for your mother of what she longs to achieve.

[JASON *and the* TUTOR *go out with the* CHILDREN.

CHORUS [*sings*].
  No longer have I any hope now for the children's lives,
  no longer. Already they are going to their death.
  The bride will accept the golden headband,
  will accept, poor woman, the destruction it conceals.
  She herself with her own hands will put the ornament   980
  of Death around her golden hair.

  The loveliness and divine brightness of the robe
  and the golden garland will persuade her to put them on.
  Now she will adorn herself as a bride for the dead below.
  Such is the trap, such the deadly fate
  into which she, miserable creature, will fall.
  She will find no escape from ruin.

  And you, wretched man, both bridegroom   990
  and curse for your new royal family,
  without knowing it you are bringing destruction
  on your children's lives,
  bringing hateful death on your wife.
  Miserable man, how far you have strayed
  from the future you foresaw.

  I share with your grief, I grieve for your pain, unhappy
    mother of boys,
  you who will murder your own children
  to avenge your bridal bed
  which your husband abandoned,
  hurting you against all his oaths,   1000
  to live in marriage with another bedfellow.

      The TUTOR *enters with the* CHILDREN.

TUTOR. Mistress, these children, I tell you, are no longer to be
  exiled and the royal bride was delighted to take your gifts
  into her hands. There it is all peace for them.* But what's
  this? Why are you standing there with such a desperate look
  when things are going well for you? Why have you turned
  your face away? Aren't you glad to hear what I have just
  said?

MEDEA. Alas!

TUTOR. Your reaction is out of harmony with what I have told
  you.

MEDEA. Alas, I say again.

TUTOR. Can it be that I am announcing some misfortune without knowing it? Am I wrong to think I have brought you 1010
good news?

MEDEA. Your news is as it is. I find no fault with you.

TUTOR. But why are your eyes downcast, and why do you shed
these tears?

MEDEA. I cannot but weep, old man—the gods and I planned
all this, my evil plan.

TUTOR. Be of good cheer. One of these days your children will
bring you home.

MEDEA. I shall bring others to peace* before I, poor creature
that I am, come back.

TUTOR. You are not the only woman who has been separated
from her children. Since we are human, we must bear our
troubles lightly.

MEDEA. Yes, and I shall do so. But go into the house and 1020
get ready what the children need to see them through the
day.

[*The* TUTOR *goes into the house.*

O children, children, you have a city and a home. You can
leave me, your mother, in my misery and pass your whole
lives far away from me. And I shall go to another land as an
exile before I can reap my reward from you and see you
prosperous, before I can get ready the lustral water and deck
the marriage bed at your weddings and adorn your wife and
hold up the torches. O, what misery my wilfulness is bringing me! It was in vain then, my children, that I nursed you,
in vain that I toiled for you and wore myself down with the 1030
strain, barren the births pangs that I endured. Many indeed
were the hopes that I, poor fool, placed in you once. I trusted
that you would care for me in my old age and that your
hands would wrap my body duly in my shroud when I died,
an enviable lot for mankind.* But now that sweet thought
is lost. Deprived of you, I shall lead a life full of grief and pain
for me. You will look upon your mother with loving eyes no
longer when your way of life has been changed.

Alas! Alas! Why do you look at me like this, my children? 1040
Why do you smile this final smile of all? Aiai, what can I do?
My heart's steel shattered, women, when I saw my chil-

dren's bright eyes. I could never do the deed. Goodbye to my former plans. I shall take my children from the land. Why should I, as I seek to pain their father through their sufferings, win twice as much agony for myself? I will not do it. Goodbye to my plans.

But what is wrong with me? Do I want to make myself ridiculous by letting my enemies go unpunished? I must face 1050 the deed. Shame on my cowardice in even letting my mind dally with these weak thoughts. Go into the house, children. Those for whom it is not right to be present at my sacrifice— that is a matter for them.* My hand will not weaken.

Ah, Ah, do not, my heart, do not do this.* Let them be, poor heart—spare the children. Alive with us in Athens, they will make you happy. By the avenging fiends below in Hades, it will never come to pass that I leave my children for 1060 my enemies to insult. There's no alternative—they must die.* And since they must, I who gave them birth shall kill them. In any case, the thing is done and the princess will not escape. Even now the garland is on her head, in the robe the royal bride is dying, I know it well. But I shall start on the cruellest of journeys and I shall send these children on one that's crueller still. And so I wish to speak to them.

Give your right hands, children, give them to your mother 1070 to kiss. O dearest of hands, dearest of lips to me, o children, so noble in appearance and so beautiful, may you find joy— but elsewhere.* Your father took away your chance of happiness here. O the sweet pressure of my children's embraces, o the softness of your skin and the delicious fragrance of your breath. Away with you; go! [*The* CHILDREN *go out.*] I can no longer look upon you but I am overwhelmed by the evils which surround me. And I know what evil deeds I am about to do, but my fury against Jason is stronger than my counsels of softness, and it is fury that leads to the greatest evils 1080 for mankind.*

CHORUS [*chants*]. Often before now I have traced
        subtler thoughts and confronted
        greater dilemmas than the female sex
        ought to explore.*
        But I found a way, for we too have a muse

which journeys with us to give us wisdom,
but not with all of us—small is the number of women
(perhaps you could find one among many)
who are not strangers to the muse.
And I say that those of mortals who have not had children* 1090
and have no knowledge of this, none at all,
win greater happiness
than those who are parents.
The childless, who have not discovered
whether children prove in the end a delight
or a sorrow for men—for they have no experience of
    them—,
are freed from many troubles.
But as for those in whose homes sweet children are born,
I see them in a state of ceaseless torment as they anx- 1100
    iously wonder
first how they can bring them up well
and in what way they can leave a means of support
for their children.
And then besides this, it is unclear
whether they are toiling for worthless children
or for good ones.
And now I shall tell one trouble, the worst of all,
which is common to all mortals.
For suppose they have found sufficient sustenance,
and their children have grown up to the fullness of youth,
and they have proved to be good.
If their fortune falls out like that, Death has gone   1110
to Hades, taking with him the children's bodies.
How then can it profit a man that,
on top of all his other griefs, the gods
should afflict him with this, the most painful grief of all,
as a price for the blessings of his children?

MEDEA. My friends, I have long been waiting to find out what
has happened. I have been waiting on Fortune to find out
how events in the palace will turn out. And now I see here
one of Jason's attendants on his way. His panting breath
shows that he has a fresh disaster to announce.   1120

The MESSENGER *enters.*

MESSENGER. Medea, unholy author of a dreadful deed, take
flight, take flight, by land or sea. Use any means of transport
you can find.*

MEDEA. What has happened to make me flee?

MESSENGER. The princess has just died—and her father
Creon—from your poisons.

MEDEA. What glorious news you bring! Henceforth I shall
number you among my benefactors and friends.

MESSENGER. What are you saying? Are you in your right mind,
not mad, lady, when you have wreaked this outrage upon 1130
the royal family and rejoice to hear of it? Do you feel no fear
at what it involves?

MEDEA. I do have something to say in answer to your words.
But take your time,* my friend, and tell me how they lost
their lives. For you will give me double the pleasure if I hear
that they have died the foulest of deaths.

MESSENGER. When your two children arrived with their father
and entered the bride's home, those of us servants who had
been distressed at your troubles were delighted. At once a
buzz of news spread through the house—you and your hus- 1140
band had made up your former quarrel. One of us kissed
your boys' hands, another their golden hair. As for myself,
my joy led me to follow the children into the women's quar-
ters. The mistress whom we now honour instead of you,
before she noticed your two sons, kept her eager eyes fixed
upon Jason. But then, when she saw the boys come in, she
put a veil over her eyes and turned away her pale cheek in
disgust. Your husband, however, tried to allay the girl's 1150
angry mood with these words: 'You must not be an enemy
to those dear to me. Lay aside your anger and turn your face
this way again. Look upon your husband's friends as your
own. Accept the gifts and beg your father to remit the sen-
tence of exile on these boys for my sake.' And when she saw
the adornments, she could not resist* but promised her husband all he asked, and before your boys and their father had
gone far from the house, she took the finely woven robe and
put it on and, placing the golden garland around her curls, 1160
she arranged her hair as she looked in a shining mirror,*
laughing at the lifeless picture of her body. And then she
stood up from her throne and walked through the house,

stepping delicately on her pale white feet, utterly thrilled by
the gifts, again and again standing on tiptoe to admire the
way the robe fell.

But what came next was a fearful sight to behold. She
changed colour and staggered back sideways, her limbs
trembling, and just managed to collapse on the throne, not 1170
fall to the ground. And one of the old maidservants, perhaps
thinking that the frenzy of Pan or some other god had come
upon her,* raised an ecstatic cry—but then she saw the
white foam coming from her lips, her eyes starting from
their sockets and her flesh drained of all its blood. Then she
changed her former cry to something very different—a great
howl. Immediately one servant rushed to her father's house,
another to the new husband to report the disaster that had
befallen the girl. The whole house resounded as everyone 1180
ran this way and that. There passed the time in which a
swift runner could have completed the final two-hundred-
yard stretch of the race track, and now she recovered the
use of her voice and sight, regaining consciousness, poor
woman, with a dreadful groan. For a double calamity was
advancing upon her. The golden garland set upon her head
was sending forth a wonder, a stream of all-consuming fire,
while the delicate robe, the gift of your children, was feeding on the wretched girl's pale flesh. Leaping from her 1190
throne, she fled, all on fire, shaking her hair and her head
now this way, now that, in her wish to throw off the garland. But the gold kept its hold firm and fast, and when she
shook her hair the fire blazed forth twice as much as before.
Overcome by calamity she fell to the ground, so misshapen
that only a loving parent would find it easy to recognize her.
Her eyes had lost their usual clear and settled look, her face
its loveliness. Blood mingled with fire dripped from the top
of her head, her flesh melted from her bones like teardrops 1200
of resin as your poisons gnawed invisibly. It was a fearful
sight.

Everyone was afraid to touch the corpse. We had what
had happened to teach us. But her poor father, still unaware
of the calamity, suddenly came into the house and fell upon
the corpse. At once he cried out in his grief, threw his hands
round her and kissed her as he spoke these words. 'Poor

child, which of the gods has destroyed you and done such dishonour to your wedding day? Which of them has taken you away from your old father, now more dead than alive? Ah me, let me die with you, my child.'* But when he had 1210 stopped his lamentations, and wished to raise his aged body, he stuck to the subtle robe as ivy clings to the shoots of the bay tree—and a terrible struggle ensued; for he wanted to lift his knee while she kept clinging to him. And if he pulled violently, he kept tearing his old flesh from his bones. But after a time the flame of his life was extinguished and the ill-fated man breathed out his spirit. No longer could he master catastrophe. They lie there corpses, the girl and her old 1220 father, near to each other, a calamity to welcome tears.

I shall say nothing of how this affects you. You will experience for yourself the penalty which will turn upon you. I have long thought that man's life is merely a shadow, and I should not fear to say that those who seem to be wise as they anxiously ponder their words of wisdom convict themselves of the greatest folly. For no man is ever truly happy. One may have better luck than another if wealth pours in—but that is not real happiness.   1230

CHORUS. It seems to be with justice that the god has clamped so many disasters upon Jason on this day. O daughter of Creon, you wretched girl, how we pity you in your catastrophe—for your marriage with Jason has brought you to the house of Hades.

MEDEA. My friends, I have now decided what to do—with all haste I shall kill my children and leave this country. I shall not delay and so surrender them to other, crueller hands to kill. There's no escape from it, none at all. They must die. 1240 And since they must, I who bore them, shall kill them. But come, my heart, arm yourself. Why do I delay to do the terrible but necessary crime? Come, my cruel hand, take the sword, take it, go forward to where life's pain begins.* Do not prove a coward, do not think how very much you love your children, how you gave them birth. Forget your feelings for them for this one brief day and then lament. For even if you will kill them, still they were born your dear chil- 1250 dren—and I am an ill-fated woman.

[*Exit* MEDEA.

CHORUS [*sings*]. O Earth and radiant brightness
  of the Sun,* look down, look on
  this accursed woman before she lays her murderous hands
  on her children and kills her own flesh and blood.
  For it was from your golden stock
  that she sprang, and now I fear that your divine blood
  may fall on the ground, spilt by a mortal.
  But, O Zeus-born light, hold her back,
  stop her, drive from the house
  this Fury,* made cruel and deadly by fiends.   1260

  Vain were your pangs in childbirth for your children, all
      for nothing,
  in vain, Medea, you bore children you loved,
  after you left the most unhospitable strait
  of the dark-blue Clashing Rocks, the Symplegades.
  You wretched woman, why has this anger fallen on you
  and oppressed your heart, and why does
  raging murder follow on murder?
  The pollution of blood shed on the ground from kin,
  I know, bears hard on mortals, and woes in answer fall
      from the gods
  on the house of the kin-slayers.   1270
CHILD [*off-stage*]. Help! Help!
CHORUS [*sings*]. Do you hear the children's cry, do you hear it?
  O woman, hard of heart, ill-fated!
CHILD A. Alas what am I to do? Where can I run to from my
  mother's hands?
CHILD B. I do not know, my dearest brother. This is our death.
CHORUS [*sings*].
  Should I go into the house? I think I should defend
  the children from death.
CHILD A. Yes, by the gods, defend us. We need your help.
CHILD B. How near we are now to the sword's snare!
CHORUS [*sings*]. Cruel woman, you must be stone
  or iron*—for you will kill your children,   1280
  the fruit your womb bore,
  bringing their doom on them with your own hand.

  I have heard of one woman of those of old,
  one who laid her hands on her dear children,

Ino,* who was driven mad by the gods,
when the wife of Zeus sent her wandering from her house.
The wretched woman flung herself into the sea
because of the impious murder of her children;
she stepped over a sea-cliff,
and killed herself, dying together with her two boys.
After that, what horror could surprise us? 1290
O love of women with its many troubles,
how vast a history of catastrophe
have you brought upon men!

Enter JASON

JASON. You women who are standing near this house, is Medea
who has done these terrible things, still inside this house or
has she fled away? She must surely hide herself below the
earth or fly with winged body into the deep heaven if she is
not to pay the penalty to the royal family. Does she really
believe that she can kill the rulers of the land and get away 1300
from this house scot-free? However, I'm not concerned about
her so much as the children. Those whom she harmed will
harm her—but it is my children's life that I have come to
save,* in case the relations of the dead do something to them
in vengeance for their mother's blasphemous act of murder.

CHORUS. Unhappy man, you do not know how far into catastrophe you have come, Jason. Otherwise you would not
have said these words.

JASON. What is it? Can she be wanting to kill me too?

CHORUS. Your children have died at their mother's hand.

JASON. Alas, what can you mean? Your words are death to 1310
me, woman.

CHORUS. You must believe that your children are no longer.

JASON. Where did she kill them? In or out of the house?

CHORUS. If you open the doors, you will see your children's
corpses.

JASON. Undo the bolts with all speed, attendants, release the
fastenings so that I can see a double disaster, those two dead
children—and take a just revenge on her.

MEDEA *appears above the palace in a chariot drawn by dragons.*
The CHILDREN'*s corpses are on the chariot.**

MEDEA. Why are you shaking these doors and trying to force
  them open as you search for the bodies and for me, the
  doer of the deed? You can cease your labours. If you have 1320
  need of me, speak if you wish, but you shall never lay a
  hand on me. Such is the chariot that the Sun, father of my
  father, has given me* to defend me against my enemies'
  hands.

JASON. You loathsome creature, hateful beyond all other
  women to the gods, to me and to the whole human race—
  you have had the ruthlessness to drive a sword into the children whom you bore. You have destroyed me and left me
  childless. You have done these things—and yet can you look
  upon the sun and earth,* you, cruel perpetrator of the most
  unholy of all deeds? My curse on you. My mind is clear now
  but it was not clear when I brought you from your home in 1330
  a barbarian land to a house in Greece, disaster that you are,
  traitor to your father and the land that nurtured you. The
  gods have launched on me the curse which should have
  punished you, swooping down on me. It was after killing
  your brother by your hearth* that you embarked on the
  Argo, that fair-prowed ship.* That was how you began, and
  then, after you had become my bride and borne me children,
  you killed them because our sex life was over. There is no
  Greek woman who could ever have brought herself to do 1340
  this—and yet I chose you before all of them as a fitting wife
  for me. A hateful marriage it proved and it has destroyed
  me. You are no woman but a lioness, more savage by nature
  than Etruscan Scylla.* But I could not wound you, however
  many insults I hurl at you, such is your brazen audacity.
  Away with you, you artist in obscenity, you polluted murderess of your children. All I can do is lament my evil destiny, for I shall reap no benefit from my new marriage, and
  I shall not have the children I begat and brought up to speak 1350
  to while they are still alive—for I have lost them.

MEDEA. I would have given a long-drawn-out answer in
  response to what you have said, did not father Zeus know
  how you have repaid me and what you have done. You
  were never going to shame our bed and lead a pleasant life
  and laugh at me—nor was the princess, or Creon, the man
  who made this marriage for you—he was not going to

throw me out of this land and get away with it. So now call
me a lioness even, if you want, and Scylla who took her
abode on the Etruscan rock. I have done what I had to—I 1360
have stung your heart.

JASON. And you too feel pain and you share in the catastrophe.*

MEDEA. You are right, but my sorrow is well repaid if you cannot laugh at me.

JASON. O children, what evil you met with in your mother!

MEDEA. My boys, how sick your father's baseness which
destroyed you!

JASON. But it was not my right hand that killed them.

MEDEA. No—it was your insulting arrogance and your new
marriage.

JASON. Did you really think my marriage a good enough reason to kill them?

MEDEA. Do you think that this is a small hurt for a woman?*

JASON. Not a woman who knows self-control. But to you it is
all the evil in the world.

MEDEA. These children are no more. This will hurt you. 1370

JASON. They live on, alas, as spirits of vengeance upon your life.

MEDEA. The gods know who began all this woe.

JASON. Yes, they know your detestable spirit.

MEDEA. Hate on. I loathe your bitter snarling.

JASON. Yes, and I loathe yours. But it is easy for us to part
company.

MEDEA. How? What shall I do? I too am eager to part.

JASON. Let me bury these bodies and lament them.

MEDEA. No, I will not, for I shall carry them to the precinct of
Hera, goddess of the Acropolis, and bury them with these
my hands—so that none of my enemies can tear up their 1380
tombs and make sport with their bodies. In this land of
Sisyphus* I shall institute a holy festival and sacred rites for
times to come in recompense for this impious murder.* I
myself shall go to the land of Erechtheus to live with Aegeus,
the son of Pandion. And you, you bad man, will—as befits
you—die a humiliating death, struck on the head by a frag-
ment of the Argo,* and see the bitter conclusion to your
marriage with me.

The rest of the play is chanted.

JASON. I pray that the Fury* roused by our children
  and Justice, the avenger of bloodshed, may destroy you.   1390
MEDEA. But which god or divine power listens to you,
  the oath-breaker, the treacherous host?*
JASON. Ah, ah, you foully polluted woman, murderer of your
      children!
MEDEA. Go to your house and bury your wife.
JASON. I am going. I have lost both my children too.
MEDEA. You are still a novice in grief. Wait till you grow old.*
JASON. O my dearest children.
MEDEA.   Dearest to their mother, not to you.
JASON. So why did you kill them?
MEDEA.   To cause you pain.
JASON. Alas, I long to kiss my children's dear lips,
  poor wretch that I am.*   1400
MEDEA. Now you want to speak to them and embrace them,
  though then you pushed them away.
JASON. In the gods' name, let me touch
  the soft skin of my children.
MEDEA. Never. Your words are wasted on the empty air.
JASON. Zeus, do you hear how I am being driven away
  and how I suffer as the victim
  of this foul lioness, the killer of her children?
  But I still lament my sorrow as much as my plight allows,
  as much as I am able, calling on the gods   1410
  to witness how you have killed my children for me
  and yet prevent me
  from touching their bodies with my hands,* or burying them.
  I wish I had never begot them
  to see them slaughtered by you.

               [MEDEA *flies off in her chariot.* JASON *goes out.*

CHORUS. Zeus on Olympus dispenses many things
  and the gods bring many things to pass against our expec-
      tation.
  What we thought would happen remains unfulfilled,
  while the god has found a way to accomplish the unex-
      pected.
  And that is what has happened here.*

                              [*The* CHORUS *goes out.*

HIPPOLYTUS

Characters

APHRODITE, goddess of love
HIPPOLYTUS, illegitimate son of Theseus
SERVANT of Hippolytus
NURSE of Phaedra
PHAEDRA, wife of Theseus and stepmother to Hippolytus
THESEUS, king of Athens and Trozen
Another SERVANT of Hippolytus
ÀRTEMIS, goddess of hunting

CHORUS OF SERVANTS OF HIPPOLYTUS
CHORUS OF WOMEN OF TROZEN

*Outside the royal palace in Trozen. On one side of the stage there
is a statue of Aphrodite, on the other one of Artemis. Enter
APHRODITE.**

APHRODITE. I am called Cypris,* a powerful goddess and not
without fame among mortals and in heaven. And of all who
dwell between the Black Sea and the bounds of Atlas* and
look on the light of the sun, I give precedence to those who
revere my power, but those who are arrogant towards me I
cast down. For this is characteristic of gods as well as mortals—they take pleasure in receiving honour from men.

Soon I shall show the truth of these words. Alone of all   10
the citizens of this land of Trozen, Hippolytus, the son of
Theseus, the child of the Amazon and pupil of revered
Pittheus,* says that I am the vilest of the gods. He spurns sex
and keeps clear of marriage. It is Artemis, sister of Phoebus
and daughter of Zeus, that he honours, holding her the
greatest of the gods. He spends all his time in the green
woods with the virgin goddess* as he empties the land of its
wild animals with his swift hounds—and it is no mere mortal that keeps him company. For that I bear him no ill will.   20
Why should I? But for his offences against me I shall in the
course of this day take revenge on Hippolytus. I have long

since started most of what is to be done—there is no need
for much exertion now.

For when he came once from Pittheus' house to Pandion's
land* to see the rites of the holy mysteries, Phaedra, the noble
wife of his father,* saw him and through my designing a terrible love seized her heart. And before she came to this country of Trozen she founded right by the rock of Pallas* a temple   30
of Cypris to look out over this land. She loved a love over the
sea and men in future times will call this the temple of Cypris
founded for Hippolytus. But then Theseus, in flight from the
pollution of the blood of the sons of Pallas,* left the land of
Cecrops,* consenting to a year's exile from his homeland, and
sailed to this country with his wife; and now the wretched
woman, groaning and maddened by the stings of love, is
dying without a word* and none of the household knows   40
what has made her sick. But her love must not end like this.
I shall reveal to Theseus what is happening* and it will all
come out. As for the young man who makes war on me, his
father will kill him, calling down one of the prayers which
Poseidon,* lord of the sea, gave to Theseus as a privilege:
three prayers in all he could pray to the god and find fulfilment. The other, Phaedra, must die—with her honour safe,*
but nevertheless die she must. I am determined to make my   50
enemy pay a penalty great enough to satisfy me—her catastrophe is a secondary consideration.

But I see the son of Theseus coming this way, exhausted
by his energetic hunting, and so I shall depart from this
place. A large and happy crowd of attendants follows him
and joins him in his song, honouring the goddess Artemis
with hymns. He does not know that the gates of Hades are
standing open and that the light of this day is the last that
he will ever see.*   [*Exit* APHRODITE.

Enter HIPPOLYTUS *and the* CHORUS OF SERVANTS *chanting.* HIPPOLYTUS
holds a garland of flowers. They go to the statue of Artemis.

HIPPOLYTUS [*chants*]. Follow me, follow,
        singing to heavenly Artemis,
    the daughter of Zeus, in whose protection we are.
HIPPOLYTUS and SERVANTS [*chant*]. Lady, lady most holy,   60
        child of Zeus,

greetings, I give you greetings, O Artemis,
daughter of Leto and of Zeus,
most beautiful of maidens by far,
you who dwell in the great heaven
in your noble father's hall,
in the house of Zeus, so rich in gold.
Greetings, o most beautiful,
most beautiful of the gods on Olympus.   70

HIPPOLYTUS. My mistress Artemis,* I bring you this woven garland which I have made for you from the virgin meadow
where no shepherd thinks it right to graze his flock, where
no scythe has ever come, but in the spring the bee flies
through its virgin greenery. Reverence tends it with water
from the rivers, so that those for whom virtue in all things
has not had its everlasting place assigned by teaching but by
nature can pick the flowers there—but it is not proper for   80
base men to do so. My dear mistress, receive this garland for
your golden hair from my reverent hand. For this privilege
belongs to me alone of mortals—I keep company with you,
I converse with you, hearing your voice but not seeing your
face. I pray that I may finish the race of my life as I began
it.*

*One of the SERVANTS approaches HIPPOLYTUS.**

SERVANT. My lord—it is right to call only the gods by the name
of master—would you be willing to listen to some good
advice from me?
HIPPOLYTUS. Certainly. If I weren't, I would look a fool.*   90
SERVANT. Well, do you know of the principle that has been
established among mortals?
HIPPOLYTUS. No I don't. Exactly what is your question about?
SERVANT. The principle that we must hate a proud and anti-
social attitude.
HIPPOLYTUS. It is a good principle. Proud men give annoyance
to their fellows.
SERVANT. And there is a charm to be found in an easy affability?
HIPPOLYTUS. Very much so, and one can profit in this way with
little effort.

SERVANT. And do you believe that this holds true of the gods as well?

HIPPOLYTUS. Certainly, if mortals live according to the same principles as the gods.

SERVANT. Then why do you not address a proud goddess?

HIPPOLYTUS. Which goddess? Be careful* you do not say some-   100
thing you will regret.

SERVANT. This goddess who stands by your door, Cypris.

HIPPOLYTUS. Since I am pure, I greet her from a distance.*

SERVANT. Yet she is proud and her fame is great among mortals.

HIPPOLYTUS. No god who uses the night to work her wonders finds favour with me.

SERVANT. My boy,* we must pay the gods their honours.

HIPPOLYTUS. We all have our likes both in gods and among men.

SERVANT. I only hope that it works out well for you, and that you get the common sense you need.

HIPPOLYTUS. Off with you, my servants, go into the house and see to your meal. When one comes back from the hunt, a   110
full table is a delight. And you must rub down the horses so that, after I have eaten my fill, I can yoke them to my chariot and get the exercise I need. As for your Cypris, I bid her a hearty farewell.*

The SERVANTS *and* HIPPOLYTUS *enter the house, but the old* SERVANT *stays behind.*

SERVANT. Because I must not follow the example of young men when they show such an attitude, I shall give worship to your image, mistress Cypris, with words that become a slave. You should forgive. If a man speaks foolishly of you in the spirited vehemence of youth, act as if you have not heard it. After all, the gods ought to be wiser than mortals.*   [*Exit*   120
SERVANT.

A CHORUS *of* WOMEN OF TROZEN *enters.*

CHORUS [*sings*].
There is a rock which they say drips water from the Ocean*
and shoots forth from the cliff face
a running stream for pitchers to draw.
And there a friend of mine.
washing crimson robes

in the water of the river,
was laying them down on the surface
of a rock warm from the generous sunlight. From there it
　　was
that the news about my mistress first reached me—　　　　130

that she keeps herself inside the house on a bed of sickness
worn down by distress,
and delicate fabrics shadow her blond head,
I hear that this is the third day
on which she has consumed no food
while she keeps her body pure from Demeter's grain,*
wishing in her secret trouble to bring her ship to shore
at the bitter journey's end of death.　　　　140

Are you wildly wandering, lady,
because Pan possesses you or Hecate
or the holy Corybantes
or the mountain mother?*
Are you wasting away from a sin which concerns Dictynna,*
mistress of many beasts—
have you failed
to pour altar offerings?
For that goddess wanders over the lagoon of the Mere
and over the sandbar, the sea's dry land
amid the eddies of the salt water.　　　　150

Or does some woman tend your husband,
the ruler of Erechtheus'* people, the son of noble fathers,*
tend him in her house
in a bed which you, his wife, cannot see?
Or has there sailed from Crete
to the harbour that gives to sailors the fairest welcome
some seafaring man
who brings news to the queen,
and is her heart gripped fast by grief for her sufferings
as she lies on her bed?　　　　160

A woman's nature is an awkward compound,
and often there dwells with it a grim and miserable help-
　　lessness
that goes with unreason and the pangs of childbirth.

Once this breeze swept through my womb,
but I called upon the heavenly goddess who eases labour,
Artemis, lady of arrows,*
and always, by the grace of the gods,
she comes to me and makes me enviable.

[*The* NURSE *enters with servants carrying* PHAEDRA *on a bed.*
But here in front of the doors is the old Nurse   170
carrying her mistress out of the palace.
A hateful storm cloud darkens on her brows.
My soul longs to learn whatever this can mean—
why has the queen's body been ravaged,
what has changed her colour?

NURSE [*chants*].

What ills we mortals suffer! How hateful are our sicknesses!
What should I do for you, what leave undone?
This is the light you wanted, here is the bright air,
now the sickbed on which you lie   180
is outside the house.
You spoke of nothing else but of coming out here,
but soon you will hurry back again into your bedroom.
You cannot go steadily for long, and take pleasure in
    nothing—
what you have fails to please you, what you have not
you hold more dear.
It is better to be sick than to look after the sick—
the former is a single thing, but the latter involves
grief for the heart and labour for the hand.
All of our human life is full of pain
and there is no rest from toil.   190
But whatever else there may be that is more dear than life,
darkness hides it, wrapping it round in clouds.
We show ourselves to be infatuated lovers
of this thing, whatever it is, that glistens here on earth,
for we have no experience of another life
and no revelation of what lies below the ground,*
but we drift on a sea of idle myths.

PHAEDRA [*chants*].   Hold up my body, keep my head upright.
All the strength in my limbs is gone.
Take my slender arms, my maids.
How heavy is the headdress I am wearing!   200

Take it off me and let my hair hang loose on my shoulders.
NURSE [*chants*]. Bear up, my child, and do not turn your body
   so unmanageably this way and that.
   You will endure your sickness more easily
   if you show a calm
   and noble spirit.
   Mortals find no escape from suffering.
PHAEDRA [*chants*]. Aiai!
   If only I could draw a draught
   of pure water from a dewy spring,
   and rest myself, lying beneath the black poplars   210
   and in the lush meadow!*
NURSE [*chants*]. O my child, what is this that you cry aloud?
   Do not say these things for all to hear,
   flinging out words that ride on madness.*
PHAEDRA [*chants*].
   Take me to the mountain! I shall go to the wood
   among the pine trees where the hounds
   which kill the wild beasts
   tread as they close on the dappled hinds. By the gods
   I beg you, take me there! I long to shout to the hounds
   and to poise by my blond hair a Thracian spear,   220
   clutching the headed missile in my hand,
   and hurl it.
NURSE [*chants*]. Whatever is it, my child, that torments you so?
   What concern have you with hunting?
   Why do you long for the flowing springs?
   Here right by the city walls is a well-watered hillside—
   you could get a drink from there.
PHAEDRA [*chants*]. Artemis, mistress of the Mere by the sea,
   of the exercise place which sounds with the hoofs of horses,
   if only I could be on the ground of your precinct   230
   taming Venetian horses.
NURSE [*chants*].
   What is this new wish you have flung out in your madness?
   Just now you were off to the mountain,
   setting out to the hunt you longed for,
   and now you yearn for horses
   on the sands where no waves break.
   It is not an easy matter to divine

which of the gods tugs at your bridle
and causes your wits to veer, my child.

PHAEDRA [*chants*]. How wretched I am! Whatever have I done?
  I have swerved aside from sanity—and where am I now?
  I have gone mad, a god possessed me and I fell.   240
  Cry alas, alas for my misery.
  Nurse, hide my head again
  for I am ashamed of what I have said.
  Hide my head, I say. A tear comes down from my eyes
  and they have taken on the look of shame.
  Sanity brings pain
  but madness is a vile thing.
  No, it is best to lose all consciousness and die.

NURSE [*chants*].
  I cover your head. But when shall death shroud my body? 250
  I have lived long and this has taught me much.
  If only mortals would mix the bowl of friendship for each
    other
  only to a moderate strength
  and not touch the deepest marrow of their soul.
  The loves of our hearts should be easy to untie,
  easy to push away, easy to tighten fast.
  But when one heart feels the pain for two,
  as I find myself grieving over her,   260
  the burden is a heavy one.
  They say that to keep to one's principles unswervingly in life
  leads to a fall more often than it brings joy
  and fights a greater war with our health.
  And so I praise excess
  less than moderation.*
  And wise men will agree with me.

CHORUS. Old woman, faithful nurse of the queen, we can see
  Phaedra's wretched state with our own eyes, but it is
  unclear to us what her sickness is. We should like to discover 270
  this from your lips.

NURSE. I do not know, even though I tax her. She is not willing to tell me.

CHORUS. And do you not know what began these troubles
  either?

NURSE. My answer to that is the same. She keeps her silence*
about all this.

CHORUS. How weak she is! How wasted her body!

NURSE. It is not surprising. This is the third day she has not
taken food.

CHORUS. Is she possessed by madness—or is she trying to die?

NURSE. To die? Well yes, the way she's starving herself will certainly lead her to her death.

CHORUS. What you say is amazing, if her husband is prepared
to tolerate this.

NURSE. That is because she hides her trouble and does not
admit that she is sick.

CHORUS. But can he not tell when he sees her face?   280

NURSE. No. He is in fact out of this country.*

CHORUS. Aren't you applying pressure as you try to discover
what her sickness is, what makes her mind go astray?

NURSE. I have done everything I can and have got nowhere.
But I shall not let my efforts to reach the truth slacken even
now,* and so you too will be able to corroborate from the
evidence of your eyes what kind of servant I am to my mistress in her troubles.

Come, my dear child, let us both forget what we said
before. You must become more cooperative, relaxing your   290
sullen frown and opening your mind. I know that previously
I was not always in harmony with you, but I too shall
change all that and embark upon another, better way of
talking to you. And if you are suffering from an illness which
cannot be spoken of, there are women here to help to cure
your sickness. But if it is proper to tell men of your affliction,
speak out so that the matter can be referred to doctors.

Well, why are you silent? You should not be silent, my
child. You should either put me right if I am saying anything
out of turn, or agree with whatever I have said that hits the
mark. Say something, look this way.   300

I am failing miserably, women. We are making all this
effort in vain. We are no nearer to success than we were
before. She was not softened by my words then and she is
not listening to me now. But know this—and then you can
become more stubborn than the sea—if you die, you will
betray your children, who will have no share in their

father's house—I swear this by the Amazonian queen, the horsewoman, who bore a master for your children, a bastard with the aspirations of the legitimate—you know him well, Hippolytus . . .   310

PHAEDRA. Alas!

NURSE. Does this touch you?

PHAEDRA. You have destroyed me, nurse, and I beseech you by the gods to say no more* about this man.

NURSE. You see? You are sane but, despite your sanity, you are unwilling to help your children and to save your life.

PHAEDRA. I love my children. I am tossed on quite another tempest of fortune.

NURSE. Are your hands pure of blood, my child?

PHAEDRA. My hands are pure, but a pollution stains my mind.

NURSE. Through spells from an enemy which have harmed you?

PHAEDRA. One dear to me destroys me. It is not what either of us wishes.

NURSES. Has Theseus done you some wrong?*   320

PHAEDRA. No. And I pray I may never be seen to harm him.

NURSE. Well, what is this terrible thing that is driving you to your death?

PHAEDRA. Let me go wrong. The wrong does not hurt you.

NURSE. No, I shall not, I will not. If I fail, it will be your responsibility.

        [*The* NURSE *kneels before* PHAEDRA *and clasps her hand.*

PHAEDRA. What are you doing? Will you try to force it out of me by clasping my hand?

NURSE. Your hand, yes, and your knees too.* And I shall never let go.

PHAEDRA. You wretched woman, it will prove calamitous for you if you find it out, calamitous.

NURSE. Why, what greater calamity could there be for me than not to have your trust?

PHAEDRA. You will be ruined. But as things stand I win honour by what I do.

NURSE. Why hide it then, when what I beg is for your good?   330

PHAEDRA. I must. I am contriving to win glory* from my shame.

NURSE. Surely you will appear the more honourable by speaking of it?

PHAEDRA. For the gods' sake, leave me and let go of my right hand.

NURSE. No. You are not giving me the gift you owe me.

PHAEDRA. I will give it, for I respect the sacred power of supplication that lies in your hand.*

NURSE. Now I shall say no more. You must do the speaking now.

PHAEDRA. O my poor mother, how terrible the love you conceived!*

NURSE. Her love for the bull, my child? What do you mean by this?

PHAEDRA. And you, my wretched sister,* wife of Dionysus!

NURSE. My child, what is the matter? Are you speaking ill of 340 your family?

PHAEDRA. And now I the third—see how I am being destroyed in my misery!

NURSE. I am alarmed by what you are saying. What are you going to tell me?

PHAEDRA. It was from their loves, not of recent date, that my troubles began.

NURSE. I still know nothing of what I want to hear.

PHAEDRA. Alas! If only you could say for me what I must say!

NURSE. I am no prophet to understand for sure what is unclear.

PHAEDRA. What is it that they mean when they say that people love?

NURSE. Something both very sweet, dear girl, and painful too.

PHAEDRA. It will be the second kind from which I suffer.

NURSE. What are you saying? Are you in love, my child? With 350 whom?

PHAEDRA. Whoever that man is, the son of the Amazon . . .

NURSE. Hippolytus do you mean?

PHAEDRA. You hear the name from your own lips, not from mine.

NURSE. Alas, what is this you say, my child? Your words are death to me. Women, this cannot be borne, no longer can I bear to live. The day I look on is hateful, hateful its light. I shall fling down my body from some high place, I shall find in death an escape from life. Farewell. I no longer exist. For the virtuous—they do not want to but still they do it—love what is base. I see that Cypris is no god—but if there be any 360 power still greater than a god, then that is what she is, she who has brought destruction on this woman and me and the whole house.

CHORUS [*sings*]. Did you hear, O did you listen to
our queen as she cried aloud
her wretched sufferings, too terrible to hear?
I hope that I may die before I come to
your state of mind, my dear one. Ah me! Alas! Alas!
O woman, pitiable in your pain!
O the troubles which have mortals in their care!
You are destroyed, you have brought catastrophe forth to
    the light.
What awaits you* as this day spins out its length?
Something unknown before will be brought to fulfilment
    for the house.   370
But it is unclear no longer where the fortune sent by Cypris
has its waning end, you wretched girl from Crete.

PHAEDRA. Women of Trozen, who live in this furthest promontory of the land of Pelops,* even before now I have at times
pondered in the long hours of the night to no avail upon the
wreck of our mortal lives. And it seems to me that people go
wrong not because of the nature of their minds—after all,
many people have sound judgement. I think we should view
the matter in this light. We understand and recognize what
is good, but we do not labour to bring it to fulfilment, some   380
of us out of laziness, some because we put something else,
some pleasure, before virtue—and there are many pleasures
in life, long conversations and indolence, that pleasing
vice—and a sense of shame. This takes two forms. One of
them is not a bad thing, but the other proves a burden upon
the house.* If the appropriate moment for each were clearly
different, these two concepts would not be spelt with the
same letters. So since this is what I really think, there is no
drug which could have made me pervert my view and
change it to the contrary.   390

    And I shall tell you of the path which my thoughts fol-
lowed. When love wounded me, I first considered how I
could best endure it. So I began with this policy—to stay
quiet* about this sickness and to keep it hidden. For there's
no trusting the tongue.* It can give counsel to other people's

thoughts, but when it speaks for itself, it brings abundant
trouble upon us. My second course was this—I planned to
conquer my madness through self-control and thus to bear
it easily. My third course—since I was failing to win victory   400
over Cypris by these means—was to resolve on death. This
was the best policy—no one will deny it. For I would not
wish any noble actions of mind to remain unsung or any
shameful deeds to have many witnesses.* I knew that the act
and the sickness brought disgrace with them and besides I
was well aware that I am a woman—an object of loathing
to all men.

May the most baleful of deaths fall on that woman who
first set about shaming her marriage bed with men who
were not her husband! It was from noble houses* that this
bane for the female sex began. And when the nobility   410
approve of what is shameful, you can be very sure that the
base will think it a truly fine standard of behaviour. I hate
those women who lay claim to virtue but in secret dare to
commit shameful deeds. How, my mistress lady Cypris, can
they ever look their bedmates in the face—how can they fail
to shudder at the darkness, their co-conspirator, in case the
very beams of their house may some time speak out? It is
this very thing which is driving me to death, my friends—
never may I be found guilty of bringing disgrace upon my   420
husband or the children I have borne.* No, may they flour-
ish as free citizens with freedom of speech as they dwell in
the famous city of Athens. May their mother's reputation
allow theirs to stand high. For even if a man has courage in
his heart, he becomes a slave when he is aware of rotten-
ness in his mother or father. They say that one thing alone
competes in life's contest, the consciousness of a just and
righteous mind within one, while time sooner or later
reveals bad men, setting its mirror before them as before a
young girl. May I never be seen in their number.   430

CHORUS. Ah! virtue, ah! I see that it is a noble quality the world
over and enjoys good repute among mortals.

NURSE. My mistress,* just now your plight made me terribly
afraid for a moment. But now I realize that I was being
small-minded. Second thoughts are better. What you have
suffered is nothing extraordinary, nothing unaccountable.

The lightning of the goddess's rage has launched itself
against you. You are in love—what is so surprising about
that? So are many other mortals. And will you then destroy   440
your life for love? It is a bad bargain for those who love those
near to them, and all those who will do so, if they have to
die. No one can bear the force of Cypris when she comes in
spate. The one that yields to her, she pursues with gentle-
ness, but whomsoever she finds arrogant or proud, she seizes
and you cannot think how violently she treats him. Cypris
roams in the air, she is in the surge of the sea, all things are
born from her. It is she who sows and gives love and it is   450
through love that every one of us on earth is created.*

Yes, and all who have the works of the artists of old and
are themselves ever interested in poetry, know that Zeus
once desired to bed Semele, they know that radiant Dawn
once snatched up Cephalus to join the gods—and all for
love.* Yet they still dwell in heaven and do not go into exile
to avoid their fellow-gods. No, they resign themselves, I
think, to the plight that has mastered them. And will you not
accept your love? If not, your father should have begotten   460
you on stated conditions or with other gods as masters if you
refuse to acquiesce in these laws.

How many thoroughly sensible men do you think don't
turn a blind eye when they see their marriages collapsing?
How many fathers do you think help their wayward sons in
love affairs? For it is a wise policy for men to let what is not
virtuous remain unseen. And mortals should not put too
much effort into achieving perfection in their lives. You
would not make a totally precise and finished job of the roof
with which you cover your house.* When you have fallen
into a stormy a sea of troubles as you have, how do you   470
think you could swim to safety? No, if you have more of
what is good than what is bad, as a mere human being you
would be fortunate indeed.

But, my dear girl, lay aside this wrong-headedness, lay
aside this wilfulness—for it is nothing other than wilfulness
to wish to be superior to the gods. Love on—go through with
it. This is what a god wished to happen. And if it makes you
sick, find a good way to control your sickness. There are
charms and words which cast a spell.* Some cure for this

sickness will be found. Men would take overlong to discover 480
the means unless we women find them.

CHORUS. Phaedra, what the nurse says is more expedient* in
your present plight, but it is you I praise. However, this
praise of mine is harder to deal with than the words of this
woman—and far more painful to your ears.

PHAEDRA. Words with too good a ring—those are what destroy
men's well-ordered cities and their homes. We must not say
things that delight the ears—but what will save our reputation.

NURSE. No more noble sentiments. It is not fine words you 490
need, it's the man. Let us make the matter clear at once and
tell the straight truth about you. If you were not living
through such a crisis and you actually were a woman in
control of your emotions, I would never have led you on to
this point for the sake of your sexual pleasure. But as things
are, there is much at stake. We are playing for your life, and
no one should think ill of us for this.

PHAEDRA. Your words are shocking. Stop your lips, woman,
and utter no more of these most shameful arguments.

NURSE. Shameful they may be, but they are better for you than 500
your fine talk. Rather the act, if the act will save you, than
reputation—your pride in that will lead you to your death.

PHAEDRA. Ah, no, I beg you by the gods—for your words are
plausible even in their shamefulness—go no further than
this. My soul is soil well turned by love for sowing, and if
you utter shameful words plausibly, I shall give way utterly
to what I now run from.

NURSE. Very well then, as you wish. You should not be in the
wrong in the first place, but as you are, do what I tell you.
A favour to me is the next best recourse. In the house I have 510
a love charm*—it has just come to my mind—a spell for love
which will bring your sickness to an end, cause you no
shame, and give your mind no hurt, if you remain steadfast.
But we need to take some token from the man you long for,
a lock of his hair or something from his clothes, to join
charm and token and win success.

PHAEDRA. Do I anoint my body with this drug, or do I drink it?

NURSE. I do not know. Wish only to succeed, my child. There
is no need for knowledge.

PHAEDRA. I am afraid that I may find you to be only too clever.

NURSE. If you fear that, you can be sure that you would fear anything. What exactly are you afraid of?

PHAEDRA. I beg you, do not mention any of this to the son of Theseus.* 520

NURSE. Do not worry, my girl. I shall set this matter right.* Only I beg you, my mistress lady Cypris, be my helper. As for all the other things I have in mind, it will be enough to tell them to our friends within.

[*The* NURSE *goes into the house.* PHAEDRA *goes to the back of the stage.*]

CHORUS [*sings*]. Eros, Eros, you who distil desire
upon the eyes and bring sweet joy
to the souls of those you war against,
may you never appear to harm me,
may you never come in discord.
For the shafts of fire or the stars are not more powerful 530
than those of Aphrodite which Eros, the son of Zeus,
lets fly from his hands.

In vain, in vain by the river Alpheus
and in the Pythian dwelling of Phoebus*
does Greece pile up slaughtered cattle,
while we pay no reverence to Eros, tyrant over mankind,
the key-holder of the most sensuous chambers 540
of Aphrodite.
It is he who ravages mortals, hurtling them
through the gamut of calamity whenever he comes.

It was Aphrodite who yoked the girl from Oechalia,*
a filly unyoked in marriage,
manless and unwed before, brought her beneath the yoke
from Eurytus' house
and gave her like a running Naiad or bacchant 550
amid a welter of blood and smoke
in a blood-stained marriage to Alcmena's son. O maiden,
wretched in your marriage!

O holy wall of Thebes,
O mouth of Dirce's* fountain,
you could confirm how Cypris comes upon one.

For it was to the fire-girt thunder that she gave as his love
the mother of the twice-born Bacchus,   560
lulling her to sleep
in a doom of blood.*
Terrible is her breath and she breathes on everything,
while she flits like a bee from flower to flower.

PHAEDRA [*by the door*]. Quiet, women.* It is all over with me.
CHORUS. What is it in the house, Phaedra, that causes you
such fear?
PHAEDRA. Wait—let me hear what those inside are saying.
CHORUS. I'll keep quiet. But what you have uttered bodes no
good.
PHAEDRA. Ah me, aiai! How miserable I am in my sufferings!   570
CHORUS [*chants*]. Your cry—what does it mean? Your shout—
what are you saying?
Tell me, lady, what words do they speak
that dart upon your mind to frighten you?
PHAEDRA. I am ruined. Stand by these doors and hear what
shouting falls upon the house.
CHORUS [*chants*]. You are by the door. It is for you to pass on
what the palace speaks.
Tell me, tell me, what disaster   580
has come upon us?
PHAEDRA. The son of the horse-loving Amazon, Hippolytus,
cries out, heaping dreadful insults on my servant.
CHORUS [*chants*]. I hear a voice, but can be sure of nothing.
Say what cry has reached you,
reached you through the doors.
PHAEDRA. Yes, and it is clear—he calls her 'bawd of vicious-
ness', 'betrayer of her master's bed'.   590
CHORUS [*chants*].
I cry alas for these evils. You are betrayed, dear lady.
What can I advise you?
For what was hidden is now revealed, and you are ruined,
Aiai, ah, ah, betrayed by a friend.
PHAEDRA. By telling of my sad plight she has destroyed me. It was
a friend's act but not a noble one to try to cure my sickness.
CHORUS. What then? What will you do? There is no help for
your sufferings.

PHAEDRA. One thing alone I know—I must die now, at once.
This is the only remedy for the woes that now beset me.   600

HIPPOLYTUS and the NURSE *come out of the house.* PHAEDRA *remains
at the back of the stage.*

HIPPOLYTUS. O mother earth and open sunlight,* what a
speech I have heard, what unspeakable words!

NURSE. Be silent, boy, before someone hears your shouts.

HIPPOLYTUS. No, I cannot be silent. I have heard terrible things.

NURSE. Silent, yes, I beg you by this strong right arm.*

[*The* NURSE *tries to take hold of* HIPPOLYTUS' *arm.*

HIPPOLYTUS. Don't touch me, and don't grasp my robes.

NURSE. O, by your knees I beseech you, do not destroy me.

HIPPOLYTUS. Why do you say that, if, as you claim, you have
said nothing that is bad?

NURSE. My boy, what I said just now was certainly not for all
to hear.

HIPPOLYTUS. It is the better course to say what is good with all   610
the world to witness.

NURSE. My child, do not dishonour your oath.*

HIPPOLYTUS. It was my tongue that swore. My mind took no
oath.*

NURSE. My boy, what will you do? Will you ruin those close to
you?

HIPPOLYTUS. Close? You disgust me. No one who sins can be a
friend of mine.

NURSE. Forgive. People are prone to make mistakes, child.

HIPPOLYTUS. O Zeus, why have you created women to live in
the light of the sun and prove a bane, a counterfeit coinage
for mankind? If you wanted to propagate the human race,
you should not have brought this about through women.   620
Rather men should deposit bronze or iron or heavy gold in
your temples as the purchase price for any offspring. They
should buy their children through a means test, each pay-
ing an appropriate sum, and they should live in their houses
free from women.* But as things are, when we are about to
take this evil into our homes, we first expend the wealth of
our houses. It is clear that a woman is a great evil—after all,
in order to get rid of it, the father who gave her life and
brought her up attaches a dowry to her when he sends her

away from home. And then the man who takes this perni- 630
cious creature into his house rejoices as he tricks out his disastrous idol with lovely jewels and decks her in robes to
perfection, poor man, as he gradually drains his house of its
wealth. He has no alternative. And so, if he has allied himself with a good family, he takes pleasure in his in-laws and
perseveres with a marriage which is bitter to him, or if he
has made a happy marriage but regards his in-laws as bad
citizens, he tries to stifle his ill fortune by focusing on what
is good.

Things are easiest for the man whose wife is a cipher.
Even so it is harmful to have a woman set up in all her silli-
ness in one's home. Yet it is the clever woman that I detest. 640
May I never have in my house a woman who is more intel-
ligent than a woman should be. For Cypris instils mischief
more into the clever ones, while a woman with no resources
stays free from folly owing to her limited intellect.

And a servant should not go in to a woman, but we
should make animals with bites but no speech live with
them so that they can neither talk to anyone nor get a
response from others. But as it is, these wicked women plot
wicked schemes in their houses and the servants carry them 650
out of doors. And this is what you have done with me, you
wicked creature. You came to me to make a match between
me and the partner of my father's inviolable bed.* I shall
wash my ears clean and wipe away the pollution of your
words with water from the running streams.* How could I
give way to sin when even to hear such things makes me
feel impure?

Be sure of one thing—it is only my piety that protects you,
woman. For if I had not been caught off my guard when I
swore my oath by the gods, I would never have held back
from telling my father this. But, as things are, as long as
Theseus is out of the country, I shall keep away from the 660
house and I shall keep my lips silent. However, I shall come
back when my father comes and I shall watch how you look
him in the face—you and your mistress too. I shall know,
because I have already had a taste of your baseness. My
curse on you both. I shall never have my fill of hating
women, not even if someone says that I am always harping

on the same old theme. Let someone either teach them to be
virtuous or allow me always to tread them underfoot.

> [*HIPPOLYTUS goes out away from the palace.*

PHAEDRA [*sings*]. How wretched and ill-starred
the fate of women!
We are lost. What plan, what words are left us now   670
to undo the knot which words have tied?
I have met with justice. O earth and light!
Wherever can I shun my fortune?*
How, my friends, shall I hide my misery?
What god could come to help me, what mortal
stand by me and assist me,
the victim of unjust deeds?* The suffering which afflicts
    me
now moves beyond the end of life in that hardest of cross-
    ings.*
Most ill-starred of all women am I.

CHORUS. Alas, alas! It is all over. Your servant's schemes, my   680
mistress, have gone awry. Disaster is here.

PHAEDRA. Vilest of women, you who destroy your friends,
what have you done to me! May Zeus my ancestor* give you
a deadly wound with his fire and rub you out root and
branch. Did I not tell you—did I not anticipate what you
planned?—tell you to be silent about the things which now
fill me with such shame? But you could not restrain yourself.
And so I shall die with my good name dishonoured.

But I must make new plans. For, thanks to your bungling
interference, this man, his heart whetted with anger, will   690
speak against me to his father, he will speak to old Pittheus
of this terrible thing that has happened, and fill the whole
land with most shaming words.* My curse on you and on all
others who are eager to serve their friends in evil ways
against their will.

NURSE. Mistress, you can find fault with the ill you claim that
I have done, since the bitterness gnawing at you is stronger
than your judgement. But I have something to say in answer
if you will listen to me. I brought you up and I am your
friend. I sought a cure for your sickness but I found what I
did not wish to find. However, if I had succeeded, I should   700

certainly have been numbered among the wise. Our wisdom
is measured by our success or failure.

PHAEDRA. What! Is this just, is this good enough for me—that
you should wound me and then use words to come to terms
with me?

NURSE. We are wasting time with our talk. I showed bad judgement. But there is a way you can be saved even from this
plight, my child.

PHAEDRA. Stop—no more words.* Your advice to me was bad
before and you put your hand to a vicious scheme. Away
with you! Go, and take thought for yourself. I shall set my
own affairs to rights.* [*The* NURSE *goes into the house.*] But I
beg you, you noble women of Trozen, grant me this favour   710
and no more. Veil in silence what you have heard here.

CHORUS. I swear by blessed Artemis, the daughter of Zeus, that
I shall never reveal anything of your tragedy to the light of
day.*

PHAEDRA. My thanks for your words. But there is one further
thing I shall tell you.* I have thought of a way out of my sad
plight, by which I may ensure a life of good repute for my
children and make for myself what profit I can in view of
what has now befallen. For I shall never disgrace the royal
house of Crete or come to look Theseus in the face after these   720
shameful deeds—simply to save one life.

CHORUS. What evil action, never to be healed, are you planning to commit?

PHAEDRA. To die. But as to how I die, I shall take my own
counsel.

CHORUS. Speak words of good omen.

PHAEDRA. Give me good advice then. But I shall delight Cypris,
the goddess who destroys me, as I leave this life on this very
day. How bitter the love which will prove to be my fall! But
through my death I shall bring calamity on another too—to
make him learn not to feed his arrogance on my tragedy. He   730
and I shall share together in this sickness, and that will
prove his lesson in virtue.*   [PHAEDRA *goes into the house.*

CHORUS [*sings*].
I wish I could be in the hidden hollows of the high cliffs,
and that there the god would make me

a winged bird
among the flying flocks.
I wish I could fly over
the sea wave of the shore of Adria*
and the waters of Eridanus,
where the wretched girls
drip the amber-gleaming brightness of their tears
into the dark river swell   740
in pity for Phaethon.*

And I wish I could make my way to where the apples grow.*
to the shore of the Hesperides, the songstresses,
where the lord of the sea's dark waters
allows no further voyaging
to sailors—
confirming the holy limits of the sky
which Atlas holds—
and divine springs flow
by where Zeus lay.
There the holy earth, bountiful in her gifts,   750
swells the happiness of the gods.

O white-winged ship of Crete,
you who brought my queen
over the thudding waves of the salt sea
from a happy home for the joy of a marriage
which has brought nothing but misery. For bad were the
    omens for her
under which she flew,
both when she left the land of Crete for famous Athens
and when they tied the twisted cable's ends to the shore   760
    of Mounichos*
and stepped upon the mainland's soil.

And therefore her soul has been broken
by the terrible sickness of Aphrodite,
an unholy love.
Foundering amid cruel calamity,
she will fasten
from the beams of her bridal chamber
a hanging noose

and slip it round her white throat 770
in shame at her hateful destiny.
She will choose honourable repute* instead
and free her soul from the pain of love.

NURSE [*off-stage*]. Ah me! Ah me! All of you near the house run
here to help! My mistress, Theseus' wife, is hanging in a noose.

CHORUS. Alas, alas, it is all over. The queen no longer lives. She
hangs suspended in a noose.

NURSE. Can't you hurry? Won't someone bring a two-edged
sword so that we can cut this rope from her neck? 780

CHORUS. My friends, what shall we do? Do you think we should
enter the house and cut the queen from the tight-drawn
noose?
—But why? Are there not young attendants there? Do not
interfere if you want to lead your life in safety.

NURSE. Lay out her wretched body. Set it straight. This is the
bitter harvest my masters have reaped from her stewardship
of the house.

CHORUS. The poor woman is dead, I hear. They are stretching
her out now as befits a corpse.

Enter THESEUS, *wearing garlands.**

THESEUS. Women, do you know what it means, this shouting 790
of servants which reverberates so deeply through the house?
For none of my household has thought to open the gates and
welcome me with the smiles due to a man who has visited
an oracle. Nothing bad has happened to old Pittheus, I hope?
He is far advanced in years by now, but even so it would
grieve me much were he to depart this house.

CHORUS. The disaster which has befallen you, Theseus, does
not concern the old. A young death* brings you pain.

THESEUS. Alas, my children—it is not they, I hope, who have
been stripped of their lives?

CHORUS. They live—but their mother has died a death which 800
will bring you dreadful anguish.

THESEUS. What are you saying? My wife dead? How did it happen?

CHORUS. She tied up a hanging noose and strangled herself.

THESEUS. Blighted with the chill of grief—or from what blow of
fate?

CHORUS. That is all we know. I too have only just come to your
house,* Theseus, to grieve over your sorrows.

THESEUS [*taking the garlands from his head*]. Aiai, why do I wear
these garlands of plaited foliage on my head? I have come
back from my mission to find disaster.

Unlock the doors that bar the portal, my attendants,
release their bolts, so that I can see the bitter sight of my wife   810
whose death has destroyed me.

> The doors open and PHAEDRA's corpse is rolled out on the
> ekkyklema. A tablet hangs from her wrist.*

CHORUS [*chants*].
Oh, oh, woman miserable in your wretched woes.
Your sufferings, your act is so terrible
that it devastates this house.
Alas for what you have had the hardiness to do—
dying a violent death in an unholy doom,
meeting it in a struggle, the work of your own wretched
hand.
Who is it, unhappy woman, that has put out the light of
your life?*

THESEUS [*sings*]. Ah me, what woes I endure! I have suffered,
poor wretch that I am, have suffered the greatest of my
sorrows.
O fortune, how heavily you have fallen upon me and my
house,
spreading a stain I had not guessed at, the work of some   820
avenging spirit!
No, it is not fortune, but the ruin of my life, a life no longer.
I look out, wretched Theseus, over so vast a sea of troubles
that never shall I swim my way back through it,
never come through this wave of disaster.
With what words, wretch that I am, with what words
can I speak of your lamentable fate and hit the mark?
For like a bird you have vanished from my hands
in your swift and sudden leap to Death.
Aiai aiai, how tragic, tragic are these sufferings.   830
From some distant past there comes back against me
a fate from the gods
through the sins of some ancestor.

CHORUS. It is not on you alone, my lord, that such disasters
   have fallen. The loss of a good wife is one you share with
   many others.

THESEUS [*sings*]. Down beneath the earth, to the gloom
      beneath the earth I wish to go from here
   to dwell in the dark after death, miserable creature that I
      am,
   for I have lost your dearest company.
   It is rather that you have killed me than died yourself.
   Who will tell me where it sprang from, this deadly hap-   840
      pening
   that came, my wretched wife, upon your heart?
   Would someone explain what has occurred—or is it for
   nothing that my royal house holds so many servants?
   Alas I cry over you.
   What a grief for the house have I seen in my wretched-
      ness.—
   grief not to be endured, not to be spoken. Oh, my life is over.
   The house is empty, and our children are orphans.
   Aiai aiai, you have left me, left me, o dearest
   and best of all the women
   whom the light of the sun   850
   and the starry radiance of the night* looks upon.

CHORUS [*chants*].
   You poor man, what calamity your house contains!
   My eyes are wet with streaming tears
   at your catastrophe.
   But I have long been shuddering at the thought of the woe
      that is to come.*

THESEUS [*noticing the tablet tied to* PHAEDRA's *hand*]. What's this?
   What is this tablet* hanging from your dear hand? Has it
   something new it wishes to impart? Can it be that the
   wretched woman has written me a message with a request
   about my marriage and our children? Have no fears over   860
   that, poor lady, for to Theseus' bed and his house no woman
   shall ever come. Yes, and here the imprint of the golden
   signet ring of her who is no more holds my gaze. Come, let
   me undo the threads which seal this tablet and see what it
   means to say to me.

CHORUS [*sings*]. Alas, alas, this is another, a new disaster

that the god brings upon us to succeed the old.
May the fate of death befall me as it has befallen the
  house.
For I speak of the house of my rulers—alas! alas!—   870
  as a ruin—it no longer exists.
O guardian angel, if it is possible in any way,
do not cause the house to fall but hear me as I beg you,
for something makes me see a bad omen, like a prophet.

THESEUS. Alas, what a disaster is here, treading upon the
  other's heels, not to be endured, not to be spoken! Oh, what
  a wretch I am!

CHORUS. What thing is this? Tell me if I may be told.

THESEUS [chants].
  It cries out, the tablet cries out a terrible message.
  How can I flee this weight of woes, I am lost and done for,
  such, such is the song that in my misery I see
  taking voice in this writing.   880

CHORUS. Aiai, the words you have spoken are the harbinger of
  horrors.

THESEUS [chants]. No longer will I keep this back within the
    gates of my mouth,
  this deadly horror, so agonizing to express.
  O citizens!
  Hippolytus has dared to lay violent hands on the partner of
  my bed; he has flouted the holy eye of Zeus.* O father
  Poseidon,* you once promised me three prayers. With one of
  them destroy my son. If the prayers you gave to me are sure,
  do not let him survive this day.   890

CHORUS. My lord, in the name of heaven take back your
  prayer. A time will come when you will see that you are
  wrong.* Listen to me.

THESEUS. I shall not. And what is more I shall banish him from
  this land. He will find himself struck by one of two fates.
  Either Poseidon will respect my prayers and send him down
  dead to the house of Hades or he will wander to a foreign
  land in exile from this country, draining the bitter dregs of
  his life.

CHORUS. Look, here he comes himself, your son Hippolytus,   900
  and at the very moment. Abate this evil passion, King
  Theseus, and take thought for what is best for your house.

HIPPOLYTUS *rushes onto the stage.*

HIPPOLYTUS. I heard your shout, father, and have come here in haste. But I do not know what it is you grieve over and would wish to hear this from you.

Oh no, what is this? I see your wife, father, lying dead. I am utterly amazed at this. I left her just now, it is only a short while ago that she looked upon the light of this day. What happened to her? How did she die? Father, I want to find out now from you. 910

You say nothing? But disaster is no time for silence.* After all, the heart that wishes to know everything will be found greedy for knowledge even amid disaster. It is simply not right for you to hide your misfortunes from your friends, father, let alone those still closer to you than friends.

THESEUS. O mankind, how much you miss your aim and come to nothing! Why do you teach countless skills? There is nothing you cannot devise or discover, and yet there is one thing that you do not understand and have so far failed to hunt down—how to teach those who have no sense to 920 think aright.

HIPPOLYTUS. It is a formidable teacher that you speak of, if he is able to force those with no sense to think sound thoughts. But it is not subtle talk that we need now, father. I fear that your misfortunes may have made your tongue talk wildly.

THESEUS. Alas, men should have some clear test of their friends* established, a way of judging their hearts, to show who is a true friend and who is not. And all humans should have two voices, an honest voice and the one they would have had anyway so that the one that speaks dishonest 930 thoughts might be convicted by the honest one—and then we should not be deceived.*

HIPPOLYTUS. Can it be that one of your friends has slandered me to your ears and your trust in me grows sick, though I have done nothing wrong? I am truly confounded. You confound me by your words which run astray from good, well-based sense.

THESUS. Alas for the mind of man—to what extremes will it go? What limit in brazen boldness will it find? For if it is puffed up with pride in the course of a man's lifetime and he

that comes next is to prove a greater villain than his prede-   940
cessor, the gods will have to attach to the world another
earth which will have space for the hordes of the unjust and
the vicious. Look at this man who has defiled my marriage,
though he is my son, and is convicted by the dead woman
as manifestly vicious. You, show me your face, since I am
polluted now in any case, and look straight at your father
here. *You* keep company with the gods, do you, as a man
out of the ordinary, you the virtuous one, unsullied by evil?
Your boasts would never convince me to be so mad as to   950
charge the gods with folly. Well, now you can vaunt yourself, now play the huckster with your vegetable diet, conduct
your ecstatic rituals with Orpheus for your master and
revere the vacuous piffle of your many screeds*—for you are
caught. To all I proclaim it—avoid such men. They hunt
their prey with fine words, while scheming shameful
schemes.

She is dead. Do you think that this will save you? Vilest of
men, it is this more than anything else that convicts you.
For what oaths, what words could be stronger than hers and   960
so acquit you of the charge? Will you say that she hated
you, and that the bastard and the legitimate are natural enemies? If so, she made a sorry bargain with her life if she
destroyed what was most precious to her in her hatred for
you. Then will you claim that men can control their sexual
urges while woman cannot?* I know well that young men
are not a whit less prone to fall than women when Cypris
troubles their heart in its youthful prime; but the fact that   970
they are male assists their defence. So now . . . But why do
I wage this war of words with you when her corpse is present to bear the clearest witness? Get out of this country! Off
with all speed into exile and go neither to the city of god-
built Athens nor anywhere within the borders of the land
ruled by my spear. For if I suffer this treatment at your
hands and let you win, never will Sinis of the Isthmus bear
witness that I killed him—it was an empty boast—while the
rocks of Sciron's sea will deny that I was a harsh enemy to   980
evil men.*

CHORUS. I do not know how I could say that any mortal is
happy when even the greatest men are overthrown.

HIPPOLYTUS. Father, the passion and intensity of your heart is
terrible. But this affair, though it prompts you with fine
words, is not at all fine if one were to open it up. I lack the
art of glib speech for addressing a crowd; I am more skilled
at talking to a few people of my own age. And this is perfectly proper, since those who are inferior when talking
among men of judgement make sweeter music for a crowd's
ears. But nevertheless, with this crisis upon us, I have no   990
choice but to speak. I shall begin my words at that point
where you first tried to trick me—intending to destroy me in
the expectation that I would not answer you.

    You see this light and earth.* In these elements, there is
no man—even if you deny it—who is more virtuous than I.
First of all, I understand how to reverence the gods and to
have as my friends those who attempt no wrong but would
also hold it shame to send evil messages to their companions
and to repay them with shameful services; I am not one to   1000
mock my fellows, father, but I stay the same to my friends,
both when they are absent and when near.

    And one thing has never touched me—the thing through
which you believe you have now caught me. To this day my
body has been pure, unsullied by sex. I know nothing of that
activity apart from what I have heard through talk and seen
in pictures. And I am not eager to look at even these since I
have a virgin soul.

    So my chastity does not convince you? Well, I'll drop that
then. But in that case you must make clear how I was corrupted. Did this woman surpass all others in physical
beauty?* Or did I hope to possess your house by marrying   1010
the heiress to it? If so, I was a fool, no, completely crazy.
Then will you say that sane men hold kingship to be a sweet
ambition? This is certainly not true, since all those who find
the idea of absolute power pleasing are mad.* For myself, I
would choose to come first as victor in the Greek games, but
in the city I would rather be in the second position, ever
prospering with the nobility as my friends. For one can
attain one's will that way, and the absence of danger
bestows greater pleasure than kingship.   1020

    I have one more thing to say—you have heard everything
else. If I had a witness of what I truly am and I were

fighting my case while this woman still lived, you would
have seen who was base simply by sifting the facts. But as
things stand, I swear to you by Zeus, the god of oaths, and
by the solid earth, that I never laid a hand on your wife, I
would never have wanted to, never would have formed the
intention. May I die with my memory and name eclipsed,
without city or home, an exile roaming round the earth, and
when I am dead may neither the sea nor the land receive 1030
my body* if I am a bad man. What fear it was that made this
woman take her life I do not know—for it is not right for me
to speak further.* She could not be virtuous, yet she acted
virtuously, while I, who have virtue, did not use it well.*

CHORUS. In swearing these oaths by the gods, no small guar-
antee of your good faith, you have delivered a satisfactory
rebuttal of the charge.

THESEUS. Is he not a sorcerer, a charlatan, this man who has
the confidence to think that he will subdue my passion by
this calm response—when he has dishonoured his father?   1040

HIPPOLYTUS. And I am utterly amazed at the same thing in
you, my father. For if you were my son and I were your
father, I would have killed you and not punished you with
exile if you had presumed to lay your hand on my wife.

THESEUS. That is just what I would have expected you to say.
No, you will not die like this—this penalty you have just proposed for yourself. For a death that is quick comes most easily to a man plunged in misfortune. But as you wander in
exile from your native country to a foreign land, you will
drain the bitter dregs of your life. This is the payment for an 1050
impious man.

HIPPOLYTUS. Alas, what will you do? Will you not let time give
its evidence about me,* but drive me from the country?

THESEUS. Yes, beyond the Black Sea and the places where Atlas
dwells* if somehow I could—so great is my loathing for you.

HIPPOLYTUS. Will you not first review the evidence of oaths, of
pledges of good faith or of prophets' utterances—but simply
cast me from the land without trial?

THESEUS. This tablet has no diviner's guess on it. Its accusation
against you is to be believed. As for the birds that flutter over
our heads, I snap my fingers at them.*

HIPPOLYTUS. O gods, why do I not unlock my lips then—since 1060

I am being destroyed by you whom I reverence? But no. There is no hope at all that I could convince the man I have to convince. And I should violate the oaths I swore—and all for nothing.*

THESEUS. Alas, your smug piety will be the death of me. Will you not leave your father's land as quickly as you can?

HIPPOLYTUS. Where shall I turn then in my misery? What guest-friend's house can I enter in my exile on this charge?

THESEUS. One who is delighted to entertain as guests those who defile women and form a vicious partnership with his wife as they look after his home in his absence.

HIPPOLYTUS. Aiai, your words strike at my heart. Here is mat- 1070 ter close to tears, if I appear a bad man and seem one to you.

THESEUS. You should have lamented, should have thought of the consequences at the time when you brought yourself to outrage your father's wife.

HIPPOLYTUS. O house, if only you could find a voice to speak on my behalf and bear witness whether I am a bad man.

THESEUS. It is a clever ploy for you to resort to a witness with no voice. But it is the deed that proclaims you a bad man— it needs no words.

HIPPOLYTUS. Alas! If only I could stand facing myself and look at myself, so that I could have wept for the ills I am suffering.*

THESEUS. You schooled yourself far more in self-regard than in 1080 the reverent behaviour towards parents that befits a just man.

HIPPOLYTUS. O Hippolyta, my unhappy mother, how bitter my birth! I pray that no one I love may be a bastard.

THESEUS. Will you not drag him off, servants? I proclaimed his exile some time ago. Didn't you hear me?

HIPPOLYTUS. Any of them who dares to lay a hand on me will regret it. You yourself must drive me out of the country, if that is what you want.

THESEUS. I shall do so if you do not obey my words. No pity for your exile steals upon my heart.

HIPPOLYTUS. It is settled then, it seems. How wretched I am! I 1090 know the truth but do not know how I can give it expres- sion.   [*THESEUS goes out.*

HIPPOLYTUS turns to the statue of Artemis.

O daughter of Leto, dearest of the gods to me, my partner,

my fellow-hunter, I shall depart in exile from famous
Athens. Farewell, city and land of Erechtheus.* O plain of
Trozen—how many delights you hold for those who pass
their youth in you—fare you well. I address you as I look on
you for the last time. Come, o my young companions from
this land, speak your farewells to me and escort me from the
country—for never will you see another man who is more 1100
virtuous, even if my father does not think so.

                    HIPPOLYTUS *goes out.*

MALE CHORUS OF SERVANTS [*sings*].
  The care of the gods for mortals, when it comes to my
      mind,*
  greatly relieves my sorrow.
  But, though I have in my heart hope of understanding,
  I fail to grasp it as I look amid men's fortunes
  and their deeds.
  For from here comes one thing, from there another, and
      man's life
  shifts round,
  ever unstable.   1110
CHORUS OF WOMEN [*sings*].
  May destiny in answer to my prayers grant me this
  from the gods,
  good and happy fortune and a heart untainted by pain.
  May the thoughts within me be neither over-rigid nor
      again fraudulent,
  may my ways be adaptable, may I always suit them to
      tomorrow's length of hours
  and join in its good fortune throughout my life.
MALE CHORUS OF SERVANTS [*sings*].
  For no longer is my mind unclouded but what I behold   1120
  belies my expectations—
  since we have seen the brightest star of Greek Aphaia,*
  seen him setting out to another land
  driven by his father's rage.
  O sand of the city's shore,
  O mountain thicket where with his swift-footed dogs
  he killed the wild beasts,
  with holy Dictynna* his companion!   1130

CHORUS OF WOMEN [*sings*].

  Never again will you mount your chariot-team of
    Venetian colts,
  holding the race-track around the Mere* with the feet
  of your racing horses.
  And the music that knew no sleep beneath the frame of
    the lyre's strings
  will sound no more in your father's house.*
  You will bring no more wreaths of victory
  to Leto's daughter* in her resting places amid the deep
    greenery.
  Your exile has brought to an end   1140
  the rivalry of the girls to be the bride for your bed.

  And because of your misfortune
  I shall live out my fated span of ill fate
  in tears. O Hippolyta, unhappy mother,
  your birth pangs were in vain. Alas,
  I rage against the gods.*
  Ah! ah!
  You Graces who dance hand in hand,
  why do you send this wretched man,
  quite innocent of this catastrophe,
  out of his fatherland, away from this his house?   1150

  Look, here I can see a servant of Hippolytus rushing towards
  the palace, and I can tell from his face that he's sad at the
  news he brings.

A SERVANT of Hippolytus comes on.

SERVANT. Where can I go to find Theseus, the king of this land,
  women? If you know, tell me. Is he inside this palace?

THESEUS comes out of the house.

CHORUS. Here he is coming out of the house.
SERVANT. Theseus, to you and to the citizens who live in Athens
  and Trozen, I bring news which calls for your concern.
THESEUS. What is it? I hope that no fresh disaster has befallen 1160
  the two neighbouring cities?*
SERVANT. Hippolytus is dead, or almost dead—it makes no odds.
  He still sees the light of day but his life is poised in the balance.

THESEUS. How did he die? Someone whose wife he raped as he
   raped his father's didn't come to blows with him, I trust?
SERVANT. His own chariot destroyed him—and the curses from
   your mouth, which you called upon your father, lord of the
   sea, to fulfil against your son.
THESEUS. O gods, and Poseidon—truly then you are a father to
   me* for you have heard my prayers. How *did* he meet 1170
   destruction? Tell me, in what way did Justice trap him and
   break him, the son who shamed me?
SERVANT. By the shore where the waves break we were curry-
   ing the horses' coats with combs, weeping as we did so. For
   a messenger had come and told us that Hippolytus could no
   longer walk in freedom in this land since you had sentenced
   him to the miseries of exile. Then he came, weeping in the
   same strain, and joined us on the shore, a vast crowd of 1180
   friends and other young men following behind him. After a
   time he ceased from his tears and said, 'Why am I so distressed? I must obey my father's orders. Harness the horses
   beneath the chariot's yoke, my servants, for this is no longer
   my city.' Then everyone set speedily to work and, more
   quickly than it would take to describe it, we got the horses
   ready and stood them right by our master. He placed his feet
   neatly in the footstalls* and took up the reins in his hands
   from the chariot rails. First of all he stretched out his arms 1190
   to the gods and said, 'Zeus, may I die now if I am a vicious
   man. And may my father see that he dishonours me—either
   when I am dead or while I still see the light of day.' And at
   once he took the switch into his hands and whipped all the
   horses with a single movement.
     We servants accompanied our master, walking below him
   by the chariot near the horses' bridles along the road which
   goes straight towards Argos and Epidaurus.* And when we
   were striking into a desolate region, there is a headland
   beyond this land of Trozen lying towards what is by now the 1200
   Saronic Gulf. From there a rumbling, like Zeus' thunder, in
   the earth unleashed a deep roar. It made us shudder to hear
   it. The horses reared their heads upright and pricked their
   ears to the sky and we were seized by a violent fear—wherever, we wondered, could the sound be coming from? As we
   looked out towards the headland where the sea beats, we

saw a wave, the work of a god, its solid mass towering
towards the sky. My view of Sciron's headland was blocked,
the Isthmus and the rock of Asclepius* were hidden. And
then all swollen up, it flung a boiling spray of foam about it 1210
while the sea snorted high as it came to the shore where the
four-horsed chariot was. And at the very moment when this
surging mountain of water was breaking, the wave sent
forth a bull,* a terrible and wondrous creature. All the land
was filled with its bellowing and we shuddered as the echoes
boomed back, while the sight that met our eyes was more
than they could bear. At once a dreadful fear took hold of
the horses. And our master, with all his experience of their
ways, seized the reins in his hands and tugged them as a 1220
sailor tugs his oar, leaning his whole weight back on them.*
But they clamped the fire-hardened bits in their jaws and
pulled him along forcibly, taking no thought for their helmsman's hand or their harness or the well-made chariot. And
if as he grasped the helm he steered the careering horses to
the softer ground, the bull would appear in front of them and
turn them back, maddening the chariot's four-horse team
with panic. But as often as they swept in their frenzy 1230
towards the rocks, it would silently keep pace with them,
closer and closer to the chariot's rail, until at last it drove
the rim of a wheel against a rock and overturned it, bringing it crashing to the ground.

All was a welter of confusion. The wheels' naves and the
axle's linchpins were leaping into the air and the driver,
unhappy man, was dragged along entangled, knotted inex-
tricably in the reins, smashing his poor head against the
rocks and tearing his flesh to shreds and crying out things
that were terrible to hear. 'Stop, horses! You were reared in 1240
my own stables—do not pulp me to nothing! Alas for the
headstrong curse of my father! Who will come to my help?
Who will save a truly virtuous man?' Many of us wanted to,
but we were too slow and fell behind. Somehow or other
Hippolytus was freed from the cut-leather thongs and fell to
the earth, still breathing the breath of life—but it will not be
for long. The horses and the bull, that fatal monster, had disappeared, where I know not, in the rocky countryside.

I am only a slave of your house, my lord, but to believe

you when you say that your son is vicious is more than I 1250
shall ever be able to do, even if the whole of the female sex
were to hang themselves and someone filled all the
pinewood on Mount Ida full of writing.* For I know that he
is a good man.

CHORUS. Aiai, a new catastrophe has come to pass, and there
is no escape from fate or necessity.

THESEUS. In my hatred of the man who has suffered this I took
pleasure in your words. But now out of respect for the gods
and that man—because he is of my blood—I feel neither 1260
pleasure nor distress* over these grim events.

SERVANT. What then? Should we bring him here—or what else
should we do to the unhappy man to please your heart?
Consider the matter. But if you follow my advice you will not
prove a cruel father to your son in his pitiable state.

THESEUS. Bring him here so that face to face I can convict him
with my words and this god-sent disaster,* convict the man
who denied that he polluted my bed.   [*The* SERVANT *goes out.*

CHORUS [*chants*].
You, Cypris, lead captive the unbending hearts of the gods,
and the hearts of men, and with you joins the bright-
    winged one,
shooting all round him with his arrows so swift.*   1270
He flies over the land
and the echoing salty sea,
and he works his spell on all whose frenzied hearts he
    assaults,
Eros, winged god of golden brightness—
on the nature of the young of the mountains and the sea,
on all that the earth breeds
and the blazing sun looks down upon,
and on men. Over all of these, Cypris,   1280
in royal honour you rule alone.

        ARTEMIS *appears above the house.**

ARTEMIS [*chants*]. You, son of Aegeus, born from noble fathers,
I bid you hear me.
It is I, Artemis, the daughter of Leto, who speak to you.
Theseus, why do you rejoice at this, you hard man,
when you have sacrilegiously killed your son,

by the lying words of your wife persuaded to believe
what was not visible? Yet only too visible is the calamity
    you have won.
Why do you not hide your body   1290
in the depths of Tartarus* in your shame,
or change to a bird and fly upwards
and soar above this woe?
For you cannot possess a share in life
among good men.

Hear, Theseus, the truth of your catastrophe. Yet I shall gain
nothing by it—rather I shall give you pain. But this is what
I have come to do, to reveal the honesty of your son's heart
so that he might die with honour, and to make known the 1300
itch of your wife's lust—or in a way her nobility. Stabbed by
the stings of that goddess most hated by all of us who delight
in the virgin life, she conceived a passion for your son. She
tried to conquer Cypris by reason but suffered ruin she did
not wish for through the schemes of her nurse who made
known her sickness to your son under oath. He—as was
right—did not fall in with her words, nor again when he
was being vilified by you did he break the pledge of his oath
since he is a pious man. But she, in fear that she might be 1310
forced to reveal the truth, wrote her lying words and
destroyed your son. It was a trick, but even so her trickery
convinced you.

THESEUS. Alas!

ARTEMIS. Does what I say sting you, Theseus? But keep quiet
so that you can hear what followed and grieve the more.
You know that you have three infallible prayers to your
father? You took one of these, you man of sin, to use against
your son when you could have aimed it at an enemy. Now
your father, the sea god, because he loved you, gave you as
much as he was bound to since he had pledged himself. But 1320
you have plainly done wrong both by him and by me—you
waited for no proof or prophetic utterance, you conducted
no investigation and allowed no long time for an inquiry,
but with needless haste you hurled the curse upon your son
and killed him.

THESEUS. I wish I might die, mistress.

ARTEMIS. You did terrible things, but nevertheless it is still possible for you to win pardon even for this. For Cypris wished
this to happen to satisfy her passion. This is the way of the
gods—none of us wishes to oppose the purpose willed by 1330
another, but we always stand off.* You can rest assured that,
if I did not fear Zeus, I should never have sunk to such a
depth of shame as to allow the dearest man to me of all on
earth to die.

As for your fault, first of all the fact of your ignorance
acquits you of wickedness. Then your wife by her death
made it impossible to question her about what she had said
and so convinced your judgement.

What a calamity has burst upon you—and has brought
me grief as well! The gods do not rejoice when pious men 1340
die.* It is the bad on whom we wreak utter destruction, on
their children, house and all.

> HIPPOLYTUS *enters, supported by his servants.*

CHORUS [*chants*].
But look, here comes the wretched man,
his youthful flesh disfigured, his blond head
in bloody ruin. Woe for the sufferings of the house!
See what has been brought to fulfilment upon these halls.
Twofold is the sorrow* sent by the gods to seize on them.
HIPPOLYTUS [*chants*].
Alas! alas!
Look upon me in my misery, my body in bloody ruin
through the unjust curse of an unjust father.
Cry alas for me, the unhappy one who is no more.   1350
Through my head darts pain
and through my brain leaps a spasm of agony.
Stop, let me rest my failing body.
Ah! ah!
O hateful horses which drew me,
fed by my own hand,
you have destroyed me, you have killed me.
Alas! alas! For the gods' sake, servants,
handle this mangled flesh gently.
Who is standing by my side on my right?   1360
Hold me up as you should, drag me along gently,

a man ill-starred and accursed
through my father's wrong-doing. Zeus, Zeus, do you see
   this?
Here am I, a god-fearing man, proud to be pious,
one who surpassed all others in virtue,
making my way, in foreknowledge of my fate, to Hades,*
my life destroyed root and branch, and it was in vain
that I laboured at the work of reverence
towards my fellow men.
Aiai, aiai!   1370
Now, yes now, the agony comes upon me, agony.
Let go of your wretched burden, let me go
and may death the healer come to me.
Finish me off, finish my misery.
I long for a two-edged blade
to cut me apart and lull my life
to sleep.
O the miserable curse of my father!
Some blood-stained evil
inherited from my ancient ancestors   1380
breaks its bounds, it does not rest within them,
and it has come against me*—but why against *me*,
a man wholly innocent
of evil?
Ah, I cry woe.
What can I say? How can I free
my life from this suffering
and find release from pain?
Would that the night-black doom
of dark Hades would lay
my wretched self to rest!

ARTEMIS. Unhappy man, locked in the embrace of this cat-
   astrophe. It is the nobility of your spirit that has destroyed 1390
   you.
HIPPOLYTUS. Ah! the fragrance of a god's breath. I recognized
   you even in my sufferings and my body's pain was lightened.
   The goddess Artemis is in this place.
ARTEMIS. Unhappy man, to you she is the dearest of the gods.
HIPPOLYTUS. Do you see me, mistress, in my wretched state?

ARTEMIS. I see you*—but it is not proper for my eyes to shed a tear.*

HIPPOLYTUS. Your huntsman and your servant is no more.

ARTEMIS. No more. But though you are dying, you are dear to me.

HIPPOLYTUS. Your groom and the guardian of your images is no more.

ARTEMIS. No, for Cypris, who will stop at nothing, planned it so. 1400

HIPPOLYTUS. Alas, I now understand what god it was that has destroyed me.

ARTEMIS. She found fault with you since you paid her no honour and your chastity enraged her.

HIPPOLYTUS. One goddess—I see it now—has destroyed the three of us.

ARTEMIS. Yes, your father and you—and the third was his wife.*

HIPPOLYTUS. Well then, I cry alas for my father's unhappy fortune too.

ARTEMIS. He was misled by the goddess's design.

HIPPOLYTUS. O you my father,* how utterly wretched you are in this catastrophe!

THESEUS. All is over for me, my child, and there is no joy left for me in life.

HIPPOLYTUS. It is you I grieve for rather than myself for your tragic mistake.

THESEUS. If only I could die instead of you, my child! 1410

HIPPOLYTUS. O the gifts of your father Poseidon, how bitter they proved!

THESEUS. How I wish that they had never found utterance on my lips.

HIPPOLYTUS. But why? You would have killed me, you were so angry then.

THESEUS. Yes, my mind was deluded by the gods.

HIPPOLYTUS. Alas, the gods! If only the race of mortal men could prove a curse to them!*

ARTEMIS. Let it be. Not even beneath the darkness of the earth shall the rage of the goddess Cypris as she works her purpose sweep down upon your body and remain unrequited—no, it shall be avenged, a reward for your reverence and your virtuous mind. No, with this hand I shall take 1420 vengeance on another man, one of hers, one who is most loved by her above all mortals, with these arrows from which there is no escape.*

As for you, wretched man, in recompense for these sufferings I shall give you the greatest honours in the city of Trozen. Unwed girls will cut their hair in tribute to you before their marriage,* and throughout the length of time you will reap your reward from the deepest sorrow of their tears. And the maidens' care for you will always find expression in song, so that Phaedra's love for you will not slip into 1430 silence* and die without a name.

You, son of old Aegeus, take your boy in your arms and clasp him tight. It was in all innocence that you destroyed him, and it is natural that men should fall into error when the gods dispense things thus. And I bid you, Hippolytus, not to hate your father. For it is your fate to have met destruction in this manner.

And now farewell. It is not proper for me to look upon the dead or to pollute my sight as men breathe their last and die.* I see that you are now near this evil fate.

HIPPOLYTUS. Go on your way, blithe maiden, and joy go with you. 1440

[*ARTEMIS leaves.*

How easily you take leave of our long companionship! Since you desire it, I call a truce to my quarrel with my father— for I have always obeyed your commands. Ah, ah! Darkness now comes to me, falling upon my eyes. Take me, my father, and compose my body for death.

THESEUS. Alas, my son, what are you doing to me in my utter wretchedness?

HIPPOLYTUS. My life is over—I see the gates of those who dwell below.

THESEUS. Will you die and leave me thus, my hands stained with pollution?

HIPPOLYTUS. No, since I free you from the guilt of my death.

THESEUS. What are you saying? Are you releasing me from the 1450 curse of bloodshed?

HIPPOLYTUS. I call Artemis, the archer goddess, to witness it.

THESEUS. O dearest son, how plainly your father can see your nobility.

HIPPOLYTUS. I bid you too farewell, O father—and fare well indeed.

THESEUS. I cry alas for your reverent and virtuous spirit.

HIPPOLYTUS. Pray that you find your legitimate sons of such a
    stamp.

THESEUS. Do not desert me my child. Endure.

HIPPOLYTUS. My endurance is at an end—my death is upon
    me, father. With all due speed place a covering my face.

THESEUS. O glorious bounds of Aphaia* and Pallas, what a man 1460
    will you lose in Hippolytus! O wretched Theseus! How often
    shall I think upon the evils wrought by you, Cypris.

　　　　[*THESEUS goes out and the body of* HIPPOLYTUS *is carried out.*

CHORUS [*chants*].

　　　　This sorrow has come against our expectation
　　　　for all the citizens to share.*
　　　　Again and again many tears will break forth.
　　　　For traditions concerning the great
　　　　have greater power
　　　　and call for grief.　　　　　　　　[*The* CHORUS *goes out.*

ELECTRA

Characters

FARMER
ELECTRA, daughter of Agamemnon
ORESTES, her brother
PYLADES, friend of Orestes
OLD MAN
MESSENGER
CLYTEMNESTRA, mother of Electra and Orestes
CASTOR and POLYDEUCES

CHORUS OF COUNTRY WOMEN

The scene is a remote farm near the borders of Argos. The time is just before dawn. The FARMER *emerges from his farmhouse.**

FARMER. O ancient land of Argos where the waters of the river Inachus flow—it was from you that King Agamemnon once set out for war* on a thousand ships and sailed to the land of Troy. He killed Priam, master of the land of Ilion, he took the famous city of Dardanus*, came back to Argos here, and fixed to our temples' towering walls countless barbarian spoils. Over there he had had good fortune; but here at home he met his death through the tricks of his wife Clytemnestra;* Aegisthus, son of Thyestes, joined her in the deed.   10

So Agamemnon is dead and no longer holds the ancient sceptre of Tantalus. Now Aegisthus rules over the land. He has taken that man's wife, the daughter of Tyndareus, as his own.* As for the children Agamemnon left at home when he sailed to Troy, the boy Orestes and the girl Electra, when Orestes was about to be killed by Aegisthus, his father's tutor smuggled him away to the land of the Phocians and gave him to Strophius to bring up.* Meanwhile Electra remained in her father's house, and when she grew to the time when   20 youth is in blossom, the leading men of Greece began to ask for her as wife. Yet Aegisthus was afraid that she might bear

to a noble husband a child who would avenge Agamemnon;
so he kept her in the house—no betrothal for her.

But this course, too, was fraught with much fear—she
might bear children to some nobleman secretly—and so he
planned to kill her. Her mother may have had a savage
heart, but even so she saved her daughter from Aegisthus'
hand. She had a pretext for her husband's death* but was
afraid that, if she killed her children, she would stir up bit-   30
ter hatred. And so Aegisthus devised the following scheme:
Agamemnon's son had left the land a runaway, and he
promised gold to whoever killed him. Electra he gave to me
to be my wife. I was born of Mycenaean* ancestry—no fault
can be found with me in that respect since, as far as birth
goes, I shine bright, but in possessions I am poor, and that's
what undermines nobility.* By giving her to a lesser man, he
thought he'd have less to fear, but if a man of rank had her,   40
he would have wakened the sleeping murder of Agamem-
non. Justice would have come to Aegisthus then.

The man who stands here has never—Aphrodite* is my
witness—shamed her in bed—she is a virgin still. I'd be
ashamed to take a child of a blessed family and then to treat
her disrespectfully—I am not worthy of her. And I sigh for
my so-called brother-in-law,* poor Orestes, in case he ever
comes to Argos and sees the unlucky match his sister has
made.

But if anyone says that I am stupid if I take a young vir-   50
gin into my house and do not lay a finger on her, let him
know that he measures good behaviour by bad standards of
judgement and that he is stupid too.

ELECTRA *enters from the farmhouse. Her hair is cropped, she is
dressed in rags, and she carries a water pitcher on her head.*

ELECTRA. Night, black night, nurse of golden stars, night in
which I carry this pitcher on my head as I go to fetch the
waters of the river's streams and send forth groans for my
father into the vast skỳ. It is not necessity that has reduced
me to such a pass. No, I want to make the gods see plainly
the brutal, impious way Aegisthus treats me.* The devilish   60
daughter of Tyndareus, my mother, has done her husband
a favour by throwing me out of my house. She has had other

children by Aegisthus—Orestes and I no longer have any
rights there.

FARMER. Unhappy woman, why do you slave away for me like
this? You were brought up for something far better. Why
don't you stop when I tell you to?

ELECTRA. A friend like the gods, that's how I look on you. I
have been vilely treated but you have shown me respect.
People are very fortunate if they find a doctor to cure mis-   70
fortune—and I find one in you. So, even though you do not
tell me to, I must lighten your work as far as I can by helping you with it. Then it will be easier for you. You have
enough to do out of doors. It is my task to see to everything
inside the house.* When a working man comes back home,
it is a pleasure for him to find things in order there.

FARMER. If this is how you feel, go on your way. In fact the river
is not far from our house. At daybreak I shall drive my oxen
into the field and sow the soil. A lazy man couldn't gather   80
together a livelihood, not even if he was always praying to
the gods. It takes hard work.   [*The FARMER and ELECTRA go out.*

From the opposite side of the stage ORESTES and PYLADES enter.

ORESTES. Pylades,* in you I see the trustiest and dearest of men,
my truest friend. You alone of those I love were willing to
show honour to Orestes here, reduced to what I am now
after my terrible sufferings from Aegisthus. He killed my
father—he and my hellish mother. Without anyone knowing, I have come from the god's holy oracle to the land of
Argos to exchange murder with my father's murderers.*
And during this very night I eluded the tyrants who rule this   90
land and went to my father's tomb. I gave him tears and
offered him a lock of my hair and slaughtered a sheep* and
shed its blood over the altar hearth. I do not set foot inside
the city walls, since it is with two aims jostling in my mind
that I have come to the borders of this land—to make a getaway to another country if anyone spots and recognizes
me—and to look for my sister. They say that she is no longer
a virgin but lives in wedlock. I want to join with her, to take 100
her as my partner in murder and to find out for certain what
is going on inside the city walls.

So now—for dawn now lifts her bright white eye*—let's

step aside from this well-worn track. Some ploughman or
slave woman will come our way and we can ask them if my
sister lives in this area.

But look, here comes a servant carrying a pitcher heavy
with water on her close-cropped head.* Let's hide and listen
to this slave woman. Perhaps we may hear something about   110
the business which has brought us to this land.

                        [ORESTES *and* PYLADES *withdraw.**

    ELECTRA *enters, her water pitcher on her head.*

ELECTRA [*sings*].
    Hasten your pace forwards—it is time to do so—oh,
    onward, onward, weeping.
    Alas for me!
    I was born the daughter of Agamemnon,
    was brought to birth by Clytemnestra,
    the hateful daughter of Tyndareus,
    and the citizens call me
    Electra the wretched.
    Alas, alas for my cruel sufferings   120
    and my hateful existence—
    while you, father, lie in Hades,
    butchered by your wife and Aegisthus,
    father Agamemnon.

    Come, awake the familiar strains of woe,
    rouse the pleasure that comes with many tears.*

    Hasten your pace forwards—it is time to do so—oh,
    onward, onward, weeping.
    Alas for me!
    to what city, to what house,   130
    my miserable brother, do you wander,
    abandoning your pitiable sister
    amid the most painful sufferings
    in our ancestral halls?*
    O come to free me,
    wretched Electra, from my miseries—
    O Zeus, Zeus*—and to champion my father
    for his blood most foully shed,
    bringing your wandering steps to shore in Argos.

Let me take this pitcher from my head and put it down   140
so that I can cry out to my father in the early morning
the laments which I pour forth all night.
I give voice to a cry, a song, a dirge
of Hades,* father, for you beneath the earth—
the laments through which I waste away without respite
day after day as I claw
my own throat with my fingernails
and batter at my close-cropped head* with my hands
in mourning for your death.

Ah, ah, let me tear my hair,   150
and as a tuneful swan
by the river's streams
calls to its much-loved father—
but he lies dead in the tricky snares of the net—,
so do I weep for you, my father,
the wretched man,*

your flesh washed in the last washing of all,
in death's most lamentable repose.*
Alas, alas I cry
for the cruel cutting of the axe,   160
for the cruel plotting,
schemed, father, for your return from Troy.
It was not with ribbons of victory that your wife greeted you
and not with garlands either.
No, she made you the victim of the grim outrage
of Aegisthus' two-edged sword*
and got a husband through guile.

*The CHORUS OF COUNTRY WOMEN enters**

CHORUS [*sings*].
O Electra, daughter of Agamemnon, I have come
to your country home.
There came to us, there came a man who drinks not wine
     but milk,*
a Mycenaean herdsman who walks the mountains;   170
he brings news that the Argives have proclaimed a festival
for two days hence,
and all the unmarried women are planning to process
to Hera's temple.*

ELECTRA [*sings*].

    It is not bright clothes, my friends,
    nor golden necklaces
    that set my wretched heart aflutter,
    and I shall not direct the dance
    among the Argive girls
    and stamp and whirl my feet.   180
    In tears I spend the night
    and tears are my concern
    every day in my misery.
    Look at my filthy hair
    and these rags that are my clothes.
    Do they befit the royal daughter of Agamemnon
    and Troy, which has cause
    to remember my father,
    its captor?

CHORUS [*sings*].

    The goddess is great. Come, let me lend you   190
    close-woven garments to wear
    and golden ornaments to set off the grace of fine
      robes.*
    Do you think, if you do not honour the gods,
    you will conquer your enemies simply with your tears?
    No, it is by showing the gods reverence
    not with groans but with prayers
    that you will find fair weather, my child.

ELECTRA [*sings*].

    None of the gods listens to the voice
    of the unhappy one, none to my father's blood
    shed long ago.   200
    Alas for the dead man
    and for the living wanderer
    who dwells somewhere in another country,
    trudging, poor man, from one workman's hearth to
      another,
    though born of a famous father—
    while I myself live in a labourer's house,
    wasting my soul away,
    an exile from my ancestral home
    up among the crags of the mountains,   210

and my mother lives in a blood-stained marriage,
the wife of another man.

CHORUS. Helen, your mother's sister, is to blame for bringing
many evils on the Greeks and your house.

ORESTES and PYLADES emerge from their hiding place.

ELECTRA. Alas! Women, I break off my lament. Here are some
strangers; they have been hiding near the house behind the
altar and are now stepping out from their place of ambush.
Let's escape from these villains—you run off down the path
and I'll rush into the house.

ORESTES. Stop, you poor woman. You need fear no violence 220
from me.*

ELECTRA. O Phoebus Apollo,* I beg you not to let him kill me.

ORESTES. There are others I'd rather kill; they are more my enemies than you.

ELECTRA. Go away. Do not touch what you have no right to
touch.

ORESTES. There is no one I would have *more* right to touch.

ELECTRA. Then why are you lurking outside my house with a
sword?

ORESTES. Stay and listen, and soon you will agree with me.

ELECTRA. I am standing still. I am utterly in your power. You
are stronger than me.

ORESTES. I have come to bring you word of your brother.

ELECTRA. O my dearest friend, is he alive or dead?

ORESTES. He is alive. I want to give you the good news first. 230

ELECTRA. My blessings on you—the reward for sweetest words.

ORESTES. May the two of us share together in those blessings!

ELECTRA. In which land does the wretched man eke out his
wretched exile?

ORESTES. From city to city he wanders as he wastes away.

ELECTRA. Surely he doesn't lack the daily necessities of life?

ORESTES. No, but a man in exile is weak.

ELECTRA. What have you come to say to me from him?

ORESTES. I am to find out if you are alive and, if so, what kind
of life you are leading.

ELECTRA. First of all then, can't you see how haggard my body
is?

ORESTES. Yes, withered away with grief—that makes me sigh. 240

ELECTRA. And my head and hair close-cropped by the razor.

ORESTES. Your brother's fate and your father's death gnaw at you perhaps?

ELECTRA. Woe is me—what is more dear to me than they are?

ORESTES. Alas, alas! Yet what is more dear to your brother, do you think, than you?

ELECTRA. He may love me, but he's far away, not with me now.

ORESTES. But why do you live here at such a distance from the city?

ELECTRA. I have married, stranger, married death.

ORESTES. I grieve for your brother's sake. Which Mycenaean have you married?

ELECTRA. Not the one my father once hoped he would give me to.

ORESTES. Tell me, so that I can hear and inform your brother. 250

ELECTRA. It's my husband's house that I live in here, far from the city.

ORESTES. Is he a labourer or a herdsman—as seems appropriate to the house?

ELECTRA. He is a poor man but a noble one and he treats me with respect.

ORESTES. What is this respect your husband shows you?

ELECTRA. He has never forced himself on me.

ORESTES. Is this because of some vow of chastity*—or does he look down on you?

ELECTRA. He didn't think it right to show disrespect to my ancestors.

ORESTES. Why wasn't he delighted to have made this match?

ELECTRA. He considers that the man who gave me in marriage had no right to do so,* stranger.

ORESTES. I understand. He is afraid that Orestes may take 260 revenge one day.

ELECTRA. He does fear that. But he also has integrity.

ORESTES. Ah! It is a noble man you are speaking of.* He must be treated well.

ELECTRA. Yes, if the man who is now away ever comes home.

ORESTES. Did the woman who bore you accept this?

ELECTRA. Women love men,* stranger, not their children.

ORESTES. Why did Aegisthus degrade you in this way?

ELECTRA. By marrying me to a man like this, he wanted to make my children powerless.

ORESTES. So that you wouldn't bear sons who would take revenge?

ELECTRA. That was his plan. May he pay me the price for this!

ORESTES. Does your mother's husband know that you are still 270 a virgin?

ELECTRA. No, we say nothing and keep him in the dark.

ORESTES. So are these women who are listening to our talk your friends?

ELECTRA. Yes, and they won't breathe a word of what we are saying to each other.

ORESTES. What then is Orestes to do in the light of all this if he comes to Argos?

ELECTRA. Can you ask this? A shameful question! Is it not now high time?

ORESTES. When he does come, how could he kill his father's murderers?

ELECTRA. By daring to do to his enemies what they dared do to his father.

ORESTES. Would you truly have the hardihood to join him in killing your mother?

ELECTRA. Yes, with the same axe* that took my father's life.

ORESTES. Do I tell him this—can he count on your cooperation? 280

ELECTRA. I would die happy if I had shed my mother's blood in revenge.

ORESTES. Ah! If only Orestes were nearby to hear these words!

ELECTRA. But, stranger, I wouldn't recognize him* if I saw him.

ORESTES. No wonder, for you were both young when you separated.

ELECTRA. Only one of my friends would recognize him.

ORESTES. Do you mean the man who they say stole him away from death?

ELECTRA. Yes, an old man, the ancient tutor of my father.

ORESTES. They killed your father—did they give him a tomb?

ELECTRA. They gave him what they gave him—he was cast out of the house.*

ORESTES. Alas, what is this that you have said! Yes, men are 290 hard hit by the awareness of other men's woes as well as their own. Speak to me, so that with the full knowledge I can take to your brother words which bring no joy, yet must be heard. Sympathy keeps no company with the boorish but only with sensitive men. Yes, and having too sensitive a spirit takes its toll on the sensitive.

CHORUS. My heart longs to hear this as well as him, for, since I live far from the city, I do not know the horrors there, and I too want to learn of them.

ELECTRA. I am ready to speak if I must—and one must speak   300
to a friend—to speak of my and my father's heavy fortunes. And since you urge me to speak, I beg you, stranger, tell Orestes of my evils and of his. Tell him first of the sort of clothes which give me shelter, of the terrible filth that cakes me, of the kind of house that is my home—though once I dwelt in a royal palace. I myself labour at my own clothes with the shuttle* or I shall have to do without them and be naked. I myself carry water from the river. I have no place   310
at festivals,* I must stand apart from the dances. I keep clear of married women since I am still a virgin, and I feel shame at the thought of Castor,* who wooed me, his kinswoman, before he went to join the gods. Meanwhile my mother sits on her throne amid the spoils of Phrygia,* and beside her seat stand Asian slave girls whom my father won when he sacked Troy, their robes from Ida's land fastened with golden brooches.* But my father's blood still rots black in the house and the man who killed him mounts his victim's chariot to   320
ride abroad. Ecstatically he clasps in his murdering hands my father's sceptre, his emblem of command over the Greeks. But Agamemnon's tomb is dishonoured. It has never yet received libations or a shoot of myrtle.* His altar is dry of any tributes. And, soaked with wine, my mother's husband, famous man, leaps, they say, upon my father's tomb and batters his marble monument with stones, and he has the face to say these words against us: 'Where is your son   330
Orestes? Isn't he here to prove a good guard for your tomb?'—these insults to an absent man.

  Stranger, I beg you, take this message back. Many bid him come—it is I who give them voice—, my hands, my tongue, my miserable thoughts, my shaven head, and he who fathered him. For, if his father destroyed the Trojans, it is disgraceful if he cannot kill one man, one to one, young as he is and the son of a better father.

CHORUS. Look, I see this man, your husband I mean. He has 340
stopped working and is on his way home.

The FARMER re-enters.

FARMER [*starts in surprise*]. What's this? Who are these
strangers I see at the door? Why have they come to our
country door? Is it me they want? It is a shameful thing, I
tell you, for a woman to stand around with young men.*

ELECTRA. My dearest husband, don't get suspicious of me. You
will discover the truth. These strangers have come to bring
me news of Orestes. Strangers, forgive what he has said.

FARMER. What news do they bring? Is he alive, still in the
upper world?

ELECTRA. That's what they tell me, and I believe their words. 350

FARMER. And does he think at all of you and your father's woes?

ELECTRA. I hope so; but a man in exile is weak.

FARMER. What news of Orestes have they brought?

ELECTRA. He sent them to see my woes.

FARMER. They can see some of them, surely? You, I suppose,
have told them the others.*

ELECTRA. They know them: nothing remains unsaid.

FARMER. Then surely you should have opened the doors to
them some time ago? Enter our house. In return for your
good words you will meet with such hospitality as my home
affords. Attendants,* bring their baggage inside our house. 360
And don't think of saying no. After all, you are friends since
you come from a man who is our friend. Even if I am poor,
I shall certainly not show a churlish nature.

ORESTES. By the gods, is this the man who makes a pretence of
marriage with you since he does not want to shame Orestes?

ELECTRA. Yes, this is the so-called husband of the wretched
woman before you.

ORESTES. Ah! There's no effective touchstone to identify a good
man. Classifying men's natures is a confusing business.
Before now I've seen the son of a noble father turning out 370
worthless, while the children of bad men prove good; I have
seen emptiness in a wealthy man's mind but a great spirit in
a poor body. So how can a man make a good judgement in
distinguishing between the good and the bad? By wealth?
But there he'll find a poor yardstick. By the lack of worldly

goods? But a sickness attends poverty and teaches a man to
be bad out of necessity. Or by considering fighting prowess?
But who can face the enemies' spears and prove a witness of
which man is brave? It is best to accept that this is all hap-
hazard and to let it alone.* This man, who is neither great   380
among the Argives nor swollen-headed because of a famous
lineage, just an ordinary man in fact, we have found to be
truly good. Give up your folly, you who are crammed with
empty ways of thought and go astray. No, you should judge
men by the company they keep and how they behave. It is
men like this who manage cities and homes well. But empty-
headed hunks* are only good for looking decorative in the
city centre. Even in battle the muscular man stands no more
steadfastly than the weak. It all comes down to one's nature 390
and courage.

   But, seeing that the son of Agamemnon, present in me
though absent in person, is worthy of it—for his sake we
have come—, let us accept the hospitality of this dwelling.
You must go inside this house, servants. I'd rather have a
poor but generous host than a rich one. I am grateful for the
way this man receives us into his home, but I could have
wished that your brother prospered and were leading me
into a prosperous house. Perhaps he may come. For the oracles of Apollo do not fail;* but by human prophecy I set no   400
store.   [ORESTES *and* PYLADES *enter the house.*

CHORUS. Now, Electra, now more than before our hearts are
   warmed with joy. For perhaps your fortune, which limps
   slowly forward, may take its stand successfully.

ELECTRA. You thoughtless man, you know the poverty of your
   house and these guests are your betters. Why have you
   invited them in?

FARMER. What's the problem? If they are noble—which they
   seem to be—surely they will be as content with the humble
   as with the great?

ELECTRA. Since you have blundered by forgetting your humble
   station, go to the dear old tutor of my father. In exile from
   the city, he tends his herds around the river Tanaus* which 410
   cuts through the borders of Argos and Sparta. Tell him that
   this man has come to our house and that he should bring
   some gifts for a meal. He'll be delighted, I tell you, and will

offer a prayer of thanks to the gods when he hears that the
boy whom he once saved is alive. We wouldn't get anything
from my father's home from my mother. We should bring
bitter news if that hard woman were to find out that Orestes
is still living.

FARMER. Well, if it seems best to you, I'll pass on this news to 420
the old man. You go into the house right away and get ready
what's inside. A woman can find plenty to add some flavour
to a meal if she wants to. And in fact we've still got enough
plain food in the house to fill these men for one day anyhow.

[*ELECTRA goes into the house.*

Whenever my thoughts turn to such matters, I see what
great power money has. It allows one to be generous to
guests and to pay the doctor to save a body which has fallen
sick. But the cost of plain food for a day doesn't come to 430
much. Every man, whether rich or poor, holds an equal
quantity in his belly when it's been filled.

[*The FARMER goes out.*

CHORUS.

Famous ships, ships which once went to Troy*
with your numberless oars,
escorting the dancing Nereids*
where the dolphin which loves the pipe*
leapt spinning
by the dark-blue prows,
taking on his way the son of Thetis,
light-footed Achilles,*
with Agamemnon to the banks
of Simois, river of Troy.   440

The Nereids, leaving the headlands of Euboea,
carried the golden shield, the golden armour,
the work of Hephaestus' anvil,*
up along Pelion, up along the sacred woods
of sheer Mount Ossa,
seeking the Nymphs where they keep their watch,
where the horseman father was rearing
the son of the sea-nymph Thetis,* swift-treading Achilles,
to be a light for Greece,   450
a help to the sons of Atreus.

I heard from a man who had come from Troy
in the harbour of Nauplia*
that on the circle of your famous shield,*
o son of Thetis,
these were emblems—terrors
to the Trojans—which had been fashioned:
on the rim which runs round its edge
was Perseus* who cut the Gorgon's throat,
carrying her head over the sea
as he flew on his winged sandals with Hermes,   460
Zeus' messenger, the rustic son of Maia.*

And on the middle of the shield there shone*
the blazing circle of the sun
with its winged horses
and the dances of the stars in the sky,
the Pleiades, the Hyades—which turned
away the eyes of Hector:*
on the helmet of beaten gold   470
were Sphinxes* carrying in their talons
the prey they had won with their song;
on the cuirass to enclose his ribs
the fire-breathing Chimaera hurried running
on its clawed feet when it saw the colt of Peirene.*

On the deadly sword leapt four-footed horses
and black dust swirled around their backs.
It was the king of such warriors
that your adultery killed, daughter of Tyndareus,*   480
schemer of evil.
For that the heavenly ones shall at some time
send you the just punishment of death.
The day will come when I shall see
beneath your throat the blood of death
spilt by the sword.

Enter the OLD MAN.

OLD MAN. Where, where* is my young lady and mistress, the
daughter of Agamemnon whom I once brought up? How
steep the approach to her house is—a difficult walk for a   490

wrinkled old man like me. Still, they are my friends and I must stagger along, back bent double, knee tottering:

Enter ELECTRA.

O my daughter—I've just seen you by the house—here I am bringing you this young offspring of my grazing flocks, which I drew from under its mother, as well as garlands and cheeses taken from the press and this hoary treasure of Dionysus* with its delicious scent—just a little, but it is pleasant to pour a cup of it into a weaker drink.* Can some- 500 one* go and take these into the house for the guests? I've made my eyes wet with weeping and want to dry them with these rags which are my clothes.

ELECTRA. Why are your eyes moist like this, old man? It's not, I hope, that my situation—you have not been here for some time—has reminded you of our unhappy story? Or do you grieve over the wretched exile of Orestes and for my father whom you once held in your arms but reared to prove no benefit to yourself* and your friends?

OLD MAN. No benefit—but still here is one thing I didn't leave undone: I made a detour on my journey and came to his grave, fell to my knees and wept to find it neglected. I undid 510 the wineskin which I am carrying for your guests, poured a libation and placed myrtle branches round the tomb. But on the altar itself I saw a slaughtered black-fleeced sheep, its blood not long shed, and shorn locks of golden hair.* And I wondered, my child, who in the world had had the courage to go to the tomb—no Argive would have done so. But per- haps it may be that your brother has come in secret and on his return paid honour to his father's sad tomb. Put this 520 lock* beside your hair and see if it proves to be the same colour as the cut hair. Usually when people are of the blood of the same father, most of their physical characteristics are similar.

ELECTRA. What you say, old fellow, is unworthy of a wise man. Do you really think that my bold brother would come to this country by stealth in fear of Aegisthus? And then how can locks of hair be compared when one has been grown by a noble man in the wrestling schools,* while the other comes from a woman who uses a comb? It's impossible. You could 530 find many people whose hair looks alike though they are not born from the same blood, old man.

OLD MAN. Well then, go and step in the footprint and see whether the imprint of the shoe matches your foot, my child.

ELECTRA. How could there be a footprint in a rocky stretch of land? And if there is one, how could the foot of a brother and a sister be the same size? The man's is bigger.

OLD MAN. If your brother has come to the land and visited the tomb,* is there not some bit of cloth woven by you by which you could recognize him—the clothing in which I once stole 540 him away from his death?

ELECTRA. Don't you know that when Orestes left the country I was still a young girl? And even if I had woven garments, how could he now wear the same clothes as then when he was a child—unless his garments had grown up with his body? But either some stranger has cut off a lock in pity of Agamemnon's tomb or some Argive has eluded Aegisthus' spies.

OLD MAN. But your guests, where are they? I want to see them and ask about your brother.

ELECTRA. Here they come, stepping quickly out of the house.

Enter ORESTES *and* PYLADES.

OLD MAN. Well, they are noble—but this can be misleading. 550 Many noblemen are in fact base.* But even so I give greetings to your guests.

ORESTES. Greetings, old man. Electra, to which of your friends does this ancient husk of a man belong?

ELECTRA. He is the one who brought up my father, stranger.

ORESTES. What is this you say? Is he the one who stole away your brother?

ELECTRA. This is the one who saved him—if he still exists.

ORESTES. Here! Why is he looking at me as if examining the bright stamp on a silver coin?* Can he think I look like someone else?

ELECTRA. You are Orestes' friend—perhaps that is why he is 560 glad to see you.*

ORESTES. Orestes is my friend. But why is he walking around me?

ELECTRA. I myself am wondering too as I see this, stranger.

OLD MAN. O mistress, daughter Electra, pray to the gods.

ELECTRA. To get or to alter what?

OLD MAN. To take a precious treasure which the god reveals to you.

ELECTRA. See, I call on the gods. Or do you mean something else, old man?

OLD MAN. Look then at this man, my child, the dearest man in the world.

ELECTRA. I've been looking for a long time. Have you gone out of your mind?

OLD MAN. Am I out of my mind as I see your brother?

ELECTRA. What are these unhoped-for words that you have 570 said, old man?

OLD MAN. That you see here Orestes, the son of Agamemnon.

ELECTRA. What proof can I see in which I may trust?

OLD MAN. A scar by his eyebrow where once, as he chased a fawn with you in your father's house, he was bloodied when he fell.*

ELECTRA. What do you mean? I do see the evidence of a fall.

OLD MAN. Do you hesitate then to embrace your dearest friend in the world?

ELECTRA. No longer, old man. My heart is persuaded by your proof. [*to* ORESTES] You have come at last—against all expectations I hold you.

ORESTES. And you are held by me at last.

ELECTRA.   I never thought it would happen.

ORESTES. I too never expected it.   580

ELECTRA.   Are you he?

ORESTES. Yes, your only friend. But if I can snare and draw in the catch I pursue . . . Still I am confident. Otherwise we must no longer believe that the gods exist if injustice is to prove stronger than justice.

CHORUS [*sings*].
    You have come, O day, at long last you have come,
    you have blazed forth, have shown to the city
    no doubtful beacon* in this man who went wandering
    long a wretched exile from his father's house.
    A god, yes, a god ushers in   590
    our victory, dear girl.
    Lift up your hands, lift up your voice,

and send forth prayers to the god,
that your brother may walk
with great good fortune in his city.

ORESTES. Well then, now I possess the precious delight of your
embraces and shall repay them in my turn in time to come.
But you, old man, you have come just at the right moment
to tell me what I must do to take revenge on my father's
murderer and on my mother, his partner in a blasphemous 600
marriage? Do I have any good friends in Argos or am I
utterly bankrupt like my fortunes? Who should I meet with?
Should we meet by night or day? What sort of road am I to
take against my enemies?

OLD MAN. My child, you have no friend in your misfortunes. In
fact it is a real godsend to find a man to share in good and
bad alike. In your friends' eyes you are utterly ruined and
you have left them no hope. So listen to me and learn. It is 610
only by your courage and your fortunes that you will win
your father's house and city.

ORESTES. Then what do I have to do to gain this end?*

OLD MAN. You must kill the son of Thyestes and your mother.

ORESTES. This is the crown* I have come for. But how can I
grasp it?

OLD MAN. You shouldn't go inside the city walls even if you
want to.

ORESTES. He has plenty of strong bodyguards to protect him?

OLD MAN. You're right, for he fears you and does not sleep
soundly.

ORESTES. Well then, you advise me on the next step, old man.

OLD MAN. Listen to what I say then—something has just
occurred to me.

ORESTES. I hope you can come up with a good plan—and that 620
I can see that it is good.

OLD MAN. I saw Aegisthus when I was on my way here.

ORESTES. This is music to my ears. Where?

OLD MAN. Near these fields on the horse pastures.

ORESTES. What was he doing? I see hope amid my helplessness.

OLD MAN. He was preparing a festival for the Nymphs,* as I
thought.

ORESTES. For his children's well being or for a birth to come?

OLD MAN. I know only one thing. He had the equipment to kill an ox.

ORESTES. How many men were with him? Or was he alone with his slaves?

OLD MAN. No Argive was there, just help from his household.

ORESTES. There is no one who will recognize me when he sees   630
me, old man?

OLD MAN. They are household slaves, and they never saw you.

ORESTES. Would they be well disposed towards us if we won?

OLD MAN. Yes, for this is characteristic of slaves—and it's advantageous for you.

ORESTES. So, however could I get close to him?

OLD MAN. By going where he will see you as he sacrifices the ox.

ORESTES. His fields are just by the road, I gather.

OLD MAN. Yes, and he will spot you from there and invite you to share in the feast.*

ORESTES. A cruel fellow-diner*—if the god so wills it.

OLD MAN. You must extemporize from then on, when you see how the dice fall.

ORESTES. That's helpful advice. But where is my mother?   640

OLD MAN. In Argos. But she will join her husband for the feast.

ORESTES. Why did my mother not set out at the same time as her husband?

OLD MAN. She fears the citizens' reproaches and stayed behind.

ORESTES. I understand. She realizes that the city eyes her askance.

OLD MAN. Something like that. People hate an unholy woman.

ORESTES. So what now? Shall I kill her and him at the same time?

ELECTRA [*suddenly interrupting*]. I shall arrange the killing of my mother.*

ORESTES. Certainly, and fortune will cause the murder of Aegisthus to succeed.

ELECTRA. Let this one man serve both of us.

ORESTES. By all means. How will you plan to murder our   650
mother?

ELECTRA. Go, old man, and say this to Clytemnestra. Tell her that I've just given birth to a boy.

OLD MAN. And that you gave birth some time ago or recently?

ELECTRA. Nine days since*—the time in which a woman in childbirth becomes purified.

OLD MAN. How can this lead to the murder of your mother?

ELECTRA. She will come when she hears that I am sick in childbirth.

OLD MAN. How can that be? Do you think she cares about you,
my child?

ELECTRA. Yes, and she will weep over my children's low birth.*

OLD MAN. Perhaps. Please bring the discussion back to the point.

ELECTRA. Well, it is clear that, once she has come, she dies.   660

OLD MAN. Very good, she will come to the doors of your house.

ELECTRA. Is it not a short journey to Hades then?

OLD MAN. If only I could see this and die.

ELECTRA. First of all then, point out the way to Orestes, old man.

OLD MAN. To where Aegisthus is now sacrificing to the god?

ELECTRA. Then meet my mother and tell her my message.

OLD MAN. I shall—so that the words seem to come from your
lips.

ELECTRA. The task is yours now. You have drawn the first lot
of death.

ORESTES. I am ready to go if someone would lead the way.

OLD MAN. And here am I to escort you willingly.   670

ORESTES. O Zeus, god of fathers and router of my enemies—*

ELECTRA. Pity us, for we have suffered pitifully.

OLD MAN. Yes, pity your descendants.

ORESTES. And Hera,* you who rule over the altars of Mycenae—

ELECTRA. Give us victory, if we pray for what is just.

OLD MAN. Yes, give these children just vengeance for their
father.

ORESTES. And you who dwell, impiously slain, beneath the
earth—

ELECTRA. And Queen Earth,* on whom I beat my hands—

OLD MAN. Defend, defend these your dearest children.

ORESTES. Come now, leading every corpse to fight alongside   680
you—

ELECTRA. All those who destroyed the Phrygians with you in
war—

OLD MAN. And all those who hate impious polluters—

ORESTES. Have you heard, you who suffered terrible things at
the hands of my mother?

OLD MAN. Your father hears all this, I know. Now it is time to
go.

ELECTRA. He hears all this, I know. This is the situation. You
must be a man. And I declare to you that Aegisthus must
die. For if you are thrown and suffer a fatal fall, I am dead
too. You are not to say that I live. I shall strike my head with
a double-edged sword. I'll go inside the house and make
things ready. And if happy news of you arrives, the whole 690
house will shout aloud for you. But if you die, things will be
very different. That is what I say to you.

You, women, be sure to raise your cry as a beacon to tell
me how this contest goes. I shall keep guard holding a sword
at the ready in my hand. If I am vanquished by my enemies,
I shall never let them violate my body in reprisal.

[ELECTRA *goes inside the house.*

CHORUS. A story is still told among the grey-haired tales*
that Pan, guardian of the fields, who breathes forth 700
sweet-sounding music on his harmonious reed pipes,*
brought from the Argive mountains
from under its delicate mother
a lamb with a beautiful golden fleece.
And a herald standing on the stone steps
shouts aloud:
'Come to the assembly, to the assembly,
Myceneans, to see
this lamb of our happy kings— 710
a fearful portent.'
And with dancing they honoured the house
of the family of Atreus.

Golden braziers were set out
and the fire on the Argive altars
blazed forth through the city;
And the pipe, servant of the Muses,*
sounds its most melodious music;
and lovely songs swelled up,
telling of the golden lamb, the possession
of Thyestes; for he wins over the dear wife 720
of Atreus with secret love
and carries off the marvellous lamb
to his house.
And going to the assembled people,

he declares that he has the horned creature
with the golden fleece in his house.

Then, then it was that Zeus
altered the shining journeys of the stars
and the radiant sun
and the bright white face of the dawn;   730
and he torments the Western regions*
with the hot flame of divine fire,
and the water-filled clouds go Northwards
and the parched lands where Ammon dwells*
wither up, drained of moisture,
cut off from the most beautiful rain showers from Zeus.

This is what they say—though it finds
small credence with me—*
that the gold-faced sun changed and reversed
his hot position in the sky   740
for mortal misfortune—
for the sake of justice among men.
But fearful myths bring gain to mortals
in ensuring service to the gods.
You did not remember them when you killed your husband,
you sister of famous brothers.

Listen! My friends, did you hear a cry—or did empty imagination suggest it to me?—a cry as of Zeus' subterranean
thunder? Listen, here is a breeze rising which brings its message. Mistress, come out of your house, Electra!   750

ELECTRA enters.

ELECTRA. My friends, what is happening? How have we done
  in the contest?
CHORUS. I know only one thing. I hear a groan which speaks
  death.
ELECTRA. I heard it too, from a distance but even so.
CHORUS. Yes, the sound travels far but is clear nevertheless.
ELECTRA. Is it Argives who groan—or my friends?
CHORUS. I don't know. The shouting is an utterly confused, dis-
  cordant noise.
ELECTRA. Your words mean death for me here. Why do I delay?

CHORUS. Wait, so that you can find out your fortunes clearly.

ELECTRA. There's no hope. We've lost. If we had won, messengers would have come.*

CHORUS. They will come. It is not a little thing to kill a king. 760

Enter MESSENGER.

MESSENGER. O maidens of Mycenae, winners of a glorious victory, I bring news to all Orestes' friends that he is the conqueror and that Aegisthus, the killer of Agamemnon, lies on the ground.* You must give grateful prayers to the gods.

ELECTRA. Who are you? How can I be sure that what you say is true?

MESSENGER. Don't you recognize me as your brother's attendant?

ELECTRA. My dearest friend, in my fear I didn't recognize your face but now I know who you are. What are you saying? Is the hateful murderer of my father dead?

MESSENGER. He is dead. I give you the same message a second 770 time—you want to hear it.

ELECTRA. O you gods, and Justice who sees all, at last you have come. In what way did he kill the son of Thyestes? What pattern did it follow? I want to know.

MESSENGER. When we had started out from your home here, we got onto the broad wagon-road and went to where the new king of the Myceneans was. He was standing on the well-watered gardens,* picking sprigs of delicate myrtle for his head.* Seeing us, he called out, 'Welcome, strangers!* Who are you? Where are you travelling from? What is your 780 native land?' And Orestes said, 'We are Thessalians, on our way to the river Alpheus* to sacrifice to Olympian Zeus.' Hearing that, Aegisthus spoke these words: 'Now you must join with us and share in our feast as our guests. It so happens that I am sacrificing an ox to the Nymphs. If you get up at dawn, staying here will make no difference to your journey. Now let us go into the house.'—and as he said these things, he took Orestes by the hand and led us off the road—'I'll brook no denial.' And when we were inside, he 790 said this: 'Can someone as quickly as possible bring purifying water for our guests so that they can take their stand by the altar near the lustral bowl.' But Orestes said, 'We have just purified ourselves* in cleansing waters from a river's

streams. If it is proper for foreigners to join in the sacrifice
with citizens, Aegisthus, we are ready and do not say no, my
lord.'

It was in the middle of the company that they exchanged
these words. But then the slaves, laying aside the spears
which guarded their master, all set their hands to the task;
some of them brought the victim, others lifted baskets,   800
others lit the fire and set up cauldrons* around the hearth.
The whole house resounded with the noise. Taking barley
meal,* the bedfellow of your mother threw it on the altars,
saying these words: 'Nymph of the rocks, may I often sacrifice oxen to you, I and my wife, the daughter of Tyndareus,
now at home, and may we fare as we fare now—but may
my enemies fare badly'—he meant Orestes and you. But my
master prayed the opposite, though he did not speak the
words aloud—that he would win his father's house.   810
Aegisthus, taking from the basket the straight-bladed knife,
cut some hair from the calf and with his right hand placed
it on the holy fire* and slaughtered the animal when the
slaves had lifted it onto their shoulders, and he said this to
your brother: 'The Thessalians' special expertise, they boast,
lies in cutting up a bull skilfully and breaking in a horse.
Take a knife, my guest, and show that what is said about
the Thessalians is true.' Orestes seized a well-made Dorian
knife in his hand, flung from his shoulders his handsome   820
cloak, chose Pylades to help him with his work and pushed
away the slave. Then taking the foot of the calf, he stretched
out his hand and laid bare the white flesh. And he skinned
the hide quicker than a runner completes twice the double
length of the hippodrome,* and he opened up the sides.
Taking the holy parts into his hands, Aegisthus examined
them. And in the intestines there was no lobe, and the portal vein and the gall bladder nearby made it clear that evil
was to attack the one who looked.* He glowered sullenly,   830
and my master asked him, 'Why are you downcast?' 'O
stranger, I shudder in fear of some stratagem from abroad.
The most hateful of men to me, the most bitter enemy to my
house, still lives, the son of Agamemnon.' Orestes said, 'Do
you fear the trickery of an exile, you who rule over a city?
Please—so that we can feast on the innards—won't some-

one bring us a Phthian cleaver to replace this Dorian knife
to break the breast bone?' And he took it and struck.
Aegisthus, taking the innards,* was scrutinizing them, sort-
ing them out. As he stooped down, your brother, standing 840
on the tips of his toes, smote him on his backbone and
smashed his spine. His whole body twisted and jerked con-
vulsively throughout its length as he died his grisly death.

His slaves leapt to their spears the moment they saw this,
a large number for a fight with two. But inspired by courage,
Orestes and Pylades stood there, brandishing their weapons
against them. Orestes said, 'I have not come as an enemy to
this city or to my servants. But I have taken vengeance on
my father's murderer, I, Orestes the wretched. Do not kill 850
me, former slaves of my father.' And when they heard his
words they held back their spears, and he was recognized by
an old, old man in the household. Immediately they gar-
landed your brother's head, raising joyous cries. He is coming to show the head to you—no Gorgon's head he brings
but Aegisthus whom you hate. The dead man has now paid
a bitter reckoning for bloodshed with his own blood.

[*Exit* MESSENGER.

CHORUS [*sings*]. Set your foot to the dance, dear girl, like a fawn 860
bounding its light leap heavenward as it sports.
Your brother is the victor; he has won the garland
for a greater victory than those by the streams of Alpheus.*
Sing a song of glorious conquest
to accompany my dance.

ELECTRA. O light, O brightness of the four-horsed chariot of the
Sun, O Earth, O Night,* on which I gazed before, now I can
open my eyes in freedom, for Aegisthus, the killer of my
father, has fallen. Come, my friends, let us bring out such 870
ornaments for the hair as I have hidden away in the house,*
and let me crown the head of my victorious brother.

[ELECTRA *goes into the house.*

CHORUS [*sings*]. You bring ornaments for his head then. We
shall continue with the dance the Muses love.
Now our beloved former rulers will be kings of our land
and justly so. They have destroyed the unjust.

Let our shout sound in harmony with the pipe as we
  rejoice.

Re-enter ELECTRA *with two garlands. Enter* ORESTES *and* PYLADES
  with the dead AEGISTHUS *on a bier.*

ELECTRA. O winner of a noble victory, Orestes, son born to a   880
father who won the conquest in the war beneath Troy,
receive this garland to bind the locks of your hair. You have
come not after running a futile furlong in the stadium.* You
have killed Aegisthus, who destroyed your father and mine.
And you, Pylades, his fellow-warrior, brought up by the
most dutiful of men,* receive a garland from my hand. You
and Orestes played an equal part in winning the contest.
May both of you always appear blessed in my sight.

ORESTES. Electra, first hold the gods the authors of this good for-   890
tune,* then praise me too, the servant of the gods and fortune. I have killed Aegisthus—no empty words but plain
fact—and have come back. But to make assurance doubly
sure I am bringing the dead man himself to you. If you wish,
fling him out for the wild beasts to snatch at or impale him
on a stake as a prey for the birds, the children of the air.*
For now he is your slave, though previously he was called
your master.

ELECTRA. I feel ashamed,* but still I want to speak.   900

ORESTES. Why ashamed? Tell me, since you have nothing to
fear.

ELECTRA. . . . ashamed to insult a corpse—in case I arouse bad
feeling.

ORESTES. There's nobody who would blame you.

ELECTRA. Our city is quick to criticize, loves to do so.

ORESTES. Speak out if you wish, sister. We made no terms with
this man when we took him on as our enemy.

ELECTRA. Well then, how should I first begin my tally of evils,
how end, what deal with in between?* Yet in the early
mornings I never stopped rehearsing what I wanted to say   910
to your face if I did become free of my former fears. So now
we are free; and I shall settle the score with you with the
words I wished to say to you when you were alive.

  You ruined me and deprived me and Orestes here of our
dear father, though we had not wronged you at all, you

made a shameful marriage with my mother and you killed her husband, the commander-in-chief of the Greeks, though you did not go to Troy yourself. And you reached such heights of stupidity that you thought that my mother, once married to you, would prove faithful,* though she betrayed 920 my father's bed. Let a man know that, when he has corrupted a man's wife in a clandestine liaison and then is forced to take her, he is a wretched creature if he thinks that a woman who did not behave well with her first husband will do so with him. Yours was a grim life though you pretended it was good. You knew, of course, that you had made an unholy marriage, and mother knew that she had won a godless man in you. Both of you were vicious and you took up each other's vicious fortunes. This was what all the 930 Argives said of you: 'he's the woman's man—she's not the man's woman'.* Yet it is disgraceful when a woman, not a man, is in charge at the house; and I detest those children whom the city calls not their father's but their mother's. When a man has married above himself in a splendid match, no one talks of the man, everyone of the woman. And—the thing that most misled you in your blindness—you vainly thought that you were somebody because of your massive wealth. But wealth is nothing—only a fleeting companion. 940 It's one's nature that one can trust in, not wealth.* Our nature stands by us always and endures misfortunes, while wealth, which dwells unjustly with fools, blossoms only briefly, then flies from the house.

As for your behaviour with women, I keep silent—it is not good for a virgin to speak of this—but I shall hint in a way that can be understood. You showed no self-control—after all, you had a royal house and your share of beauty. But I hope to have no girlish-looking fellow as my husband—but a real man. The children of such men lay their hand to 950 war—good looks are merely decorative at dances.

Away with you! You know nothing of how time found you out and made you pay. So let no criminal think, even if he has got off to a good start, that he is outrunning Justice. Let him wait till he comes near the finish, on the last lap of life.*

CHORUS. He did terrible things and terrible is the penalty he has paid to you and to this man. Justice has great might.

ELECTRA. Well then, we must carry his body inside the house
  and stow it in the dark, slaves, so that when mother comes   960
  she may not see the corpse before we slaughter her.

The body of AEGISTHUS *is carried off.*

ORESTES. Wait. There's something else we must talk about.

ELECTRA. What! You don't see a rescue party from Mycenae?

ORESTES. No, I see the mother who gave me birth.

ELECTRA. Perfect—she is coming into the centre of our net.*
  Look how she glitters—both her chariot and her dress.

ORESTES. What are we to do?* Are we going to kill our mother?

ELECTRA. Surely pity can't have overcome you now that you
  see our mother in the flesh?

ORESTES. Alas, yes! For how can I kill her, the woman who
  bore me and brought me up.

ELECTRA. Kill her as she killed your father and mine.   970

ORESTES. O Phoebus, your pronouncement was full of folly.

ELECTRA. When Apollo is a fool, who can be wise?

ORESTES. Apollo, you who proclaimed that I must kill my
  mother, you were wrong.

ELECTRA. How can you be harmed if you avenge your father?

ORESTES. Now I shall stand trial for matricide; then I was
  unpolluted.

ELECTRA. If you do not avenge your father, you will be unholy
  then too.

ORESTES. I know it. But shall I not pay the penalty for my
  mother's murder?

ELECTRA. But what if you let slip vengeance for your father?*

ORESTES. Did a fiend speak this oracle in the likeness of the god?

ELECTRA. Sitting on the holy tripod?* I do not think so.   980

ORESTES. I cannot believe that this oracle was spoken well.

ELECTRA. Watch that you don't unman yourself and play the
  coward. Go and set up the same trap for her as she used
  against her husband for Aegisthus' sake.

ORESTES. I shall go inside. I am taking a step into the terrible,
  and I shall do terrible things. If the gods think them good,
  so be it. But the struggle is a bitter one, not sweet to me.

                    [ORESTES *and* PYLADES *go into the house.*

Enter CLYTEMNESTRA *on a chariot with her retinue of Trojan slaves.*

CHORUS [*chants*]. O lady,
  queen of the Argive land,
  daughter of Tyndareus
  and sister of the good sons of Zeus*   990
  who dwell in the flaming sky amid the stars
  and have it as their function
  to save mortals amid the breakers of the sea—
  greetings—I reverence you as much as the blessed gods*
  for your wealth and your great happiness.
  Now, O queen, is the moment
  to give due respect to your fortunes.

CLYTEMNESTRA. Get down from the chariot, Trojan girls, and
  take my hand so that I can step out of this carriage. While 1000
  the temples of the gods are adorned with the spoils of Troy,
  I have these girls, the pride of the Trojan land, a small prize
  in comparison with the daughter I lost,* but decorative for
  our house.

ELECTRA. Should not I, a slave thrown out of my father's house
  and living in this miserable house—should not I, mother,
  take the hand of a blessed queen?

CLYTEMNESTRA. There are these slaves here. Don't put yourself
  out for me.

ELECTRA. Why not? I am your prisoner whom you have driven
  from my home; my house has been captured and I have
  been captured like these girls, and left orphaned of a father. 1010

CLYTEMNESTRA. Well, this is the result of your father's plots
  against those of his friends who least of all deserved them. I
  shall speak out. And yet when bad reputation lays hold of a
  woman, a certain bitterness infects her tongue—which in
  my opinion does not reflect badly on her. When you know
  the facts, if you can then loathe a woman with justice, it is
  right to hate her, but if not, why hate at all? Tyndareus gave
  me to your father not so that I or my children should die.
  But he lured my daughter* with the hope of marriage to 1020
  Achilles and went off taking her from home* to Aulis where
  the fleet was held and there he stretched her over the sacrificial altar and slashed the white throat of Iphigenia. If he
  had killed her to avert the capture of our city or to benefit
  our house and save the other children, one for the sake of

many, it would have been forgivable. But as things were, because Helen was a slut and her husband did not know how to control a treacherous wife, for those reasons he killed my girl.

Well, though I was wronged in this, I did not turn wild 1030 and I would not have killed my husband. But he came back to me with his girlfriend, a mad prophetess, and brought her into our marriage bed and he kept two wives together in the same house.* Women are flighty creatures,* I grant you that. But, since this is the case, when a husband is at fault and thrusts aside his home marriage, a woman likes to imitate the man* and take another friend, and then criticism of us flares up while the men who caused it all keep their good 1040 name. If Menelaus had been secretly snatched from his house, ought I to have killed Orestes* so that I could save Menelaus, my sister's husband? How could your father have put up with that? Was it not then right for him, the killer of my child, to die if it would have been right for me to suffer death* at his hands. I killed him, I turned the one way I could travel—to his enemies. After all, which of his friends would have joined me in killing your father?

Speak if you wish and argue against me with complete freedom.* Say how it was wrong for your father to die.   1050

CHORUS. What you have said is just, but it is a shameful justice. A sensible wife ought to go along with her husband whatever happens. A woman who thinks otherwise seems to me beneath consideration.

ELECTRA. Remember, mother, what you said just now when you gave me permission to speak freely to you.

CLYTEMNESTRA. I say it again. I do not go back on it, my child.

ELECTRA. Might you listen, mother, and then hurt me?

CLYTEMNESTRA. I won't. I shall humour you.

ELECTRA. I shall have my say and I'll begin like this. If only you 1060 had better judgement, mother. For, while your beauty deserves to win praise, yours and Helen's, you are truly two sisters, both of you vicious and unworthy of your brother Castor. Helen, though snatched away, went willingly to her ruin, while you destroyed the best man of Greece and hid behind the pretext that you killed your husband for your daughter's sake. And some believe you, for they do not

know you as well as I do. You! Before your daughter was
killed, when your husband had only recently set out from 1070
home, you decked out the blond locks of your hair before a
mirror. A woman who makes herself look beautiful when
her husband is away from home, write her off as a bad lot.
There's no need for her to show a beautiful face out of doors
unless she's after some mischief.

I know that you alone of all Greek women were happy if
things went well for the Trojans, while if they were losing,
your face clouded over since you didn't want Agamemnon
to return from Troy. Yet it would have been perfectly possi- 1080
ble for you to behave well. You had a husband who was not
inferior to Aegisthus, a man whom Greece chose to be its
general.* And, since your sister had behaved so scan-
dalously, you could have won great glory. After all, the bad
offers a standard of comparison for the good to notice.

But if, as you say, father killed your daughter, how have
I and my brother done you wrong? Why, when you killed
your husband, did you not give us our father's house? No,
you gave away our property as your dowry and you brought 1090
your marriage for a price. Your present husband is not in
exile because he exiled your son and he hasn't been killed
for killing me, killing me twice as much as my sister in a living death. If murder sits in judgement and demands murder
in requital, I shall kill you, I and your son Orestes, in
vengeance for our father. If the one murder is just, so is the
other.

A man who marries a bad woman from considerations of
wealth or high birth is a fool. For it is better to live in a humble and respectable marriage than a great one.

CHORUS. Chance rules when one marries a woman. I have seen 1100
some marriages working out well and others badly.

CLYTEMNESTRA. My child, your instinct has always been to love
your father. This is the way of things. Some are their fathers'
children while others love their mothers more than their
fathers. I shall pardon you. I'm not so very pleased, my child,
at what I've done.* Ah, how I suffer for what I plotted. I
pushed my anger against my husband further than I should 1110
have.

ELECTRA. Your sorrow comes too late—now there is no cure.

Yet, though father is dead, why do you not bring back your
son, a wanderer in foreign lands?

CLYTEMNESTRA. I am afraid and it is my own good that I look
after, not his. He is angry, they say, at the murder of his
father.

ELECTRA. Then again, why do you let your husband be so cruel
to me?

CLYTEMNESTRA. That's what he's like. And you are stubborn.

ELECTRA. Yes, for I'm unhappy. But I shall stop being angry.

CLYTEMNESTRA. Then he will no longer be harsh with you.

ELECTRA. He is proud, for he dwells in my house.*   1120

CLYTEMNESTRA. You see? Yet again you fan the flames of hatred.

ELECTRA. I am silent. For I fear him—as I fear him.

CLYTEMNESTRA. That's enough on this subject. Tell me, why
did you call me here, my child?

ELECTRA. You heard, I think, that I had given birth. Sacrifice
for me in thanks for my safe delivery—I do not know how—
on this tenth day after the child's birth, as is the custom. I
have no experience since this is my first child.

CLYTEMNESTRA. This is not my task but your midwife's.

ELECTRA. I bore the child, I was midwife, I alone.

CLYTEMNESTRA. Is your house so remote from friendly neigh-   1130
bours?

ELECTRA. No one wants to have poor people as friends.

CLYTEMNESTRA. You've just given birth—how filthy you are,
how poorly dressed! Yes, I shall go so that I can make the
tenth-day sacrifice to the gods for your child. When I have
done you this favour, I shall go to the country where my
husband is sacrificing to the Nymphs. Attendants, take the
chariot and put the horses at the mangers. When you think
that I have finished this sacrifice to the gods, be back here.
For I must do my husband this favour.   [*The slaves take off*
                                              the chariot.

ELECTRA. Come into my poor home. Please be careful that the   1140
soot-stained house does not blacken your clothes.* You will
make the kind of sacrifice you should make to the god.

                    [*CLYTEMNESTRA goes into the house.*

The basket is prepared and the sacrificial knife is sharpened,
the knife which killed the bull* near whom you will fall
when you are struck.* In Hades' halls too you will be the

wife of the man you slept with in the light. So great is the favour I shall give you, so great the penalty you will pay for my father.

[ELECTRA *enters the house.*

The characters all sing until 1232.

CHORUS. Here is the payment for evils. The winds of the house
veer round and blow a different way. Then in his bath
my ruler, my ruler fell,
the roof and the stone cornice cried aloud   1150
as he said this, 'O cruel woman,
why will you murder me on my return
to my dear fatherland in the tenth seed time?'

Just punishment for her adultery flows back, bringing to
    judgement
the woman who herself, sharp-edged weapon in hand,
killed her husband when he came at last
to his house and the heaven-high walls
upreared by the Cyclopes*—she took up the axe
in her hands. Unhappy husband,   1160
whatever the madness was that possessed
the remorseless woman.
Like a mountain lioness ranging
the oak coppices of the water meadows*
she did this deed.

CLYTEMNESTRA [*from within*]. O children, by the gods, do not
    kill your mother.
CHORUS. Do you hear a shout from the house?
CLYTEMNESTRA. Oh, woe is me!
CHORUS. I too cry woe as your children overpower you. God
    hands out justice at the due time. You have suffered cruelly, 1170
    but what you did to your husband, hard-hearted woman,
    was unholy.

ORESTES and ELECTRA *come out of the house with the bodies of*
CLYTEMNESTRA and AEGISTHUS *on the* ekkyklema.*

But here they come out of the house, bespattered with their mother's blood, just shed—(and there lies her body), their trophy, proof of hideous slaughter. There is no house more wretched than that of Tantalus' descendants—and there never was.

ORESTES. O Earth and Zeus* who sees all the cares
of mortals, behold these bloody,
polluting deeds, these two bodies
lying on the ground, struck   1180
by my hand in payment for my wrongs.

ELECTRA. All too worthy of weeping—my brother—and I am to blame. In my hardness of heart I was on fire with hate against my mother here, who bore me, her daughter.*

CHORUS. Oh, I bewail your fate, a mother, a mother
who has suffered fearful miseries and worse
at the hands of your children.
But you have paid justly for the murder of their father.
ORESTES.
O Phoebus, the justice you proclaimed was mysterious,   1190
but clear are the woes you have brought to fulfilment.*
You have given me a murderer's lot
in exile from the land of Greece.
What other city can I go to?
What host, what pious man
will look on me,
the mother-slayer?
ELECTRA. Oh, woe is me! I too, where shall I go, in what dance
shall I join, what marriage* can I find? What husband will
take
me into his marriage bed?   1200
CHORUS. Your thoughts have changed back, shifting back
with the winds.
Your thinking is pious now, though previously
not so, and you did terrible things,
dear girl, to your brother, the reluctant one.
ORESTES.
Did you see how the wretched woman tugged her breast
from her robes and showed it as I killed her—
Oh, woe, woe—as she set the limbs which gave me birth
on the ground? Faintness drained me.
CHORUS. I know it well. You passed through agony   1210

when you heard the cry of woe
of the mother who bore you.

ELECTRA.
She put her hand to my chin* and screamed this shout:
'My child, I beg you.'
She hung from my cheeks—
and I dropped the sword from my hands.

CHORUS. The wretched woman. How could you endure
to look upon the murder of your mother
as she breathed out her life in your sight?   1220

ORESTES. I threw my cloak before my eyes*
and with the sword I made the sacrifice
driving it into my mother's neck.

ELECTRA. And I urged you on
and held the sword with you.
I wrought the most terrible of sufferings.

ORESTES. Take this cloak, cover the body of my mother with it,
and close her wounds.
And so you bore your own murderer.

ELECTRA. Look, we who loved you, and did not,   1230
put this cloak around you—*
here is the end of great sorrows for the house.

CASTOR *and* POLYDEUCES *come into view above the house.**

CHORUS [*chants*]. But here above the very top of the house
come some divine spirits
or heavenly gods—human beings do not travel
through the sky. Why do they come so clearly
to mortal sight?

CASTOR. Son of Agamemnon, hear me: the two Dioscouri, sons
of Zeus, call you—the brothers of your mother, Castor and 1240
his brother Polydeuces here at my side. We have just stilled
the sea's swell,* fearful to ships, and come to Argos when we
saw the murder of our sister here, your mother. Well, she
has justice—though you have not acted justly. But Phoebus,
Phoebus—yet he is my lord and so I say nothing. He is wise
but what he proclaimed to you was not.* But we must put
up with this. As for the future, you must fare as Fate and
Zeus have determined for you. Give Electra to Pylades* to

take to his house. And you must leave Argos. It is not right 1250
for you, the murderer of your mother, to walk in this city.
The terrible Furies,* the dog-faced goddesses, will drive you
spinning as you wander, a madman. When you come to
Athens, embrace the holy image of Pallas.* She will prevent
them from touching you as they flicker with their terrible
serpents, holding her gorgon-faced shield above your head.
There is a hill of Ares where the gods first sat with their voting pebbles to try homicide when savage Ares killed 1260
Halirrhothius, son of the ruler of the sea, in anger at the
unholy union with his daughter—here from this time on
men cast their votes most honestly and steadfastly.* There
you too must stand trial for murder. Equal votes will be cast
and will save you from the penalty of death; for Apollo will
take the blame on himself since he proclaimed that your
mother must be murdered, and it will be established as the
law for posterity that the defendant will always be acquitted
when the voting is equal. So the terrible goddesses, hard hit 1270
with grief for this, will sink into a chasm by the hill itself,*
which will prove a holy oracle for pious mortals. But you
must dwell in an Arcadian city by the streams of Alpheus
near the Lycaean shrine.* The city will be called after you.
This is what I have to say to you.

The citizens will hide the corpse of Aegisthus here in a
grave. As for your mother, Helen and Menelaus, who has
reached Nauplia only now long after capturing the land of
Troy—they will bury her. She has come from the house of 1280
Proteus from Egypt—she did not go to Troy. Zeus—to cause
strife and killing around mortals—sent an image of Helen to
Ilium.*

Let Pylades take Electra, virgin and married woman, as his
wife, and let him leave the land of Achaea and bring her to
his home. And let him take the man whom they call your
brother-in-law to the land of the Phocians and heap him
with wealth.

Now you must walk along the neck of the Isthmian land*
and go to the blessed hill of the land of Cecrops. For once 1290
you have fulfilled the fate allotted you for this murder, you
will be happy and cease from these sufferings.

The rest of the play is chanted.

CHORUS. O sons of Zeus, is it right for us
    to approach you and talk to you?
CASTOR. It is right, because you are not polluted with these
    murders.
CHORUS. Since you are gods and the brothers
    of the murdered woman, why did you not keep
    the Furies away from the house?   1300
CASTOR. Fate and Necessity and the unwise utterances
    of Phoebus' tongue led to what must be.*
ELECTRA. Can I address you, sons of Tyndareus?
CASTOR. You too—I shall lay the responsibility
    for this bloody deed on Phoebus.
ELECTRA. What Apollo, what oracles ordained that I
    should be the murderer of my mother?
CASTOR. You acted together, your fates are one,
    the single doom of your fathers*
    crushed you both.
ORESTES. O my sister, I have seen you after so long,
    yet I am so soon deprived of the charms of your love.
    I shall leave you—you will leave me.   1310
CASTOR. She has a husband and a house. She has not suffered
    pitiful things—save that she is leaving
    the city of the Argives.
ELECTRA. And what greater cause for groaning is there
    than to pass the borders of one's native land?
ORESTES. But I, I shall leave my father's house
    and undergo trial for matricide,
    in the power of foreigners' votes.
CASTOR. Be confident. You will come to the holy city
    of Pallas. Be strong.   1320
ELECTRA. Hold me breast to breast,
    my dearest brother.
    The bloody curses of our mother
    are driving us away from our father's halls.
ORESTES. Fling yourself into my arms. Cry a lament
    as if I were dead and you were at my tomb.
CASTOR. Ah! Ah! Those words are terrible
    even for the gods to hear.

For in me too and the heavenly ones
  there is pity for mortals with their many labours.   1330
ORESTES. I shall see you no longer.
ELECTRA. And I shall not come near your grave.
ORESTES. These are my last words to you.
ELECTRA. City, farewell.
  And, women of my city, a long farewell to you.
ORESTES. O most faithful one, are you going already?
ELECTRA. I am going, tears welling in my soft eyes.
ORESTES. Pylades, good luck go with you,   1340
  marry Electra.
CASTOR. Yes, marriage will be their concern. But you
  flee these dogs and make for Athens.
  For the Furies, with snakes as hands* and black of skin,
  are tracking you fast with terrible steps,
  to reap their harvest of dreadful pains.
  We two are hurrying off to the Sicilian sea*
  to look after the ships on the main.
  As we go through the tract of the sky,
  we give no help to polluters,   1350
  but those to whom what is holy and just
  is dear in their lives, these we protect,
  freeing them from difficult struggles.
  And so let no one choose to do wrong,
  let no one sail with oath-breakers.
  I speak as a god to mortals.
CHORUS. Farewell. The man who can fare well
  and does not bend beneath any misfortune
  fares well indeed.   [*All depart.*

HELEN

Characters

HELEN, daughter of Zeus and Leda
TEUCROS, a Greek archer
MENELAOS, king of Sparta, husband of Helen
OLD WOMAN
SERVANT of Menelaos
THEONOE, sister of Theoclymenos
THEOCLYMENOS, king of Egypt
SERVANT of Theoclymenos
MESSENGER
CASTOR and POLYDEUCES

CHORUS OF GREEK SLAVE WOMEN

Outside a palace near the coast of Egypt. HELEN *has taken refuge
at the tomb of Proteus.**

HELEN. These are the streams of the Nile, the river of fair virgin nymphs* which waters the soil of Egypt's fields not with
with rain from heaven but with melting white snow.*
Proteus, while he lived, was the king of this land. He dwelt
on the island of Pharos and ruled over Egypt, and he married Psamathe, one of the maidens whose home is the sea,
when she had renounced her husband Aiacos.* She bore
him two children in this house, a boy called Theoclymenos,*
so named since he lived his life in reverence to the gods, and   10
a noble girl called Eido, the apple of her mother's eye while
she was a baby. But when she came to the lovely time when
youth is ripe for marriage, they called her Theonoe*—since
she knew all that the gods will for the present and for the
future. She had inherited this privilege from her grandfather
Nereus.*

As for myself, my fatherland is no obscure place. It is
Sparta, and my father is Tyndareos, though there is of
course a story that Zeus transformed himself into a bird,
a swan, and flew to my mother Leda. He pretended to be

fleeing an eagle's pursuit and consummated his love through   20
a trick—if this tale is true.* I was given the name Helen, and
I shall tell you of the misfortunes I have suffered. In a contest over their beauty three goddesses came to Alexandros*
in a deep valley on Mount Ida, Hera and Cypris and the
maiden born from Zeus.* They wished judgement to be pro-
nounced on their figures. And Cypris offered my beauty as a
bait—if what has proved disastrous can be beautiful. She
promised that Alexandros should marry me, and won the
contest. So Paris of Mount Ida left his ox-stalls and came to
Sparta to get me as his wife.   30

   Then Hera, taking it amiss that she had not won the
divine beauty contest, turned my marriage to thin air for
Alexandros and gave to the son of King Priam not my real
self but a breathing phantom which she had moulded in my
likeness from heavenly ether; and he believes he possesses
me—but it is a vain belief, for he does not. And then again
the plans of Zeus renew themselves to work in harmony
with these woes. For he brought war upon the land of the
Greeks and the wretched Trojans so that he could lighten   40
mother earth of the superflux of human population and
bestow fame upon the strongest man of Greece.* And in the
war with the Trojans I was set up as the prize for the spears
of the Greeks—or rather not I but my name.

   As for my real self, Hermes took me up and hid me in the
clouds in the upper air's embrace—for Zeus did not cease to
care about me—and brought me to live in this house of
Proteus, the man he had judged the most virtuous of all
mortals, so that I could keep my marriage with Menelaos
undefiled. And I am here, but my wretched husband mus-   50
tered an army and went to the towers of Ilion* to hunt down
his ravished wife. Many souls of men have died on my
account by the streams of Scamander.* I am the long-suffering one, and yet men curse me, for, as it seems, I have
betrayed my husband and started a great war for the Greeks.

   Why then do I still live on? I heard this declaration from
the god Hermes—that I shall yet dwell on Sparta's famous
plain with my husband, when he discovers that I did not go
to Troy, if I keep myself from an adulterous bed. So then, as   60
long as Proteus looked upon this sunlight, I was safe from

marriage. But now that he is hidden in earth's darkness, the son of the dead man hunts me—he wants to wed me. In honour for my husband of old I come as a suppliant to this tomb of Proteus and kneel before it, praying that he may keep my bed unsullied for my husband, so that, even if I have a shameful reputation throughout Greece, my body may remain free from disgrace here in Egypt.

Enter TEUCROS *with his bow and arrows.**

TEUCROS. Who is the lord of this mighty house? Yes, it is a house worthy to be compared with that of Ploutos, god of wealth, with its royal circuit and corniced pile. But look! O 70 gods, what is this I see? My eyes behold the murderous image of a most loathsome woman, a woman who has ruined me and all the Greeks. May the gods spit you out, so close is your likeness to Helen! If I were not treading upon foreign soil, you would have died from this arrow's deadly aim as your reward for your likeness to the daughter of Zeus.

HELEN. Whoever you are, you wretch, why do you turn from me and hate me for that woman's misfortunes?*

TEUCROS. I was wrong. I gave way to anger more than was 80 right for me. You see, all of Greece hates the daughter of Zeus. Pardon me for what I have said, lady.

HELEN. Who are you? Where have you come from to reach the soil of this land?

TEUCROS. I am one of the Greeks, lady, those poor wretches.

HELEN. It is no wonder then that you hate Helen. But who are you and where are you from? Whose son must I call you?

TEUCROS. My name is Teucros, the father who begot me is Telamon,* and Salamis was the fatherland that reared me.

HELEN. Then why have you come to these fields of the Nile?*

TEUCROS. I have been driven out of my fatherland as an exile. 90

HELEN. Poor sad man! Who drove you out of the land?

TEUCROS. My father Telamon. Whom could you find closer to me than that?

HELEN. Why? What you tell me hints at a deeper calamity.

TEUCROS. It was my brother Aias who destroyed me when he died at Troy.

HELEN. What do you mean? Surely you did not cut short his life with your sword?

TEUCROS. He flung himself on his own sword—that was how he died.

HELEN. Had he gone mad? Who in his right mind would bring himself to do that?

TEUCROS. Do you know a man called Achilleus, the son of Peleus?

HELEN. Yes. He once came as a suitor of Helen—as I hear.*

TEUCROS. He died, and this led to a struggle for his armour   100 among his friends.

HELEN. And how did this lead to disaster for Aias?

TEUCROS. Another* took the arms and he left this life.

HELEN. It's because of his woes then that you suffer so?

TEUCROS. Yes, because I did not die together with him.

HELEN. Does that mean, stranger, that you went to the famous city of Troy?

TEUCROS. Yes—and my reward for joining in its sack is my own destruction.

HELEN. So it has already been set ablaze and wiped out by fire?

TEUCROS. So effectively that not a single trace of its walls can be seen.

HELEN. O wretched Helen, it was because of you that the Trojans met their deaths.

TEUCROS. And the Greeks too. Great are the evils that have   110 been brought to pass.

HELEN. And how long is it since Troy was destroyed?

TEUCROS. Nearly seven revolving years have run their course.

HELEN. And how long was that other stretch of time that you spent at Troy?

TEUCROS. Many were the months as ten whole years went by.

HELEN. And did you capture the woman from Sparta?

TEUCROS. Menelaos seized her by the hair and led her off.

HELEN. Did you see the wretched woman? Or do you speak from hearsay?

TEUCROS. I saw her just as clearly as my eyes see you now.*

HELEN. Is it possible that it was something that the gods made all of you imagine?

TEUCROS. Talk about another subject—forget about her.

HELEN. Do you believe that what you believe you saw actually   120 happened?

TEUCROS. Yes, for I witnessed it with these eyes. My mind saw through my eyes.

HELEN. Is Menelaos now at home with his wife?

TEUCROS. Well, he is not in Argos at least, nor on the banks of the Eurotas.*

HELEN. Alas! You bring sad news for those whom your sad news affects.

TEUCROS. I tell you that he and his wife are said to have disappeared.

HELEN. Did not all the Argives cross back to Greece together?

TEUCROS. Yes, but a storm drove them apart in all directions.

HELEN. On the back of which sea's salt waters were they sailing?

TEUCROS. They were in the middle of their journey across the   130
Aegean.

HELEN. And after this happened no one is aware that Menelaos arrived in Greece?

TEUCROS. No one. Throughout Greece they say that he is dead.

HELEN [aside]. Then it is all over for me. [to TEUCROS] Is the daughter of Thestios alive?

TEUCROS. Leda, do you mean? She is no more, she is dead.

HELEN. I hope that Helen's notoriety did not lead to her death.

TEUCROS. It did, so they say. She tied a noose around her noble neck.

HELEN. Are the sons of Tyndareos* still alive—or are they dead?

TEUCROS. They are dead and not dead. There are two different stories.

HELEN. Which is the truer? Oh, how unhappy I am in these miseries!

TEUCROS. Men say that they are gods—they have been trans-   140
formed into stars.

HELEN. These are fair tidings. What is the other story?

TEUCROS. That they have cut off the breath of their life because of their sister. But enough of words—I do not wish to live through these sorrows a second time. Now for the reason why I have come to these royal halls: I wish to see the prophetess Theonoe, and you must act as an intermediary for me so that I can win her guidance over how to sail my ship to the sea-girt land of Cyprus with a fair wind. It is there that Apollo commanded me to live, giving it the island name of Salamis, since Salamis is my fatherland.   150

HELEN. The voyage itself will show you how, stranger. But you must run off and leave this land before the son of Proteus,

the ruler of this country, catches sight of you. He is away
hunting, slaughtering the wild beasts with the help of his
dogs.* Any foreigner from Greece he catches, he kills. You
must not seek to discover the reason for this* and I shall not
tell you. What help would I be to you?

TEUCROS. Your advice is good, lady. May the gods grant you
good fortune in return. You are like Helen in your physical   160
appearance but not in your heart. There you are very different. May she die a miserable death and never reach the
streams of Eurotas!* But may good fortune always be with
you, lady.   [*Exit* TEUCROS.

HELEN [*chants*]. Ah, as I lay down the ground bass for my
          dirge, so full of lamentation, so full of woes,
     how am I to make my sorrow fully heard? Or what music
          could I find
     for my tears, my keenings or griefs? Alas!

[*sings*]
     Winged maidens,
     virgin daughters of Earth,
     Sirens,* if only you would come   170
     bringing a Libyan flute to second my laments,
     or pipes or lyres,
     if only you would send
     tears to harmonize with my sorrowful dirge,
     your suffering to fit with mine,
     your songs in tune with mine,
     your music to accord with my laments—
     so that down in her night-dark halls
     Persephone* could receive from me
     a bloody, unwelcome paean* accompanied by my tears
     over the dead that are gone.

          The CHORUS OF GREEK SLAVE WOMEN *enters.*

CHORUS [*sings*]. By the dark-blue water*
     I happened to be drying my purple robes   180
     on the tangled branches
     in the golden rays of the sun
     by the youthful shoots
     of the bulrushes.

From there I heard my mistress's pitiful lament,
a song of grief not apt for the lyre—
whatever it was she cried out
in wailing lamentation, like a nymph of the rivers
pouring forth her song of grief as she flees in the mountains
and cries out against her union with Pan,*
howling beneath the hollows of the rocks.   190

HELEN [*sings*]. O, maidens of Greece,
  prey of marauding barbarian* ships,
  an Achaean* sailor has come, has come bringing me tears
  to add to tears. Burning fire does its work
  on the ruins of Troy
  because of me, the killer of so many,
  because of my name, so full of pain for men.
  And Leda has chosen death,   200
  strangling herself
  in grief over my disgrace.
  And my husband is dead and gone
  after all his wanderings over the sea.
  Vanished, vanished
  are Castor and his brother,*
  the twin glory of their fatherland—
  they have left the plains where the horses' hooves thud
  and the wrestling place
  by the reedy Eurotas
  where the young men exercise.   210

CHORUS [*sings*]. Alas, I cry out over your doom of many woes
  and your destiny, lady.
  You had as your lot, your lot,
  a life that is no life, when Zeus,
  snow-white with swan down, winged in clear view
    through the sky
  and begot you upon your mother.*
  Is there any evil you have not suffered,
  any agony of life you have not endured?
  Your mother is dead
  and the two dear sons of Zeus   220
  are happy no more,
  and you do not look upon your fatherland,
  and through the cities runs the rumour

that assigns you in marriage, lady,
to a barbarian*—
while your true husband has left this life
amid the waves of the sea and never again
will he bring happiness to your father's halls*
and to Athena, the goddess with the house of bronze.*

HELEN [*sings*]. Alas, alas, which of the Trojans
    or who from the land of Greece   230
    cut the pine, with all its tears for Troy?
From that tree the son of Priam constructed
the deadly ship and sailed with his foreign oars
to my hearth,
to my beauty, source of so much woe,
to win it
by marrying me. And scheming Cypris,
the murderous goddess, sailed with him,
bringing death to Greeks and Trojans—
O, how wretched I am in my sorrows!   240
But seated on her golden throne,
Hera, proud bedfellow of Zeus,
sent Hermes, the swift-footed son of Maia,*
and while I was picking the fresh sprigs of roses
and filling the lap of my dress
so that I could visit Athena in her house of bronze,
he snatched me up through the sky
and carried me to this luckless land—
and he set up for the sons of Priam a sorrowful strife,
strife with Greece.
And by the streams of Simois*   250
the name of Helen
has won a false report.

CHORUS. Your plight is pitiful, I know. But, believe me, it would
    be best to bear what cannot be avoided in this life as lightly
    as you can.

HELEN. Dear women, what is this fate of mine, my yokefellow?
    What did my mother bear when she produced me? A freak
    for men to wonder at! For no woman, whether Greek or bar-
    barian, has given birth to her children in a white eggshell,
    and it was in an eggshell that they say say Leda bore me to

Zeus.* For my life and situation are freakish, partly through 260
Hera's work, partly because of my beauty. Ah, if only I had
been wiped clear like a painting and had begun again with
an uglier appearance in place of this beauty—and then the
Greeks could have forgotten the evil fortune which now I
have and might remember the good and not—as now they
do—the evil that is mine.

When one centres one's thoughts on a single fortune and
is injured by the gods, it is a heavy blow, but even so it must
be endured. But I am the victim of many catastrophes. First 270
of all, though I have done nothing wrong, all speak ill of me.
And this is a greater blow than the truth itself—when one
has endured blows that do not belong to one. Then, the gods
have removed me from my fatherland and exposed me to a
barbarian civilization.* I have lost my friends and, though
from a free nation, I have been reduced to slavery. For
among barbarians all save one are slaves. And as for the
only anchor which held my fortunes fast—the hope that my
husband would one day come and free me from my woes—
since he is dead, that hope is dead too.

My mother is no more and it was I that killed her—the 280
guilt for this is my own, though I am guiltless. And the girl
who was our house's jewel and mine, my daughter, is husbandless and grows grey in her virginity.* My two brothers,
called the Dioskouroi, the sons of Zeus, are no more. In all
this desolation of my fortunes, I am as good as dead and yet
I am alive. And there is one final thing—if I were to go to
my fatherland, the gates would be barred against me—they
would think that I was Helen of Troy who had come with
Menelaos. If my husband were alive, I should have been rec- 290
ognized through recourse to tokens which would have given
clear proof to us alone.* But as it is, this is not possible and
he can never return safely.

Why go on living then? For what fate am I reserved? Shall
I choose marriage in exchange for my woes and lead my life
with a barbarian, sitting at his lavish table? But when a
woman dwells with a husband she hates, she hates herself
too. The best course is to die. How then could I die nobly?
To hang oneself in mid-air is undignified—even among 300
slaves it is unseemly—while to stab oneself is not without

honour and nobility and the moment when one shuffles off
this life is a small consideration. Into such an abyss of disaster have I fallen. Other women find a blessing in their
beauty—yet it is this very beauty that has ruined me.

CHORUS. Helen, do not believe that everything the stranger
who came to you has spoken is true, whoever he may be.

HELEN. But he stated clearly that my husband has died.*

CHORUS. Much that is clear can be spoken and in fact be false.

HELEN. And much that is unclear can be spoken and be true.   310

CHORUS. You swerve towards misfortune and away from happiness.

HELEN. Yes, fear engulfs me and causes me this dread.

CHORUS. How sympathetic to you are the people in these halls?

HELEN. Everyone is friendly to me except the one who hunts me
for his wife.*

CHORUS. Then this is what you must do. You must leave the
tomb where you are sitting . . .*

HELEN [alarmed]. What are you going to say? What advice will
you give me?

CHORUS. Go into the house and find out about your husband
from the daughter of the sea-born Nereid, the maiden
Theonoe who knows everything—is he still alive or has he   320
departed this light? Once you have heard her certain answer,
you can fit your emotions to your fortunes—to joy or to
mourning. But before you know everything clearly, what can
you profit from grieving? Do what I say. Leave this tomb and
talk with the maiden. You will find out everything from her.
When you can find someone to tell the truth in this palace,
why look further? I too am willing to go into the palace with
you and join you in learning the maiden's prophetic words.
We women should share in each other's sufferings.

HELEN [chants]. My friends, I accept your advice.   330
                    Go, go into the palace
                    to learn within
                    the truth about my trials.

CHORUS [chants]. Willingly. You will not have to ask me twice.

HELEN [chants]. O day of sadness!
                    What words, what tearful words
                    shall I hear in my grief?

CHORUS [*chants*]. Do not foretell sorrows, my dear,
   and lament in anticipation.
HELEN [*chants*]. What fate has my wretched husband endured? 340
   Does he look upon this light
   and the four-horsed chariot of the sun
   and the paths of the stars,
   or does he spend eternity
   in his fate among the dead beneath the earth?
CHORUS [*chants*].
   Look optimistically on what the future will bring.
HELEN [*chants*]. You I call, Eurotas, by you I swear,
   river green with your water-reeds—
   if this report that my husband is dead   350
   is true—
   I cannot understand all this—,
   I shall stretch a deadly noose tight around my neck,
   or, with a sword's killing thrust
   to my throat streaming blood,
   drive the steel eagerly with my own hand
   to pierce and probe my flesh,
   a sacrifice to the trio of goddesses
   and to Priam's son
   who once dwelt in the caves of Ida
   by his ox-stalls.*   360
CHORUS [*chants*]. I pray that these evils may turn elsewhere
   and your own lot may prove happy.
HELEN [*chants*]. O miserable Troy,
   it is because of deeds never done that you met destruction
   and endured much sorrow. Cypris' gift of me
   gave birth to much blood,
   to many a tear. Troy has won
   woes upon woes, tears upon tears, sufferings upon suffer-
      ings.
   And mothers have lost their sons
   while maidens, sisters of the dead,
   have thrown their shorn hair
   by Troy's surging river Scamander.   370
   And Greece has raised a cry, a cry,
   has burst into wailing,
   and has set her hands against her head

and drenched the tender skin of her cheeks with blood
as her fingernails strike at it.

O happy Callisto,* once a maiden in Arcadia,
who climbed from Zeus's bed on four paws,
how much better was the fate you found than mine—
for you took the shape of a shaggy-limbed wild beast,
the form of a wild-eyed lioness,
and laid down your burden of grief.   380
Happy too was the one whose beauty once caused Artemis
to drive her from her sacred band
in the form of a hind with golden horns, the Titan-born
     daughter of Merops.*
But my beauty has brought ruin on Troy's citadels,
ruin on the Greeks as they fall in death.

> [HELEN *and the* CHORUS *go into the palace.*

> MENELAOS *enters from the sea-coast.**

MENELAOS. O Pelops, you who once raced the famous chariot race
     with Oinomaos at Pisa, if only you had departed this life at the
     time when you were served up as a meal for the gods,* before
     you begot my father Atreus, who from his marriage to Aerope   390
     begot Agamemnon and myself, Menelaos, a famous partner-
     ship. For I think it was the biggest expedition ever—and I say
     this not as a boast—that I took over to Troy by sea—and I was
     no despot* leading his army by force but the commander of
     young Greek volunteers. It is possible to reckon up the num-
     ber of those who are dead and those who to their great relief
     escaped the sea and brought the names of the dead back home
     with them. But I, poor wretch, have been wandering over the   400
     swelling waves of the grey salt-sea ever since I sacked the tow-
     ers of Troy and, though I long to return to my native land, I
     am not thought worthy by the gods to achieve this. But I have
     sailed to all the desolate and inhospitable beaches of Libya, and
     whenever I am near my fatherland, the wind's breath drives
     me away again. No favourable breeze has ever billowed out
     my sail to bring me to my homeland.

          And now I have been cast adrift onto this land, a poor
     shipwrecked man who has lost his friends. My boat has been
     broken up on rocks into many fragments of wreckage. From   410

that skilful construction only the keel was left intact and it
was on this that against all expectation I proved fortunate
enough to survive—it was by the skin of my teeth—and
Helen, whom I had dragged from Troy, was with me. I do
not know what this land and this people are called. I felt
ashamed at the prospect of meeting a crowd of them and facing their questions about my ragged state and my sense of
shame made me conceal my plight. Whenever a high-born
man suffers misfortunes, he finds himself in an unfamiliar
state which is worse for him than for a man long acquainted
with misery.

It is need that oppresses me. I have no food, and no clothes   420
on my body. You can guess this from the bits of flotsam from
the ship which I am wearing. The sea has swallowed my former clothes, garments so bright, so luxurious. I have hidden
the woman, the cause of all my sorrows, deep in a cave,
have given my surviving companions firm instructions to
keep guard on this wife of mine, and have made my way
here. I come on my own in search of provisions for my
friends there—maybe I can find something to lay my hands
on. I saw this palace surmounted by coping all round the top   430
of its walls, saw its proud gates. It belongs to a prosperous
man, and here I have come. From a wealthy house I can
hope to be given something for my sailors. But from those
who do not have enough to live we wouldn't get anything,
even if they wanted to help us.

Hey there! Is there a doorkeeper? If so, come out of the
house and report my message of disaster inside.

Enter OLD WOMAN.*

OLD WOMAN. Who is at our gates? You'd better get away from
the palace. Don't stand at our front gates and annoy our
master with your uproar. Otherwise you'll be executed as a   440
Greek—they have no business here.

MENELAOS. Old woman, you might use politer language. For I
shall do what you say. Don't be so angry.

OLD WOMAN. Off with you! For it is my task, stranger, to make
sure that no Greek approaches the palace.

MENELAOS. Ah, don't wave your fist at me and drive me away
by force.*

OLD WOMAN. It's your fault, for you are not doing as I tell you.

MENELAOS. Announce to your master inside . . .

OLD WOMAN. I think that I would rue it if I delivered a message
from you.

MENELAOS. I have come here a shipwrecked stranger—such
men are guaranteed protection.*

OLD WOMAN. Then go off to some other house and don't stay   450
here.

MENELAOS. No, I shall come inside. And you, do what I say.

OLD WOMAN. You're being a nuisance, I tell you, and soon you
will get driven off forcibly.

MENELAOS. Alas, where is my glorious army?

OLD WOMAN. You may have been a great man somewhere or
other—but you aren't one here!

MENELAOS. O god, what indignities have I suffered, and how
undeservedly!

OLD WOMAN. Why these watery eyes, these tears? Whom do
you call upon so piteously?

MENELAOS. Upon my former happy fortunes.

OLD WOMAN. Then clear off and present your tears to your
friends.

MENELAOS. What country is this? Whom does this palace
belong to?

OLD WOMAN. This is Proteus' house, and the land is Egypt.   460

MENELAOS. Egypt? Oh what a misfortune to have sailed here.

OLD WOMAN. What do you find to criticize about the glorious
river Nile?

MENELAOS. I make no criticism of that. It is my own fortunes
that I lament.

OLD WOMAN. Many people are down on their luck, not just you.

MENELAOS. So is King What's-his-name in the palace?

OLD WOMAN. This is his monument. His son rules the land.

MENELAOS. Then where might *he* be? Is he in the palace or
somewhere else?

OLD WOMAN. He is not at home. But he is a most bitter enemy
to the Greeks.

MENELAOS. How very helpful for me! What reason does he have?

OLD WOMAN. Helen, the daughter of Zeus, is in this palace.   470

MENELAOS. What do you mean? What is that you said? Tell me
again.

OLD WOMAN. The daughter of Tyndareos who once lived in Sparta.

MENELAOS. Where did she come here from? What can this mean?

OLD WOMAN. She came here from the land of Lacedaimon.*

MENELAOS. When? [*aside*] There's surely no way I can have been robbed of my wife whom I hid in the cave?

OLD WOMAN. She came here, stranger, before the Achaeans went to Troy. But go away from this palace. For things have taken a turn in there which has thrown the royal household into confusion. You have come at a very bad time and if my master lays hold on you, your gift from your host will be   480 death.* I am well disposed to Greeks, despite all the bitter words I spoke out of fear for my master.

                    [*The* OLD WOMAN *goes out, shutting the doors.*

MENELAOS. What should I think? What can I say? Now I hear of another grim misfortune keeping me company after those I suffered before—that is if, as seems to be the case, I have come here bringing the wife I took from Troy and she is being kept safe in a cave while another woman who has the same name as my wife is living in this palace. She said that she was the daughter of Zeus. Can there be any man living   490 by the banks of the Nile who has the name of Zeus? There is only one Zeus, he who dwells in heaven. And where in the world is there a Sparta except where the streams of the Eurotas flow, the river of lovely reeds, and there alone? Are there two men called by the name Tyndareos? And does any land share the names Sparta and Troy? I do not know what I should say. Well, many people in the wide world, as it seems, do have the same names—cities share names and so do women. So there is nothing to be surprised at now. I shall   500 not run away at the servant's frightening words either. Lives there a man of so savage a spirit that he will not give me food when he hears my name? The fire that burned down Troy is famous, and famous am I who lit it, Menelaos. My name is well known throughout the world. I shall wait for the lord of this palace. This will give me two prospects of safety. If he does have a cruel spirit, I shall remain in concealment and go off to the wreck of my ship. But if he shows any signs of compassion, I shall ask him for what my present quandary demands. This is the final blow for me in my   510

misery—that I, a king, must ask for the means of survival
from other monarchs. But necessity dictates. It has been
wisely said—the words are not mine—that nothing is
stronger than dire necessity.

Enter the CHORUS.

CHORUS [*chants*]. When I approached the royal house
   I heard the prophetic maiden declare what I wanted to
      hear,
   that Menelaos does not lie hidden in the earth;
   he has not yet gone
   to darkly-gleaming Erebos*—
   still on a shattering voyage
   over the salt surge of the sea,   520
   he has not yet reached the harbours of his native land,
   the wretched victim of a lifetime's wandering,
   a man utterly unfriended
   as he skirts many a different country's soil,
   rowing his sea-borne ship from the land of Troy.

Enter HELEN.

HELEN. Now I can go back again to my place of refuge at this
   tomb. I have heard the precious words of Theonoe who   530
   knows the truth of everything. She says that my husband
   lives in the sunlight and looks upon the brightness of day.
   He wanders here and there, sailing through numberless
   straits but, though worn down by his voyaging, he will come
   to this place when he reaches the end of his troubles. There
   is one thing, though, that she did not say, and that is
   whether he will survive when he gets here. I held back from
   asking this straight question in my joy when she told me
   that he was safe. She said that he was somewhere near this
   land,* a castaway shipwrecked with a few companions. Alas,
   when will you come? How I long for the moment. [*seeing*   540
   MENELAOS] Ah, who is this?* Have I fallen into an ambush, a
   plot of Proteus' impious son?* Why don't I run to the tomb
   like a swift filly or a raving bacchant?* This man who wants
   to lay his huntsman's hands* on me has a savage look.
MENELAOS. You there, racing so frantically to the tomb's solid
   structure before which burnt offerings are made—stay

where you are. Why do you run off? Ah! Now that I look
upon you, I am struck speechless with amazement.

HELEN. Protect me from harm, women! This man is stopping   550
me from reaching the tomb. He wants to take hold of me and
give me as wife to the king whom I was trying to escape.

MENELAOS. I am no thief, no agent of evil.*

HELEN. Yet the clothes you wear are wild and unsightly.

MENELAOS. Lay your fear aside and stop running.

HELEN. Now I shall stop—I have laid my hands on this tomb.*

MENELAOS. Who are you? What face is this that I see here, lady?

HELEN. And who are you? We both have the same question to
ask.

MENELAOS. I never beheld a closer resemblance.

HELEN. I salute the gods. For a god is present when we recog-   560
nize our loved ones.

MENELAOS. Are you a Greek woman or a native of this country?

HELEN. A Greek. But I want to know who you are too.

MENELAOS. You look exactly like Helen, lady.

HELEN. And you like Menelaos. I do not know what to say.

MENELAOS. You have rightly identified a most unhappy man.

HELEN. Oh, now you have come to your wife's embrace at last!

MENELAOS. What do you mean, *wife*? Do not touch my clothes!

HELEN. The wife that my father Tyndareos gave you.

MENELAOS. O torch-bearing Hecate,* send me kindly visions.

HELEN. It is no creature of the night, no attendant of the god-   570
dess of the crossroads, that you see in me.

MENELAOS. No more am I, I swear, the husband of two wives.

HELEN. But who is this other wife whose lord you are?

MENELAOS. The woman whom the cave conceals, the one I am
taking back from the Trojans.

HELEN. I am the only wife you have.

MENELAOS. Am I in my right mind—and is it my eyes that are
diseased?

HELEN. When you look on me, do you not think you see your
wife?

MENELAOS. You look the same, but I cannot be sure.

HELEN. Look at me. What clearer proof do you need?

MENELAOS. You are like her, I shall not deny that.

HELEN. Trust your eyes. What other teacher can you find?   580

MENELAOS. The trouble is that I have another wife.

HELEN. I did not go to Troy. It was a phantom.

MENELAOS. And who can create living bodies?

HELEN. The gods created a second wife for you from the air.

MENELAOS. Which of them moulded her? What you say is beyond belief.

HELEN. It was Hera. She made this substitute so that Paris could not take me off.

MENELAOS. How so? Were you here, then, and in Troy at one and the same time?

HELEN. My name could be in many places but not my body.

MENELAOS. Let me go. I had enough trouble when I came here.   590

HELEN. Will you leave me and take away your phantom wife?

MENELAOS. Yes, and I bid you farewell with a blessing since you look like Helen.

HELEN. I am lost. I found my husband but shall not keep him.*

MENELAOS. The vast weight of my sufferings at Troy convinces me, not you.

HELEN. Cry woe for my plight. Who has ever been more wretched than I am? The man I love abandons me and I shall never rejoin my fellow Greeks, never reach my native land again.

As MENELAOS *attempts to leave. a* SERVANT *enters.*

SERVANT. Menelaos, what difficulties I have had in finding you! I was sent by the companions you left behind, and have wandered over the whole of this savage land in my search for you.

MENELAOS. What is it? Have you been raided by barbarians?   600

SERVANT. I bring news of a miracle—though miracle is too weak a word.

MENELAOS. Tell me. Your urgency makes it plain that you have some strange news.

SERVANT. I say that the countless labours you endured were all in vain.

MENELAOS. These are old woes that you lament. What is your news?

SERVANT. Your wife is gone. She was lifted up and disappeared into the air's embrace. Now she is hidden in the sky. As she left the sacred cave* where we were guarding her, this is what she said: 'O you miserable Trojans and all you

Achaeans, it was on my account that you died through 610
Hera's trickery on the banks of the Scamander. You thought
that Paris possessed Helen when he did not. But as for
myself, since I have stayed on earth all the time that was
prescribed for me and have fulfilled what fate ordained, I
shall go off to the sky my father.* All men speak ill of the
wretched daughter of Tyndareos, yet they are wrong. She is
totally innocent.'

Hail, daughter of Leda, so you were here then. I brought
the news that you had gone to a hidden place among the
stars, but I was quite unaware that you had a body which
could fly. I shall not allow you to make fools of us like this 620
again,* for you caused your husband and his comrades troubles enough at Troy.

MENELAOS. Now I see it all. Everything makes sense to me
now—what she said was true. O day that I longed for, day
that has given you back to my arms for the taking!

HELEN. O dearest of men, Menelaos, the time of waiting has
been long, while our joy is new-found, but it is here.

HELEN and MENELAOS chant until 697.

With what joy I embrace my husband, friends,
I hold him in my loving arms
after the dawnings of so many bright suns!

MENELAOS. And I clasp you. I have so much to say about what 630
has happened since we were last together that I do not know
where I should now begin.

HELEN. Ecstasy sweeps over me, my hair stands on end upon
my head,
tears drop from my eyes,
and I have thrown my arms around your body, o my husband,
so that I can grasp my joy.

MENELAOS. O dearest vision, I find no fault with you.
I hold my wife, the daughter of Zeus and Leda . . .

HELEN. whom my brothers, those young men on white horses,
proclaimed happy, happy in the torchlight procession . . .* 640

MENELAOS. long ago. But god* took you away from my house,
yet now he is leading you towards a different fortune,
better even than this.

HELEN. Blessed the blow of fate that has brought you back to
    me, my husband.

We were apart so long—but now we are together. May I
    live to enjoy my fortune!

MENELAOS. May you indeed! I join with you in the same prayer.

There are two of us and if one is unhappy, so is the other.

HELEN. My friends, my friends, no longer do I sigh,

    no longer do I grieve over the past.

    I hold him, hold my husband, so long-awaited.   650

    After all these years he has come from Troy.

MENELAOS. You hold me and I hold you. O the toil and pain
    of all those countless days I endured! But now I under-
    stand

    the part played by the goddess.*

HELEN. My tears spring from joy.

    They are tears more of delight than of sorrow.

MENELAOS. What can I say? What mortal could ever have
    hoped for this?

HELEN. I hold you to my breast as I never dreamed I would.

MENELAOS. And I hold you, the woman who appeared to go
    to the city beneath Mount Ida and the doomed towers of
    Ilion.

    Tell me, with the gods to witness, how you left my house.   660

HELEN.

    Ah, ah! You take us back to the bitter start of everything.

    Ah, ah! Bitter is the story you seek to hear.

MENELAOS. Tell me. It must be heard. It was all the gift of heaven.

HELEN. I detest the words, the words I shall utter.

MENELAOS. But speak them even so. It is pleasant to hear of
    troubles that are past.

HELEN. I did not rush to wed a barbarian youth

    on the wings of the oar,

    on the wings of desire for a sinful marriage . . .

MENELAOS. What god, what destiny took you off from your
    native land as spoil?

HELEN. The son of Zeus, the son of Zeus and Maia,*   670

    brought me, my husband, here to the Nile.

MENELAOS. A miracle! Who sent him? What a wondrous tale!

HELEN. I sob and make my eyelids wet with tears.

    It was the wife of Zeus that ruined me.

MENELAOS. Hera? What disaster did she wish to bring on us?

HELEN. Alas for those springs where the goddesses bathed
  and caused their loveliness to glow
  when they came to the beauty contest.

MENELAOS. Why did Hera harbour such rancour against you
    over the contest?*

HELEN. She wanted to keep me from Paris.   680

MENELAOS.   What do you mean?
    Tell me.

HELEN. It was to him that Cypris had promised me.

MENELAOS.   O pitiable woman!

HELEN. Pitiable, pitiable indeed—and Hera brought me here to
    Egypt.

MENELAOS. And then she gave Paris a phantom instead, as you
    tell me.

HELEN. O my mother, I cry alas for your sufferings,
  your sufferings within your halls.

MENELAOS.   What are you saying?

HELEN. My mother is no more. Because of the shame of my
    unholy marriage.
  she tied fast a strangling noose.

MENELAOS. Alas. And is there any word of our daughter
    Hermione?

HELEN. Unmarried and childless, my husband,
  she grieves for my marriage which was no marriage.*   690

MENELAOS. O Paris, you destroyed my house utterly, root and
    branch!

HELEN. This has ruined you too,
  has ruined countless Greeks with their brazen armour.
  And the god cast me from my fatherland, me the accursed
    one,
  doomed to disaster, cast me from my city and from you—
  when I left our halls and our marriage bed,
  but it was not for a shameful love that I left them.

CHORUS. If it should prove that you meet with happy fortune in
  the future, this would make up for the past.

SERVANT. Menelaos, let me too share in your and Helen's joy.   700
  I can see how you feel for myself, but I do not fully understand.

MENELAOS. Yes, old man, you too must share in our story.

SERVANT. Was not this woman the author of our sufferings at
Troy?

MENELAOS. It was not her. The gods deceived me and I grasped
a cloud image, the cause of so much woe, in my arms.

SERVANT. What are you saying? Were all our toils in vain then,
all for a cloud?*

MENELAOS. This was the work of Hera. It sprang from the contest of the three goddesses.

SERVANT. What is this? So the woman here is your real wife?

MENELAOS. She is. You can take my word for it.   710

SERVANT. O daughter, how many-sided is god, how difficult to
interpret! Somehow he directs all things for the best this way
and that and changes what they are. One man works hard
while another does no work and later comes horribly to
grief, finding no security in fortune as it stands at any one
time. For you and your husband had your share of troubles,
you as the victim of report and he in his zest for fighting. But
all his struggles then availed him nothing while now he has
made no effort and yet has won the greatest happiness.

So you didn't disgrace your aged father or the sons of   720
Zeus, your brothers, after all, and you didn't do the sort of
things people say you did. Now I bring back your wedding
to my mind and I remember the torches which I carried as
I ran beside the team of four.* You were in the chariot with
Menelaos here, a bride leaving your happy home. Base is the
man who shows no respect for his master's fortunes and
does not share in his rejoicing and grieve at his sorrows.
Even if I am a slave, I hope I may still be numbered among
those slaves with noble hearts, and though I am called a   730
slave, at least may I have a free man's thoughts. Better so
than that I, a single individual, should suffer a double misfortune—to have a base spirit and to obey the orders of my
fellow-men as a slave.

MENELAOS. Come, old man, you who have completed so many
hard undertakings in the battleline as you toiled for me, now
you must take your share in my good fortune too. Go to the
friends you left behind and tell them the situation as you
have found it here. Say how our fortunes stand. Instruct
them to remain on the shore and to wait eagerly for the   740

challenges that I anticipate await me, in the event that somehow we can steal my wife out of this land. And bid them look out for a way in which we can join together in one good fortune and, if it proves possible, get safely from the barbarians.

SERVANT. I shall do this, my lord. But I now see what a worthless business prophecy is, how full of lies. So there was nothing real at all about the sacrificial flames or the cries of the birds. It is sheer naïvety to think that birds can help men. After all, Calchas said no word, gave not a hint to our army, though he saw his friends dying for a cloud. Nor did Helenos.* 750 No, his city was stormed and all for nothing. You may say, 'Was it because the gods did not wish them to?' But why then do we traffic in prophecy? We should sacrifice to the gods and pray for blessings and bid farewell to the prophet's art. This was invented simply to trap men with the bait of success. Divination has never made an idle man wealthy. Wise thinking and sound judgement—these are the true prophets.

CHORUS. My opinion of prophecy is the same as the old man's. If you win the gods as your friends, you will have supreme 760 prophetic skill in your house.   [*The* SERVANT *goes out.*

HELEN. Well then, up till now everything has gone well. But tell me, you man of sorrows, how you came safely from Troy. I know I shall gain nothing from discovering this, but I feel the longing of a lover to hear a loved one's troubles.

MENELAOS. One question quickly put—yet you ask me to unfold a lengthy tale. Why tell you of the shipwrecks in the Aegean, of the Euboean beacons of Nauplios and the cities of Crete and Libya that I visited on my wanderings, and the look-out place of Perseus?* I should not give you your fill of stories, and as I told you my grim tale, I should still be feeling the 770 pain as I did when I bore it in actual experience. I should grieve twice over.

HELEN. Your answer is fuller than my question. Let all the rest alone and tell me just one thing. How long were you tossed so ruinously as you wandered over the back of the briny sea?

MENELAOS. I endured seven revolving years at sea to add to the ten at Troy.

HELEN. Alas, alas! You tell of a lengthy time indeed, you

long-suffering man. But though you escaped safely from there, you have come here to be murdered.

MENELAOS. What are you saying? What can you mean? Your words are death to me.

HELEN. Leave this country. Run away as fast as you can. You   780 will die at the hands of the lord of this palace.

MENELAOS. What have I done to earn this fate?*

HELEN. Your unexpected arrival will interfere with his plan to marry me.

MENELAOS. Does someone want to marry my wife?

HELEN. Yes, forcing himself upon me, and I should have had to endure it.

MENELAOS. Acting with private authority—or does he rule the land?

HELEN. It is the son of Proteus, king of this country.

MENELAOS. This solves the riddle which I heard from a door-keeper.

HELEN. At the gates of which house in Egypt did you stand?

MENELAOS. This one—from which I was being driven away like   790 a beggar.

HELEN. You were surely not begging for food? Oh, my miserable fate!

MENELAOS. That is what it amounted to, but I did not call myself a beggar.

HELEN. It seems that you know all about my marriage then.

MENELAOS. Yes, but I do not know if you tried to escape this match.

HELEN. Rest assured that I have remained chaste, reserved for you alone.

MENELAOS. How can you convince me of this? What you say is welcome if it is true.

HELEN. Do you see this wretched place where I sit by the tomb?

MENELAOS. You poor woman, I see a bed of leaves. What has it to do with you?

HELEN. It is here that I was taking refuge from this marriage as a suppliant.

MENELAOS. Is there no altar—or is this the barbarians' custom?   800

HELEN. This gave me as much protection as the temples of the gods.

MENELAOS. So can I not take you home by ship?

HELEN. The sword awaits you rather than my bed.

MENELAOS. Then I should prove the most wretched of all men.

HELEN. So feel no shame, but fly from this land.

MENELAOS. And leave you? It was for you that I sacked Troy.

HELEN. Yes, leave me—better so than that my marriage* should kill you.

MENELAOS. You tell me to act like a coward, unworthily of Troy's conqueror.

HELEN. You may be eager to kill the king—but you will never succeed.

MENELAOS. Why? Is his body so invulnerable to steel?   810

HELEN. You will know soon enough. No wise man dares the impossible.

MENELAOS. Should I meekly hold out my hands for him to bind then?

HELEN. You have reached an *impasse*. We must find some clever ruse.

MENELAOS. Yes, death comes more sweetly to those who act rather than do nothing.

HELEN. We have one hope of safety, one alone.

MENELAOS. Do we rely on bribes, daring, or a glib tongue?

HELEN. There would be hope for us if the king did not find out that you have come here.

MENELAOS. He will not know who I am, I am sure of that. And who will tell him?

HELEN. Inside he has an ally inferior to no god.

MENELAOS. Does he have a private oracle hidden within his   820 house?

HELEN. No, but he has a sister. They call her Theonoe.

MENELAOS. The name is certainly oracular.* Tell me what she does.

HELEN. She knows everything, and she will tell her brother that you are here.

MENELAOS. That's the end of me! For it is impossible for me to keep my presence secret.

HELEN. Perhaps we could persuade her if we both supplicated her . . .*

MENELAOS. To do what? What hope are you fostering in me?

HELEN. Not to tell her brother that you are here in this land.

MENELAOS. And if we persuaded her, we could flee from the country?

HELEN. Easily if we had her help. It would be impossible if we tried to do it secretly

MENELAOS. This is your job—woman to woman is a suitable   830
line of approach.

HELEN. Rest assured that my hands will touch her knees.

MENELAOS. But what if she will not listen to our appeal?

HELEN. You will die, and I, poor wretch, shall be forced into marriage.

MENELAOS. False woman! You are saying 'forced' to excuse what you really want.

HELEN. No, I swear a sacred oath by my Menelaos.

MENELAOS. What are you saying? That you will die? And you will never abandon your marriage?

HELEN. Yes, die by the same sword as you. And I shall lie in death near you.

MENELAOS. To ratify this oath then, touch my right hand.

HELEN. I touch it—and swear to leave this light of day when you are dead.

MENELAOS. When I lose you, I swear that I too shall end my   840
life.

HELEN. How then shall we die and still win glory by our deaths?

MENELAOS. I shall kill you on top of the tomb and then kill myself. But first we shall join in a great contest for your hand in marriage. I dare all comers! For I shall not tarnish the glory that I won at Troy. I shall not return to Greece and suffer everyone's abuse as the man who orphaned Thetis of Achilleus and saw Telamonian Aias' butchery and Neleus' son* made childless. Shall I not hold it my duty to die for my   850
wife? It is, and I shall do it. For if the gods are wise, they cover a brave man who has been killed by his enemies' hands in a tomb with a light-lying covering of earth, but they fling cowards onto a ridge of hard rock.*

CHORUS. O Gods, may good fortune at last come to the house of Tantalos!* Put an end to its disasters.

HELEN. Ah, I cry woe, as fits my present fortune. Menelaos, all is over for us. The prophetess Theonoe is coming out of the palace. The building echoes with the noise of bolts shot   860
back.* Run away! But what point is there in running? Whether she is present or not she knows that you have come here. I call out in my misery—I am lost. You came safe

from Troy, from a barbarian land, and yet you will still fall
by a barbarian sword.

Enter THEONOE *with two handmaids holding torches.*

THEONOE. You, lead the way, bringing the torches' flame and
fumigate the heaven's air in the holy rite, so that we may
receive the breath of the sky in all its purity.* And you as
well—if any have polluted our path by treading here with
impious step—sweep it with the cleansing flame and shake 870
the pine-wood torch before me so that I may pass. And when
you have paid this my customary service to the gods, carry
the firebrand again to the palace hearth.

Helen, what of my oracles? What fulfilment have they
found? Your husband Menelaos has come. He is here for all
to see. He has lost his ships and the phantom replica of you.

You wretched man, what perils you escaped on your travels, and you do not know whether you will return home or
stay here. For this very day the gods will hold an acrimo-
nious meeting about you in the presence of Zeus. Hera, who 880
previously was your enemy, is now well disposed towards
you and wishes to bring you safely to your fatherland with
Helen here so that Greece may know that her union with
Paris, the gift of Cypris, was an empty shadow of a marriage.
Cypris, however, wishes to frustrate your return lest she be
shown up for what she is—as the goddess who bought the
prize for beauty by a marriage that, so far as Helen was concerned, was a sham. The decision rests with me whether, as
Cypris wishes, I should tell my brother that you are here and
destroy you, or take my stand with Hera and save your life
by keeping this from my brother, who has ordered me to tell 890
him when you have come to this land.

[*To the* CHORUS] Which one of you will go and tell my
brother that Menelaos is here? This is the way to ensure my
own safety.

HELEN. O maiden, I fall a suppliant* at your knees in a posture
that reflects my sad fortunes. I appeal to you both for myself
and for Menelaos whom I have won at last after so much
pain—and now at this critical moment I must face the risk
of seeing him killed. Do not tell your brother that my dearest
husband has come back to my embrace but keep him safe, I 900

beg you. Never traduce your own piety* for your brother's
sake, buying from him a gratitude which would be both
wicked and unjust. For the god hates violence, and he for-
bids all to use unlawful violence in gaining their possessions.
One must give up wealth that is wrongly won. All mortals
have a share in the heaven and in the land—and so, when
they fill their houses, all men on earth should not get hold
of others' possessions by violence. It was a timely interven-
tion—though an unhappy one for me—when Hermes gave   910
me to your father to keep me safe for my husband who
stands by me here and wishes to take me away. How could
he receive me back if he were dead? And how could your
father ever give back the living to the dead? Now is the time
for you to consider what matters to the god and to your
father. Would heaven and would the dead man wish to
return to their fellow-men what belongs to them, or would
they not? I think they would. You should not defer more to
your wrong-headed brother than to your good father.* If
you, a prophetess, who believes in the gods, are to pervert   920
your father's justice, you will keep intact your brother's
injustice. It is shameful that you should know all the will of
the gods, all that is and all that shall be, yet not know what
is just. And to leave justice on one side, save this wretched
woman from the miseries that engulf her. There is no one
on earth who does not hate Helen. Throughout Greece I am
known as the woman who betrayed my husband and lived
in the halls of the Phrygians* with all their gold. If I go to
Greece and tread on Spartan soil again, they will use the evi- 930
dence of their ears and eyes and realize that all those deaths
were due to the scheming of the gods and that I was not a
traitor to my husband after all, and they will restore me
again to my virtuous name. And I shall betroth my daughter, whom now no one will marry, put a stop to my bitter
exile here, and enjoy the wealth in my own home. If my
husband had been killed and his butchered corpse laid on
the pyre, I should have paid him his due of tears even
though he was far away. Now that he is alive and safely
back, shall I have him torn away from me?

No, maiden, no. This is my supplication to you. Grant me   940
this grace and follow your just father's nature.* For the

highest glory that can be won by children is that the offspring of a good father equals his parents' virtue.

CHORUS. The words you have spoken openly here call for pity—
and you too deserve our pity. I now wish to hear how
Menelaos will plead for his life.

MENELAOS. I could never bring myself to fall at your knees or
to fill my eyes with tears. If I became a coward, I should
bring the greatest disgrace upon Troy.* And yet they say 950
that it is proper for a noble man's eyes to shed tears in the
midst of disasters. Even so, I shall not prefer heroic tears—if
heroic they be—to a stout heart. But if you think it right to
save me, a foreigner justifiably seeking to regain my wife,
give her back to me and save us as well. And if you think it
wrong, this would be far from the first time that I have been
sunk in misery—and you will be revealed as a weak woman.
But what I consider worthy of myself and just and what will 960
most touch your heart, I shall say, falling at the tomb of
your father.*

MENELAOS goes to the tomb.

You, old man, who dwell in this tomb of stone, give me
back my wife. I ask you to give her back. Zeus sent her here
for you to keep safe for me. I know that you yourself will
never return her to me—you are dead. But Theonoe here
will never think it proper that her father, whom I call upon
in the underworld, a man formerly supreme in his reputation for piety,* should have his good name tarnished. For
now it is she who has the power to act.

O Hades,* god of the lower world, I call on you too to help
me. From me you received many bodies which fell by my 970
sword because of this woman. You have your payment.
Either restore them to life again or compel her to prove even
more effective than her pious father and to give me back my
wife.

But if you and your brother will despoil me of my wife, I
shall now tell you what Helen omitted to say to you. I must
tell you, maiden, that I am bound fast by oaths, first of all to
join in combat with your brother. He or I must die. That
is that. However, if he will not face me in a hand-to-hand 980
fight and tries to starve us* while we crouch at the tomb as

suppliants, I am resolved to kill her and then to thrust this two-edged sword into my liver on top of this monument so that streams of blood will drop down your father's tomb. We shall lie side by side, two corpses on this monument of stone. This will cause you an eternity of grief and bring infamy upon your father. For neither your brother nor anyone else will marry this woman. No, I shall take her away with me, if not to our home, at least to where the dead dwell. 990

Why waste words? I should have won more pity by resorting to tears like a woman than by this show of boldness. Kill us if you think it right. For you will not be killing people of low repute.* Yet rather listen to my words. If you do, you will be just and I shall win my wife.

CHORUS. It lies with you, young maiden, to weigh up these arguments. You must make a decision that will please everybody.

THEONOE. It is my nature and my wish to show piety, and I have a proper self-regard, and I could not bring myself to 1000 sully the good repute of my father or to do a favour to my brother which would bring a stain on my good name. Justice has a great shrine in my heart. And since I have inherited this from Nereus,* Menelaos, I shall try to keep it undefiled. I shall cast my vote with Hera since she wishes to show you kindness. I pray that Cypris may prove gracious to me, although she has no treaty with me and I shall try to remain a virgin for ever. As for the reproaches you have uttered over this my father's tomb, I echo them. I should be com- 1010 mitting a sin if I do not restore your husband to you. For had my father been alive, he would have given you to each other to have and to hold.

Yes, all men, whether in the world below or here on earth, are accountable for such matters. When they die, their individual mind does not live on, yet it has an immortal consciousness by merging with the immortal air.*

To keep my counsel brief, I shall say no more of what you have asked of me through your supplication, and I shall never join in my brother's foolish plots. For though it does 1020 not appear so, I am doing him a favour if I convert him to piety.*

But you must find a way to escape for yourselves. I shall not interfere. I shall leave you and keep silence. Begin with

the gods. Beseech Cypris to allow you to return to your
fatherland and pray to Hera that she may remain steadfast
in her intention to save you and your husband.

And you, my dead father—I shall do all in my power to
ensure that your pious name receives no taint of what is
impious. [THEONOE *goes out into the palace.*

CHORUS. No unjust man has ever met with success. The hope 1030
of safety lies in the justice of the cause.

HELEN. Menelaos, the maiden has assured our salvation. The
next step is for the two of us to put our heads together* and
contrive a scheme which will lead to us both escaping.

MENELAOS. Listen then. You have been in the palace for a long
time and have grown familiar with the king's servants.

HELEN. What do you mean by that? You give me hope that you
will bring help to both of us.

MENELAOS. Could you persuade one of those who are in charge
of four-horsed chariots to give us one of them? 1040

HELEN. I could, but how are we going to make our escape, since
we know nothing of the plains of this savage land?

MENELAOS. Put like that, it is impossible. Well, what if I were
to hide in the palace and kill the king with this two-edged
sword?

HELEN. If you planned to kill her brother, his sister would not
tolerate it and would break her silence.

MENELAOS. Well, we certainly have no ship either, in which we
could escape to safety. The sea has the one we had.

HELEN. Listen to me—if a woman can make a good suggestion.
Are you willing to be spoken of as dead though you still live? 1050

MENELAOS. The words are ill-omened,* but if I shall profit
through them, speak on. I am ready to be spoken of as dead
though I still live.

HELEN. And I shall bewail you as women should—with shorn
hair and laments—before the impious king.*

MENELAOS. What remedy lies here to bring us safety? This is not
the most original of ideas.*

HELEN. I shall ask the king of this land for permission to bury
you, the supposedly dead man, at sea in an empty burial.

MENELAOS. Suppose that he grants this. Even then how shall 1060
we two reach safety without a ship as we consign my absent
corpse to its empty grave?

HELEN. I shall tell him to give me a ship from which I shall have adornments for your grave thrown down into the sea's embrace.

MENELAOS. An excellent suggestion save in one respect. If he orders you to conduct the burial on land, your stratagem will lead nowhere.

HELEN. But we shall claim that it is not the custom in Greece to bury those who have died at sea on dry land.

MENELAOS. Another problem successfully solved. Then I shall sail with you and shall put the ornaments in the same ship.

HELEN. Yes, it is absolutely vital that you are there—you and your sailors who escaped from the shipwreck.   1070

MENELAOS. And if I can get hold of a ship at anchor, my men will stand side by side sword in hand.

HELEN. You must make all the decisions.* I pray only that following breezes may swell the sail and the ship run with god's blessing.

MENELAOS. It will. The gods will bring my toils to an end. But who will you say has told you I am dead?

HELEN. You. And you must claim that you alone escaped death as you sailed with the son of Atreus, and that you saw him die.

MENELAOS. And surely these wrappings round my body,* shreds and tatters from the ship, will give testimony in support of 1080 your story.

HELEN. Now they have proved useful, though then it seemed an untimely loss. What then appeared simple wretchedness may perhaps be crowned with success.*

MENELAOS. Should I go into the house with you or sit here quietly by this tomb?

HELEN. Stay here. If he does treat you as he should not, this tomb and your sword will protect you. I shall go into the house and cut off these locks. I shall exchange my white robes for black and tear my cheeks with my fingernails, making the skin bloody.* We are embarking upon a great 1090 struggle and I see two ways the scale could tip. Either I must die if I am found out in my plotting—or save my Menelaos and go to my fatherland.

O lady Hera who lies on the bed of Zeus, give two miserable mortals release from their sufferings, we beg you as we

cast up our arms to the sky where you dwell amid the tapes-
try of stars. And you who won the prize for beauty at the
price of my union with Paris, Cypris, daughter of Dione,* do
not destroy me. You heaped injuries enough upon me before
when you set the name of Helen, though not her body, in a 1100
barbarian land. If you wish to kill me, let me die in my
native country. Why is your appetite for evil never slaked as
you traffic in loves, betrayals, tricks, intrigues, and love
charms that stain bodies with blood? If only you knew moderation!—in all other respects you are the sweetest of gods,
I cannot deny it.*   [HELEN *goes into the*
                                                   palace.

CHORUS [*sings*]. To you let me raise my cry,
   you who dwell in your haunts beneath the foliage of the
      trees
   where you perch in the halls of the muse,
   you, the most tuneful of all the birds that sing,
   O sorrowing nightingale.*   1110
   Come trilling
   through your throbbing throat
   and join in my lament
   as I sing Helen's miserable agony
   and the tear-filled fate
   of the women of Troy,
   victims of the Achaeans' spears,
   when he sped over the surging grey sea
   in a barbarian ship, the man who came,
   came bringing you, Helen, from Lacedaimon,
   you his bride, cause of woe for Priam's sons,
   he, Paris of the deadly marriage,   1120
   and Aphrodite escorted him.

Many of the Achaeans breathed their last
slain by the spear or by a hurtled rock
and have their grim fate in Hades.
Their wretched widows have shorn their hair,
and their homes lie husbandless.
Nauplios* rowed out alone,
kindled his beacon of dazzling fire by sea-girt Euboea
and took his toll of many more Achaeans,

dashing them on the Capherean rocks
as he flashed his treacherous star
by the headlands of the Aegean sea.   1130
And then to the wretched, harbourless regions
sped Menelaos on the storm-gusts far from his native land,
carrying on his ships the prize of the voyage against the
    barbarians,
no prize for the Greeks, simply strife for them,
Hera's creation, the sacred phantom.

What is god, or not god, or what is in between?
Which of mortals can say after searching?
He who can see the divine   1140
leaping this way and that and back again
in contradictory unexpected shifts of fortune,
he it is who has got furthest towards an answer.
You, Helen, are the daughter of Zeus.
For your father became a bird and sowed the seed
in Leda's womb.
And then you were proclaimed throughout the Greek world
a traitor, faithless, lawless, godless.
And I can find no certainty among men,
no true report, about the gods above.   1150

All of you are mad, all who win glory in war
and at the mighty spear's point,
clumsily trying to resolve your troubles.
For strife, if the contest of blood is to settle it,
will never end in the cities of men.
Through strife the Trojans left their bedchambers
in the land of Priam,
when words could have settled the quarrel,* Helen, over you. 1160
But now they are in the care of Hades below,
and the blazing flame, like Zeus' bolt, hurtled upon the
    walls,
and you cause sufferings upon sufferings
in a miserable, lamentable welter of catastrophe.

Enter THEOCLYMENOS *with attendants, hounds, and hunting-gear.**

THEOCLYMENOS. Hail, tomb of my father.* I buried you, Proteus,
  by the doors from my palace so that I could easily address

you. Every time I leave and every time I enter my palace, I, your son Theoclymenos, speak to you, my father.

You my servants, take the dogs and the hunting nets into 1170 my royal house.   [*The attendants go out.*

I have often reproached myself for my complete failure to punish wrongdoers with death. And now I have been told that some Greek has come to my land as large as life and has eluded my guards. He is either a spy or he is trying to steal Helen. He shall die, if only we can catch him. But look! It appears that I have returned to find the whole business completed, for the daughter of Tyndareos has abandoned her place of refuge at the tomb* and has been carried from the land. Hey there, unbolt the doors. Open the stables, atten- 1180 dants, and bring out my chariots! It shall not be for want of effort on my part if the wife whom I long to possess gives me the slip and is smuggled from this country. But stop! I see that the woman we pursue is here in the house. She has not got away.

Enter HELEN, *dressed in black with her hair cropped.**

You, Helen, why have you changed your white robes and draped your body in black? Why have you used the knife to crop the hair from your royal head? And why do you weep, bathing your face in dewy tears? Have your dreams at night 1190 led you to lament? Or have you heard some news from home that has broken your heart with grief?

HELEN. O my master*—for now I call you by that name—my life is over. All is finished for me and now I am nothing.

THEOCLYMENOS. What catastrophe afflicts you? Tell me what has happened.

HELEN. My Menelaos—alas, how can I say it?—he is dead.

THEOCLYMENOS. I take no joy in your words, but they bring me good fortune. How do you know this? Has Theonoe told you?

HELEN. She has, and one who was present when he died told me too.*

THEOCLYMENOS. Has someone come here with certain news of 1200 this?

HELEN. Yes, someone has come. If only his journey would take him where I wish him!

THEOCLYMENOS. Who is he? Where is he? Tell me, to make the news doubly sure.

HELEN. It is this man who sits crouching by the tomb here.

THEOCLYMENOS. Apollo! how his tattered clothing marks him out!

HELEN. Alas, I think that my husband also looks like this.

THEOCLYMENOS. From what country is he? And where did he sail from to our land?

HELEN. He is a Greek, one of the Achaeans who sailed with my husband.

THEOCLYMENOS. How does he say that Menelaos died?

HELEN. In the most pitiable of all deaths, in the sea's watery billows.

THEOCLYMENOS. Where was he travelling on barbarian seas?   1210

HELEN. He was cast up on the harbourless rocks of Libya.

THEOCLYMENOS. And how did this man, his fellow-voyager, not meet his death too?

HELEN. Sometimes the low-born have better fortune than the great.

THEOCLYMENOS. But where did he leave the wreckage of his ship before he came here?

HELEN. There where I pray it may be accursed—and where I wish Menelaos had not died.

THEOCLYMENOS. Menelaos is dead. In what ship did the man come here?

HELEN. Sailors happened to find him, he says, and they took him up.

THEOCLYMENOS. And where is that abomination that was sent to Troy instead of you?

HELEN. You means the cloud-phantom? It has vanished into air.

THEOCLYMENOS. O Priam and the land of Troy, you were 1220 destroyed for nothing.

HELEN. I too played a part in the disaster which befell the sons of Priam.

THEOCLYMENOS. Did he leave your husband unburied or did he hide in the ground?

HELEN. Unburied, yes. I cry woe for all my misery and suffering.

THEOCLYMENOS. Was it for this that you cut off the locks of your blond hair?

HELEN. Yes, because he is as close to me as ever he was.

THEOCLYMENOS. It is natural that you should weep for this sad fortune.*

HELEN. It is an easy business, I suppose, to delude your sister?

THEOCLYMENOS. Indeed it isn't. But what now? Will you continue to live at your place of refuge by this tomb?

HELEN. Yes, I keep my faith with my husband by shunning 1230 you.

THEOCLYMENOS. Why do you make a mockery of me? Let the dead man rest.

HELEN. I shall shun you no longer. Now you can start to prepare for our marriage.

THEOCLYMENOS. It is late in coming, but even so I rejoice at this.

HELEN. Now do as I tell you. Let us forget what is past.

THEOCLYMENOS. On what terms? Let one favour be answered by another.

HELEN. Let us make a truce. Be reconciled to me.

THEOCLYMENOS. I lay aside my quarrel with you. Let it take wing and fly away.

HELEN. Then by your knees I beseech you, since you are my friend . . .

THEOCLYMENOS. What is it that you seek as you stretch out your arms in supplication to me?*

HELEN. I wish to give my dead husband burial.

THEOCLYMENOS. What is this? Can there be a grave when there 1240 is no corpse? Or will you bury a shadow?

HELEN. The Greeks have a custom that anyone who dies at sea . . .

THEOCLYMENOS. What do they do? Pelops' house is wise in such matters.*

HELEN. They bury them in an empty shroud of woven cloth.

THEOCLYMENOS. Bury him with due honours then. Pile up a tomb wherever in my land you wish.

HELEN. It is not in that way that we bury sailors lost at sea.

THEOCLYMENOS. How do you bury them then? I have no knowledge of Greek customs.*

HELEN. We take out to sea all that is needful for the corpse.

THEOCLYMENOS. What then can I provide you with for the dead man?

HELEN. This fellow knows. I have no experience of the ceremony, since before now my life was happy.

THEOCLYMENOS. Stranger, you have brought news which is 1250 happy for me.

MENELAOS. But not for me and not for the man who has died.

THEOCLYMENOS. How do you bury the dead who are lost at sea?

MENELAOS. It varies from one man to another depending on their wealth.

THEOCLYMENOS. As far as money is concerned, say what you want. For her sake I'll give it.

MENELAOS. First blood is shed, an offering to those below the earth.

THEOCLYMENOS. From what victim? You tell me and I shall do your bidding.

MENELAOS. Decide for yourself. Whatever you give will do well.

THEOCLYMENOS. Among barbarians the custom is to sacrifice a horse or a bull.

MENELAOS. Do not give anything unworthy of your royal birth.

THEOCLYMENOS. There is no lack of such gifts among our rich 1260 herds.

MENELAOS. And we carry a covered bier without a corpse.

THEOCLYMENOS. It shall be arranged. What else is it customary to offer?

MENELAOS. Arms of bronze,* for he loved the spear.

THEOCLYMENOS. The arms we shall give him will be worthy of Pelops' line.

MENELAOS. Also all the beautiful fruit and flowers that the earth brings forth.

THEOCLYMENOS. What then? How do you let these offerings 1270 down into the sea?

MENELAOS. We must have a ship with its complement of rowers.

THEOCLYMENOS. And how far from the shore should the vessel sail?

MENELAOS. Its wake should scarcely be visible from the coast.

THEOCLYMENOS. Really? Why do the Greeks observe this particular rite?

MENELAOS. So that the sea should cast nothing polluted back upon the land.

THEOCLYMENOS. A swift-sailing Phoenician ship* shall be provided.

MENELAOS. That would be splendid—and would do grace to Menelaos.

THEOCLYMENOS. Is it not enough that you should perform this ritual without Helen?

MENELAOS. It is the duty of a mother or a wife or child.

THEOCLYMENOS. From what you say, it is her task to bury her husband.

MENELAOS. Yes, the rite demands that we do not rob the dead of their due.

THEOCLYMENOS. Let her go with you. It is right that I should foster piety in my wife. [to MENELAOS] Go into the house and take out what you need to adorn the dead. And I shall not 1280 send you empty-handed from my land, since you have done this in kindness to Helen here. For bringing me this good news, I shall give you fine clothing in place of these rags*— and food too, for I can see how hard put to it you are at the moment. With this help from me you will reach your fatherland.

And you, poor woman, do not pine away in endless sorrow. Menelaos has met his doom. Your laments cannot bring the dead man back to life again.

MENELAOS. Young lady, you know what you have to do. You must be content with the husband who is here before your eyes and bid farewell to the one who is no more. This is what 1290 is best for you in the present circumstances. And if I find safety and come to Greece, I shall lay to rest the infamy which stained your name before—if you prove the kind of wife you should be to your husband.

HELEN. I shall prove so, and my husband will never find fault with me. You yourself who are nearby will be sure of this.

But now, you wretched man, go inside, have a bath and change your clothes. I am not going to see to your comforts just to cause delay; for you will perform what is due to my dearest love Menelaos with all the more affection if you meet 1300 with your due from me.

MENELAOS, HELEN, and THEOCLYMENOS enter the palace.

CHORUS [*sings*]. Once in the mountains, the Mother of the Gods*
        rushed on speeding feet
        through the wooded glens
        and the streams of the rivers' waters
        and the deep-roaring waves of the sea

in longing for the one who had gone,
her daughter with the name that must not be spoken.*
And the noisy cymbals
cried out
as they flung forth their piercing din,
when the goddess had yoked wild beasts   1310
to her chariot*
to search for her daughter
snatched from the dancing circles
of the maidens,
and there followed her swift as the storm winds
Artemis with her bow and grim-eyed Athena
with her spear and her full suit of armour.
But Zeus saw it all from his dwelling in the sky
and brought a different fate to fulfilment.*

And when the mother gave up her wanderings,
so fast, so wide, so effortful,   1320
gave up her search for her daughter
seized by trickery,
she crossed over the snow-clad look-out places
of the Nymphs of Ida
and in grief threw herself down
in the rocky woods deep in snow.
To mortals she brought no fruitfulness* from the plough,
she withered the green from the plains of the earth,
she called a halt to the generations of men.
She caused no fresh   1330
leafy tendrils to grow
for the flocks to graze on,
and the cities were dying.
There were no sacrifices to the gods,
no burnt offerings on the altars.
She stopped the flow
of the fresh, bright waters of the springs
in her unforgettable grief for her child.

But when the Mother had brought all feasting to an end
for gods and for the race of men,
Zeus spoke
to soothe her hateful anger: 1340

'Go, you holy Graces,
go and with loud cries
banish grief from the heart of Demeter
as she rages over her daughter.
Go too, you Muses, with your songs and dances.'
Then* first of all Cypris, fairest of the blessed gods, took hold
of the cymbals with their rumbling voice of bronze
and the kettledrum, its skin tight-stretched.
And the goddess smiled
and took into her hands   1350
the deep-sounding pipe,
thrilled by the music's loud clamour.

You, Helen, did not observe these rites*
and you lit no holy flame in your house
and so, my child, you incurred the wrath
of the Great Mother, for you paid
no reverent sacrifice to her godhead.
There is great power
in the dappled fawnskins,
in the garlands of green ivy   1360
wreathed around the sacred fennel stalks,
in the shaking and the whirling round and round
of the bull-roarer up in the air,
the bacchanal's hair flying loose for Bromios,
and the night-festivals of the goddess.
The moon has passed gently over them
with its radiance.
But you gloried only in beauty.

HELEN enters.

HELEN. All has gone well for us in the palace, my friends. For
when she was questioned, the daughter of Proteus helped to   1370
conceal my husband's presence and told her brother nothing about it. For my sake she said that he lies dead in the
earth and does not see the sunlight. My husband very expe-
ditiously seized his chance. He himself is carrying the arms
which he was supposed to cast down into the sea. He thrust
his noble arm behind the shield's band and took the spear in
his right hand, pretending that he was helping Helen to do

grace to the dead man. And he covered his body with
armour which will prove convenient for the fight. He will be
able to vanquish countless barbarians single-handed when 1380
we embark on the oared ship. I changed his castaway's rags
and dressed him in fine clothes,* and I bathed his body with
fresh water from the river—something he has not experienced for a long time. But I must be silent, for the man who
thinks he has our marriage in his grasp is coming out of the
palace. [*to the* CHORUS] And I beg you to remain loyal and
keep a check on your tongues in the hope that if we escape
safely we can one day bring you to safety too.

*THEOCLYMENOS enters with attendants. MENELAOS is with them.**

THEOCLYMENOS. File off, my servants, as the stranger ordered, 1390
carrying the funeral gifts for the sea. And you, Helen, if I
may not seem to you to speak amiss, obey me and stay
here. You will honour your husband equally whether you
are there or not. I am afraid that a sudden longing may
sweep over you and move you to throw yourself into the
surging sea, distraught with fond memories of your former
husband. For though he is missing, you still mourn him
excessively.

HELEN. O my new husband, I have no choice but to honour my 1400
first marriage when I was a maiden bride. And I would
indeed die with him, such is my love for my husband. But
what favour would it be to him for me to join him in death?
No, allow me to go and give the grave-offerings to his body
myself. May the gods grant you all that I wish—and grant
it to the stranger here too for all his help in this ritual. You
will have in me the kind of wife it is fit that you should have
in your palace since you are doing such a favour to
Menelaos and myself. All this is leading to a happy outcome.
Instruct someone to give us a ship in which we can take 1410
these offerings. With this kind deed you will crown the
favours you have done me.

THEOCLYMENOS. Go, you, and give these people a fifty-oared
Sidonian* ship with its complement of rowers.

HELEN. Shall not the man who is in charge of these funeral rites
command the ship?

THEOCLYMENOS. He shall. My sailors must obey this man.

HELEN. Repeat your order to make sure that they understand you clearly.

THEOCLYMENOS. I give the order a second time—a third time too if you wish.*

HELEN. Blessings on you—and on my plans!

THEOCLYMENOS. Do not spoil your cheeks with too many tears.

HELEN. This day will show my gratitude to you. 1420

THEOCLYMENOS. The dead are nothing. Labour spent on them is wasted.

HELEN. My words have meaning both here and for the dead below.

THEOCLYMENOS. In me you shall have a husband in no way inferior to Menelaos.

HELEN. I find no fault with you. All I need is for things to turn out well.

THEOCLYMENOS. This lies with you—if you will give me your love.

HELEN. I need no teacher now to tell me to love my friends.

THEOCLYMENOS. Would you like me to help you and escort you on your voyage?

HELEN. No, no. Do not be a slave to your slaves,* my lord.

THEOCLYMENOS. Very well. I need think no more about the rites of the Pelopid line.* My palace is unpolluted. Menelaos did 1430 not die here. Let someone go and tell my officers to bring their wedding gifts to my palace. My whole land must ring with joyous songs so that men may envy my wedding with Helen.

And you, stranger,* must go and give to the sea's embrace these offerings for the man who was once the husband of Helen. Then hurry back to the palace with my wife so that you can join with me in our marriage feast and then be sent 1440 on your way home—or stay here and live in happiness.

[*THEOCLYMENOS goes into the palace.*

MENELAOS. O Zeus whom men call father and wise god, look down upon us and grant us a change from our troubles, join with us as we drag our misfortunes up a rocky slope, give us your strong support. It needs but a touch of your finger-tip and we shall arrive at the good fortune we wish for. The calamities we suffered before have been enough. You gods, I have called you many slighting and abusive names. Surely I do not have to be in misery all the time. Can I not succeed

at last? If you give me this one favour, you will make me 1450
happy for the rest of my life.

[MENELAOS *and* HELEN *go out.*

CHORUS [*sings*]. O swift ship of Phoenician Sidon,
  voyaging vessel
  dear to the billows of Nereus,
  ship which leads the dance
  of the lovely-leaping dolphins
  when the breezes fall and the sea is windless
  and the goddess of calm,
  the grey-green daughter of the Sea, says,
  'Cease to manage the sails with ropes.
  Let them hang down freely—you have left the sea breezes   1460
    behind.
  Take up your oars of pinewood,
  o sailors, sailors,
  as you steer Helen to those shores with their splendid har-
    bours,
  the shores of the land which Perseus founded.'*

Perhaps she may find by the surging river*
or before the temple of Pallas
the daughters of Leucippos
as after so long she joins in the dancing
or the revels for Hyacinthos
for merriment at night.   1470
He it was that Phoebus killed
with the round discus
after the god challenged him to see who threw it farthest,
and his is the day
when oxen are sacrificed in the land of Sparta.
The son of Zeus ordered this holy ritual.
Perhaps you will find your daughter,
Hermione whom you left at home. Still she waits
for the pinewood torches to blaze at her wedding.

If only we could find ourselves flying
through the air
wherever in Libya the bird formations go   1480
as they leave the winter's storms,

obeying the piping of their eldest leader
who shrieks while he flies
over the rainless and the fruitful tracts of land.
O long-necked cranes,
who keep pace with the scudding clouds,
fly below the Pleiades at their zenith
and Orion at night!   1490
Bring the news
as you settle by the Eurotas
that Menelaos who took the city of Dardanos*
will be coming home.

And now hasten through the sky
along your horse-track,
you sons of Tyndareos* who dwell in heaven
beneath the whirling of the radiant stars.
Twin saviours of Helen,   1500
come over the green salt swell
and the white-foaming crests of the dark breakers of the sea
as you send to sailors
fair-breathing winds from Zeus.
Cast off from your sister
the infamy of marriage to a barbarian,
the shame she won when she was punished
for the strife on Ida,*
though she never went to Apollo's towers*   1510
in the land of Troy.

Enter from one direction THEOCLYMENOS *and* SERVANT, *from another*
the MESSENGER.

MESSENGER. My lord, we have uncovered base treachery in
    your house—how strange are the tidings of woe you will
    soon hear from my lips.
THEOCLYMENOS. What has happened?
MESSENGER. You must try to win another woman by your woo-
    ing—for Helen has left this country.
THEOCLYMENOS. How? Did she fly away or go off by land?
MESSENGER. Menelaos has taken her from this country by ship.
    He was the one who came with the news of his own
    death.

THEOCLYMENOS. Your message appals me. What ship took her 1520
  from this land? I cannot believe what you say.
MESSENGER. The ship you gave the stranger. To cut a long story
  short, he has gone off and killed your sailors too.
THEOCLYMENOS. How? I am eager to learn. For I never dreamt
  that the hand of one man could outstrip all those sailors you
  were sent to sea with.
MESSENGER. When the daughter of Zeus left this royal palace
  and set out for the sea, with the greatest cleverness she pro-
  ceeded to raise a lament over her husband, stepping delicately in time with it—but he was in fact there nearby and
  not dead at all. And when we came to the harbour where 1530
  your dockyards gird the bay, we dragged down a brand-new
  Sidonian ship with fifty benches and fifty rowers. We performed the various tasks in order. One man put on board the
  mast, another set ready the flat-bladed oars. The white sails
  were furled and the rudders were lowered by their ropes.
    And while we were working at this, Greek men, Menelaos'
  fellow-sailors—we later realized that they had been watching out for this—came to the shore, dressed in clothes from
  the shipwreck—handsome men they were,* yet they looked 1540
  filthy, caked with brine. When he saw that they were there,
  the son of Atreus spoke to them, cunningly acting a pitiable
  scene for us to witness: 'You poor men, which Achaean vessel are you from? How have you come here after your shipwreck? But come, join us in burying the son of Atreus who
  is dead. The daughter of Tyndareos here is giving him burial though we have no body.'
    And they went onto the ship, shedding counterfeit tears
  as they carried their sea-offerings for Menelaos. This made
  us suspicious and we murmured to each other about how 1550
  many of these extra passengers there were. Nevertheless we
  held our silence in obedience to your instructions, for by
  ordering that the stranger should have command of the vessel you put all of us there into confusion.
    And everything else was manageably light and so we
  stowed it in the ship with ease. The bull, however, refused
  to walk straight ahead up the gangway but bellowed as it
  rolled its eyes in a circle. Humping its shoulders and squint-
  ing along its horns, it kept us from handling it.* But Helen's

husband called out: 'O you who sacked the city of Troy, 1560
come on, snatch up this bull bodily onto your youthful
shoulders as the Greeks do it, fling it onto the prow, this sacrificial offering for the dead Menelaos.' And as he spoke he
raised his drawn sword.

They came to do his bidding and seized the bull, lifted it
on board and set it down on the deck. But as for the horse,
Menelaos stroked its neck and forehead and wheedled it onto
the ship.

Finally when everything was stowed in the vessel, Helen
stepped up the rungs of the ladder with her delicate feet and 1570
sat down in the middle of the quarter-deck, and the reportedly dead Menelaos sat near her. The other Greeks sat shoulder to shoulder along the sides, lined up equally to right and
left with swords hidden beneath their clothes. The surge was
filled with our shouts as we took up the boatswain's call.

When we were a moderate distance from the shore, the
helmsman asked, 'Should we sail still further, stranger—or
is this far enough? For you are in charge of the ship.' And 1580
Menelaos said, 'This is far enough for me.' And clasping his
sword in his right hand he went to the prow and took his
stand to slaughter the bull. He prayed as he cut its throat
but made no mention of anyone among the dead: 'O
Poseidon, sea-dwelling lord of the deep, and you holy daughters of Nereus, bring me and my wife safely from this land of
Egypt to the shore at Nauplia.' Spurts of blood gushed forth
into the sea's swell—a favourable omen for the stranger.
And someone said, 'This sea-journey is all a trick. We must 1590
sail back. You steer us to starboard, you turn the rudder.'
After killing the bull, the son of Atreus called out to his companions from where he stood: 'My men, the flower of Greece,
why hesitate to butcher the barbarians,* to kill them and
fling them from the ship into the sea's swell?' And the
boatswain shouted out orders to your sailors to counter his:
'Come on, some of you lift up an end timber, others break
up the benches, others seize the oars from their tholes.
Bloody the heads of these foreigners, our enemies.'

Everyone immediately leapt up, some of them clasping 1600
swords, others bits of ship's timber in their hands. The vessel was awash with blood. Then Helen's exhortation rang

from the prow: 'Where is the name for courage that you
won at Troy? Show these barbarians that it was justly
earned.' Eagerly they came to blows. Some fell, some staggered up, others you could have seen lying there dead.
Holding his arms, Menelaos looked out for where his comrades were in difficulties and there he appeared, his sword in
his right hand—and so your sailors dived from the ship and
he cleared the benches of them. Then he went up to the 1610
helmsman and told him to steer the ship for Greece. They
raised the mast and favourable breezes sprang up.

They have gone from this country. I escaped death and let
myself down into the sea by the anchor. When I was already
tiring, a fisherman took me from the water and set me
ashore to tell you this story. A prudent scepticism is the most
profitable quality a man can have.

[*The* MESSENGER *goes out.*

CHORUS. I still don't believe, my lord, that Menelaos was here
and remained unmasked by you or me—and yet he was.* 1620

[THEOCLYMENOS *and* SERVANT *sing until* 1641].

THEOCLYMENOS.
Alas! I am the miserable victim of a woman's trickery.
My bride has fled from me. And if the ship could be pursued
and taken,* I would have spared no effort but speedily
caught the foreigners.
As things stand, however, I shall take vengeance on my
sister who has betrayed me.*
She saw Menelaos at my palace and did not tell me.
For this she will never live to trick another with her
prophecies.

SERVANT [*stepping forward and calling*].
O, you there, my master,* where are you rushing? What
act of murder will you commit?

THEOCLYMENOS. I go where justice bids me. Out of my way!

SERVANT.
I shall not let go of your robes. For what you are so eager
to do is terribly wrong.

THEOCLYMENOS. You are a slave. Will you seek to rule your
master?

SERVANT. Yes, for I have your interests at heart.   1630

THEOCLYMENOS. Not my interests if you will allow me . . .

SERVANT.   No, I shall not allow you.

THEOCLYMENOS. . . . to kill my sister, that most wicked woman . . .

SERVANT. most pious rather.

THEOCLYMENOS. She betrayed me . . .

SERVANT.   To do what is right makes betrayal a good deed.

THEOCLYMENOS. . . . when she gave my bride to another.

SERVANT.   To someone with a greater right.

THEOCLYMENOS. Who has rights over my possessions?

SERVANT.   The man who took her from her father.

THEOCLYMENOS. But fortune gave her back to me.

SERVANT.   And necessity took her away from you.

THEOCLYMENOS. It is not for you to give me lessons.

SERVANT.   It is, if my words are more full of sense.

THEOCLYMENOS. I am a subject then, not a king.

SERVANT.   Your royal power should be used for right, not wrong.*

THEOCLYMENOS. You seem to be in love with death.

SERVANT.   Kill me.
You will kill your sister over my dead body. For good ser-   1640
  vants
the noblest of deaths is to die for their masters.

The DIOSCOUROI *appear.**

CASTOR. Calm the rage which sweeps you on against all justice, Theoclymenos, king of this land. We who speak your
name are the twin sons of Zeus whom Leda once bore at the
same time as Helen who has fled from your home. Your
anger is over the loss of a marriage which was not fated for
you, and your sister Theonoe, the maiden born from the
divine daughter of Nereus, has done you no wrong in honouring the will of the gods and her father's pious commands.

It was necessary for Helen to dwell in your house for all 1650
this time up to the present. But when Troy's foundations
were destroyed and she had finished lending her name to the
gods, this ceased to be the case. She must be joined once
more in her old marriage, return home, and live with her
husband. But do not blacken your sword with a sister's
blood. You must see that she showed good judgement in
what she did. We would have saved our sister long ago since

Zeus made us gods, but we were weaker than fate together 1660
with the gods, who decided that this should be.

That is what I have to say to you. And I say to my sister,
'Sail on with your husband. You will have fair winds. We,
your two saviour brothers, will escort you to your fatherland
as we ride on horseback over the sea. And when you reach
the end of the course of your life, you will be hailed as a goddess and will have your share in libations with the sons of
Zeus and receive guest-gifts from mortals with us. For this is
the will of Zeus. And as for the place where the son of Maia, 1670
after lifting you up from Sparta, first set you down as you
flew through the air, and hid your body so that Paris should
not marry you—I am speaking of the long low island which
guards Acte*—this shall be called Helene* among men for
the rest of time, since it gave you shelter after you were
stolen from your home. And Menelaos the wanderer shall
dwell on the island of the blessed*—so the gods will dispense
his fate. It is not that they hate the nobly-born, but those
have more labours to endure than the common run of men.'

THEOCLYMENOS. O sons of Leda and Zeus, to please you both I 1680
shall lay aside my previous quarrels over your sister.* Let
Helen go to her home if that is the gods' will. And I no
longer wish to kill my sister. You can rest assured that you
are blood-brothers of one who is both the best and the most
virtuous of sisters. And go on your way rejoicing in the sur-
passing nobility of Helen's heart. Not many women are her
equal in this.*

    [*The* DIOSCOUROI. THEOCLYMENOS, *and* SERVANT *go out.*

CHORUS [*chants*]. The divine will manifests itself in many forms,
    and the gods bring many things to pass against our expec-
      tation.
What we thought would happen remains unfulfilled,   1690
while the god has found a way to accomplish the unex-
      pected.
And that is what has happened here.*

                      [*The* CHORUS *goes out.*

EXPLANATORY NOTES

MEDEA

1–6   *How I wish . . . for Pelias*: Medea's Nurse, a slave, refers to the legendary journey of Jason and the Argonauts. King Pelias, who had usurped the kingdom of Iolkos from Jason's father, sent the hero to fetch the golden fleece from Colchis on the east of the Black Sea. The craftsman Argos built a magical ship called the Argo with wood from Mount Pelion in Thessaly. It carried Jason and his crew through the Clashing Rocks (in the Bosporos). The fleece was guarded by a dragon, but the Colchian princess Medea fell in love with Jason and helped him with her magic to take it. She then fled with him to Iolkos.

9–10   *persuaded the daughters of Pelias to kill their father*: on the pretext that if they chopped their father up and boiled him in a cauldron he would be rejuvenated. But in revenge for Pelias' treatment of Jason and his father, Medea misled his daughters, who thus simply killed him. The inhabitants of Iolkos were appalled at what Medea had done in revenge for Pelias' treatment of Jason and his father, and she and Jason fled to Corinth. Euripides spares us the gory details. He may want us to warm to the humanity of Medea at the play's outset.

11   *husband and children*: according to Apollonius of Rhodes (third-century BCE), Medea went through a marriage ceremony with Jason. In Euripides' Athens, a marriage with a foreigner would have no legal validity and Jason certainly does not feel tied by it. They have had two children.

17   *Jason has betrayed his own children*: Jason does, in fact, feel some sense of responsibility for them (559–68).

18   *beds down in a royal match*: Jason has married Glauce, the daughter of Creon, the king of Corinth. The match should give him security—and presumably will assure him of the kingship when Creon dies.

36   *she hates her children*: Medea's reactions to her children, threatening at the moment, provide one of the play's major sources of emotion. The children are in danger because they are the tokens of Jason's false marriage to her.

46–7   *here comes the children . . . races*: the children have been innocently playing.

48   *s.d.*: the Tutor is another slave. Euripides establishes a feeling of unheroic domestic realism at the start of the tragedy. From this

familiar atmosphere, the Greek audience would find itself led into
a world of inhuman cruelty.

57   *the earth and sky*: she has come outside to escape the claustro-
        phobic tensions within. While it is conventional in Greek tragedy
        for troubled characters to declare their grievances to these ele-
        ments, the Earth and the Sun prove to be of great significance
        in the course of *Medea*. See nn. at 1251–2, 1321–2, and
        1327–8.

65   *I entreat you by your chin*: this refers to the Greek custom of sup-
        plication. If one established physical contact with someone from
        whom one wanted a favour, the latter would feel under an
        obligation to grant it. The appropriate parts of the body to touch
        were the chin and the knees.

68   *draughts*: again a note of unheroic realism (though Protesilaus
        played this game on the Trojan expedition (Euripides, *Iphigenia
        at Aulis* 195–6) and Achilles and Ajax are shown dicing on a
        famous Exekias vase in the Vatican).

69   *Peirene*: a fountain in Corinth.

85–8   *is anyone . . . marriage*: the Tutor is worldly-wise and cynical.

92   *like a bull's*: a dangerous animality flashes forth from Medea.

114   *may the whole house fall in ruin*: Jason's desertion has dislocated
        the structure of the household. Medea's wish here builds on that
        idea.

119   *Our royal masters have dangerous spirits*: the Nurse observes her
        great mistress from an ordinary person's viewpoint.

125   *Moderation*: one of the ideals of Greek life. Inscribed on Apollo's
        temple at Delphi were the words 'Nothing in excess' (cf. 127).
        Excess can rouse divine resentment (cf. 129).

130   *s.d.*: the Chorus of Corinthian women is sympathetic to Medea.

148   *Earth and Light*: cf. 57 and the references given there.

157   *Zeus will be your advocate here*: Zeus, the supreme god, should
        assert the claims of Justice and support oaths. However, he—and
        the other gods—prove to be conspicuously absent from this play.

160   *Themis*: the goddess of Law, who maintains the sanctity of
        prayers (169) and oaths (209). *Artemis*: protects marriage.

167   *I, the killer of my brother*: while fleeing from her father Aeetes in
        the Argo after Jason's theft of the fleece, Medea cut her young
        brother Apsyrtus into pieces and flung them into the sea to delay
        the pursuit, for the pious Aeetes had to stop to gather up the
        remains of his son. (But see n. at 1334.) Again (cf. n. at 9–10)
        Euripides does not mention the horrific details of this episode. At
        the moment we are given a sympathetic view of Medea. But even
        so this is a sinister hint of what she is capable of doing to chil-
        dren.

173–5   *I wish . . . offer them*: the warm and ready sympathy of the
          Chorus is well brought out.

187–8   *she darts . . . the wild glance of a lioness with young*: the Greek lit-
          erally means: 'she becomes a bull with the look of a lioness with
          young.' Again (cf. 92) we see the animal within Medea.

192–201   *they discovered . . . to the feast*: the Nurse goes against a common
          Greek view when she says that all that music offers is trivial
          entertainment. Music was considered an important part of Greek
          education since it promoted harmony in the human soul.
          However, the Nurse is here showing (*a*) that she cannot relate
          to the old aristocratic lifestyle in which great poetry such as
          Homer's was sung to deeply appreciative audiences, and (*b*) that
          she does grasp how far beyond any possible psychological har-
          mony Medea has now moved.

213–24   *Women of Corinth . . . perversity*: an eminently reasonable Medea
          feels that she has done all she can to fit in with the life of a
          strange Greek city in which she is a resident alien (a metic).

227   *my friends*: while Medea calls the members of the Chorus her
          friends, they never do so in return, preferring to address her as
          'lady'. Is this a mark of respect, or is S. L. Schein right when he
          suggests that it 'reflects their sense of her as just too far out, too
          inhuman for their complete solidarity' ('*Philia* in Euripides'
          Medea', in M. Griffin and D. Mastronarde (eds.), *Cabinet of the
          Muses* (Atlanta, Ga., 1990), 65).

230–51   *Of everything that is . . . bear one child*: the most famous feminist
          statement in ancient literature. The comments on marriage are
          a reflection of the reality for Athenian—and no doubt
          Corinthian—women of Euripides' day, though they scarcely
          apply to Medea, who made a dowryless marriage for love. The
          point that men, but not their wives, can escape the stifling claus-
          trophobia of the home is well taken. And the final comparison
          between fighting in war and giving birth is an arresting and
          challenging one for any audience, especially the largely or exclu-
          sively male one of the Attic theatre.

255–8   *I, a desolate woman without a city . . . no relative at all*: as a resi-
          dent alien (a metic), Medea needs a male citizen to act as her
          sponsor. In fact, she has no male to protect her, and it is obvi-
          ously impossible for her to turn to her family. She is without a
          city to call home, a tragic lot in the Greek world.

260–4   *If I can find some means . . . to keep silence*: the Chorus agrees to
          keep silence and thus feels that it has no choice but to stand by
          helplessly when Medea's scheming takes its horrific turn. This
          causes it to become very like the audience of the play, who also
          must look on, unable to intervene.

265–6   *when she is wronged . . . more murderous*: the idea of the woman
        who is sexually slighted is a powerful one in the play.

267   *you will be right to exact vengeance from your husband*: the Chorus,
        like all ancient Greeks, accept the revenge ethic.

271–6   *Medea . . . borders of this land*: King Creon speaks decisively, say-
        ing that there is no appeal against his command. His withdrawal
        from this position reveals him as blustering and weak.

278–9   *My enemies are sailing against me . . . escape ruin*: the nautical
        imagery is an important feature of this play and is appropriate
        to Corinth with its two harbours and its *diolkos*, a kind of rail-
        way line for winching ships across its narrow isthmus (see Map
        of the Greek World p. xlvi). It is a place for short-term residents,
        for birds of passage.

285   *You are a clever woman*: Medea answers this charge in her next
        speech. However, Creon proves to be only too justified in his fear
        of her subtle brain.

286   *You are distressed . . . loss of your groom*: the theme of the sexu-
        ally slighted woman.

294–9   *Any man who is sensible . . . useless and idiotic*: Aristophanes' com-
        edy *Clouds* (423 BC) is perhaps the most notorious expression of
        the Athenians' suspicion of the Sophists, whose ingenuity
        allowed them to make the worse case appear the better. For an
        admirably positive estimate of the Sophists, see E. R. Dodds, *The
        Greeks and the Ancient Concept of Progress* (Oxford, 1973), ch. 10.

324–39: *No, I beseech you . . . letting go of my hand*: frequently in Greek
        tragedy there are passages in which two characters address each
        other in single lines. This device, called *stichomythia*, is partic-
        ularly effective in scenes of confrontation. See Introduction,
        p. xxxii.

324   *knees*: see n. at 65.

329   *my children apart, I love my country far above all else*: Creon here lets
        Medea know that the way to hurt him is through his daughter.

338   *I shall go into exile*: Medea shifts her ground.

339   *and not simply letting go of my hand*: Medea is still maintaining
        the physical contact that denotes supplication.

362–3   *an overwhelming sea of woes*: nautical imagery. Cf. n. at 278–9.

371   *he has plummeted to such depths of stupidity*: Creon was aware that
        he was making a mistake in allowing Medea to stay (350). She
        has played extremely effectively on his paternal feelings.

373–4   *he has granted me this one day . . . husband*: the action of most
        Greek tragedies takes place in a single day, which is frequently
        a source of dramatic intensity. *husband*: in the event she leaves
        him alive, his life in ruins.

385   *kill them with poison*: poison is a device favoured by women in

Greek tragedy, but it may be that here we have a glimpse of Medea as the exponent of witchcraft.

397   *Hecate*: the witchcraft theme now comes into the open, for Hecate was the goddess who presided over magic and was linked to the world of the Shades. When Medea invokes her as her co-worker and lets us know that she keeps the goddess's image in a recess of her hearth, we may feel that she is beginning to lose contact with her humanity. Lines 394-8 have left their mark, through an English translation of Seneca's version, on Shakespeare's Lady Macbeth (*Macbeth*, I. v. 39 ff.).

405   *that traitor Sisyphus*: Sisphyus was the founder of Corinth and his name was a byword for treachery, for which his punishment was to roll a stone up a hill for eternity in the Underworld, only to have it run down before it could reach the top.

406   *grandchild of the Sun*: two of the Sun's children were Aeetes, Medea's father, and the witch Circe. The flying chariot in which Medea makes her getaway is a present to her from the Sun (1321-2). Medea's descent from him endows her with an elemental force.

408-9   *women . . . of all bad deeds*: the sympathetic assessment of women in Medea's first great speech (214-66) is here reversed.

410-45   the Chorus's confident belief that women will win honour while men will assume the reputation of faithlessness, like its picture of Medea as a pathetic victim, will not be confirmed by the play's action.

421-6   *the Muses of yesteryear's poets . . . lyre-song*: there is certainly misogynistic Greek poetry by male poets. Yet the chorus ignores the fact that a number of Greek poets were women, i.e. Sappho, Corinna, Praxilla, and Telesilla, and these naturally wrote from the female point of view.

446-64   *I have noticed . . . badly towards you*: Jason's speech is of an ineffable smugness. Presumably Euripides is aiming to enhance sympathy for Medea.

478-9   *you were sent . . . field of death*: Aeetes had said that he would give Jason the Golden Fleece if he yoked two fire-breathing bulls and ploughed a field and sowed it with dragon's teeth (which Jason was unaware would produce a crop of armed men). Medea saw him safely through these ordeals.

486   *I killed Pelias*: see n. at 9-10.

519   *on the body put no stamp*: the metaphor is from the stamp on a coin. The difficulty of assessing a man's true nature is a common theme in Euripides (e.g. at *Electra*, 367-90).

523-5   *escape the wearisome storm . . . edges of his sail*: more nautical imagery. See n. at 278-9.

527   *Aphrodite*: Helen in the *Trojan Women* used this argument
           (940–50). According to her, it was not she who caused the
           Trojan War but the force of love represented by Aphrodite.

536–8   *you live in the land of Greece ... whim of the mighty*: Euripides'
           Athenian audience would have had much sympathy with
           Jason's argument here. Yet its response would surely have been
           coloured by the fact that it finds expression on the lips of so
           unsympathetic a character.

543   *Orpheus*: the most magical of singers, Orpheus had been with
           Jason on the Argo.

555   *It was not ... that I hated sleeping with you*: the theme of the sex-
           ually slighted woman. to be developed devastatingly at the end
           of the speech (568–75). Jason's insensitivity is breathtaking.

563–7   *by producing brothers ... those that are to be born*: a Greek audi-
           ence would have found Jason's argument here unconvincing.
           The legitimate family would have sought ways of marginalizing
           the illegitimate one. Cf. *Hippolytus*, 305–10.

573–4   *The human race ... free from every evil*: cf. *Hippolytus*, 616–24.

613   *tokens of introduction*: these were knuckle-bones cut in half. Your
           host could see if his half fitted with the one given to you by the
           friend who had passed it on to you.

618   *A bad man's gifts can bring no good*: proverbial.

627–42   *When love comes ... women's marriages*: 'moderation in all things'
           is a common Greek tenet. The Chorus can see where Medea's
           intemperate love has led her. (See n. at 125.) Cypris is another
           name for Aphrodite. See n. at *Hipploytus* 2 (p. 180).

642   *a sharp judge*: and so able to distinguish the unions free from war
           and spare them from attack.

663   *s.d.*: Aegeus, king of Athens, passes through Corinth on his way
           back from Apollo's oracle at Delphi. He has probably come by
           boat from Itea, the port below Delphi. His arrival is very happily
           timed from Medea's point of view.

667–707   *stichomythia*: see Introduction, p. xxxii.

668   *the navel of the earth*: Zeus is said to have released two eagles
           from opposite ends of the earth. They met above Delphi, which
           was thus regarded as at the centre of the earth, just as the navel
           is at the centre of the body.

669   *I wanted to know how I could beget offspring*: is it Aegeus' child-
           lessness that gives Medea the idea for her terrible revenge (cf. n.
           at 329)?

679–81   *Not to unloose ... the hearth of my fathers*: Aegeus must abstain
           from sexual intercourse until he reaches home.

683   *Trozen*: see Map of the Greek World p. xlvi.

694　　　*a woman who supplants me*: the theme of the sexually slighted woman.

710　　　*this your beard and your knees*: see n. at 65.

730　　　*I want to be . . . and my hosts alike*: if she contrives to make her getaway from Corinth, Medea will be Aegeus' guest. At the moment, since Aegeus is in Corinth, Creon is his host.

743　　　*It is indeed safer for me . . .*: Aegeus is convinced by Medea's prudent argument.

746–7　　*Swear by the land of the Earth and . . . the Sun*: Medea chooses these two elemental gods for Aegeus to swear by. Cf. nn. at 57 and 406.

764　　　*light of the Sun*: see previous n.

769–70　*haven . . . stern-cable*: nautical imagery. See n. at 278–9. At this pivotal moment of the tragedy, the nautical imagery is suddenly halted. Medea has resolved upon her grisly plot, and now a new theme enters the play, that of hands (785, 857, 899, 940, 959, 1071, 1141, 1206, 1234, 1245, 1284, 1309, 1365, in addition to the references below). This will lend a ghastly intimacy to the rest of the tragedy. Earlier Medea has used her own, and her children's hands, exploitatively, to lay claim to the ties of friendship through supplication (324, 339, 709–10; cf. 898–9). Already she has amorally abused that key Greek concept. But now, possessed of an appalling certitude, she uses her hands to furnish the props for her own grim play. She hands over to her children the fatal gifts (956), which they proceed to hand over to Glauce (973). With her own hands she murders her children, whose hands she has earlier kissed (1070). And she will not allow Jason to touch their corpses with his hands (1412), though she will bury them with hers (1378). Formerly adrift, she is now triumphantly in control. The play's focus has narrowed from the wide world of Medea's uncertainties, which had centred on Corinth, to the horrific actions of her hands. (See n. at 1122–3 for the renewal of the theme of travel.)

773　　　*Don't expect to receive my words with pleasure*: Medea knows full well that the Chorus will be appalled at her plans.

792–3　　*I shall kill the children, my own ones*: a chilling statement, yet with a stab of poignancy.

809　　　*dangerous to my enemies and good to my friends*: D. L. Page quotes Lessing: 'Moral excellence in ancient Greece consisted no less in unremitting hatred of your foes than in unalterable love towards your friends.' See n. at 267.

813　　　*I forbid you to do this*: the voice of the Chorus, hitherto so supportive, comes across here with great moral authority (cf. 853–5).

824–50 *Descendants of Erechtheus . . . give you a home*: the Chorus sings in celebration of Athens, where all is wisdom, culture, and love. Athens had looked at the end of the Aegeus scene as if it would assure a happy ending for the play, but now it seems likely to be forced to shelter a polluted infanticide. Erechtheus was an Athenian hero; the nine Muses, the inspirational forces behind all the arts, lived on Mount Helicon in Boeotia but proved to be at the height of their powers in Athens; the Athenian river Cephisus is associated with Aphrodite, the goddess of fertility and flowers. Can this joyously civilized city receive an unholy child-murderer? The response of the first Athenian audience to this Ode in praise of their city sung by actors portraying Corinthian women would have been a complex one, for Athens and Corinth were the bitterest of enemies in 431 BC.

869 *Jason*: she could not bring herself to say his name in their first scene together. Now she can use it to suggest that there is still sympathy between them.

899–905 *Ah me! . . . fill with tears*: a passage of enormous pathos. Medea weeps for her children, who will not live a long life. Jason will not die today but they will.

910 *a husband who traffics in contraband love*: the theme of the sexually slighted woman.

916–24 *I think that you will yet live . . . what I have just said*: the dramatic irony is particularly intense here as Jason visualizes a fulfilled and successful life for the children and Medea knows that she will cut short the possibility of such a future (cf. 930–1, 1029–35).

943–4 *Certainly . . . I think I shall persuade her*: supremely confident in his skills as a charmer, he has no idea of where his male vanity is leading him.

956 *hands*: the theme of hands, with the terrible intimacy of human contact, now comes into the ascendant. See n. at 769–70.

1002–4 *Mistress . . . all peace for them*: the Tutor's blithe cheerfulness carries a poignant charge of irony.

1015–16 *your children will bring you home . . . I shall bring others to peace*: there is a subtext here which is hard to reproduce in translation. The Greek for 'bring you home' could mean 'bring you down to the Underworld'. Medea then hints that it is others, i.e. her children, whom she herself will bring to the Underworld.

1035 *an enviable lot for mankind*: in the ancient world parents felt the desire that their children would outlive them particularly strongly, since they would thus be assured of the proper burial rites which would admit them to the Underworld.

1053–5   *Those for whom . . . a matter for them*: in a grimly horrific touch
           Medea here adapts the formula that preceded a ritual, warning
           unsuitable persons to keep away. It is a blasphemous distortion
           of the real nature of this act of vengeance upon Jason for her to
           regard the murder of her children as a sacrifice.

1056–80   *Ah, Ah, do not . . . the greatest evils for mankind*: I do not agree
           with the editor of the Oxford Classical Text that these lines are
           inauthentic. They seem to me totally in accord with the emo-
           tional fluctuations which make this great speech so moving. A
           strong case for the defence, which even so acknowledges the
           problems, is B. Seidensticker, 'Euripides, *Medea* 1056–1080, an
           Interpolation?' in *Cabinet of the Muses: Essays on Honor of T. G.
           Rosenmeyer* (Scholars Press, Atlanta, Ga., 1990).

1062   *There's no alternative—they must die*: Medea feels that, now that
           the children have returned from giving their gifts, they will fall
           victims to retaliation from the Corinthians and so she may as
           well kill them herself (cf. 1236–41). But is she right in this?
           Their involvement in her plot was totally innocent, and, had
           Medea spared them, Jason could surely have protected them. See
           1303–5.

1073   *elsewhere*: i.e. the Underworld.

1080   *it is fury that leads to the greatest evils for mankind*: Medea's final
           words in this speech make it clear that she is fully aware that
           her rage against Jason has driven her on an evil course.

1083–4   *greater dilemmas than the female sex | ought to explore*: the femi-
           nist voice that spoke so loudly earlier in the play (see e.g.
           410–30) is now distinctly muted.

1090–111   *And I say that those of mortals . . . of his children*: the Chorus
           deals with the tragic consequences of having children. It has
           been reduced to extreme pessimism.

1122–3   *take flight . . . Use any means of transport you can find*: the theme
           of travel is renewed (see n. at 769–70). Medea is, of course,
           going to flee neither by land nor by sea but through the air, the
           element of the divine. As the tragedy opens out again from its
           intense concentration on Medea's hands, it defines her anew, no
           longer as a woman but as a demon. See nn. at 1260, 1278–80,
           1316 s.d., 1342–3.

1133   *But take your time*: she wishes to savour the grisly story, and the
           Messenger's speech is certainly replete with gory detail. The
           gloating Medea is a repellent figure.

1156   *And when she saw the adornments, she could not resist*: the vacu-
           ous and childish Glauce is well characterized.

1161   *a shining mirror*: made of highly polished metal.

1171–2   *perhaps thinking . . . had come upon her*: the old maidservant immediately assumed that Glauce's frantic rush for the throne to support herself and her near-collapse were caused by a sudden frenzy sent by a god—most naturally Pan, a rustic deity, but possibly any god.

1210   *let me die with you, my child*: a wish that is only too speedily fulfilled.

1245   *where life's pain begins*: the Greek uses the metaphor of the post which marked both the start and the finish of a running race. The child-murder is both an end (of the children's lives) and a beginning (of Medea's grief for them).

1251–2   *O Earth and radiant brightness | of the Sun*: the Earth and the Sun, the Zeus-born light (1258), are here invoked at the tragedy's climactic moment. Will these elemental forces intervene to stop the unholy slaughter? The answer is no. The play is emptied of any divine force working for good. See n. at 57.

1260   *Fury*: Medea is seen no longer as a woman but as a Fury, one of a number of hideous divinities who lived in the Underworld and punished offences against the family. Medea is indeed punishing Jason's offences against her family, but only by destroying it herself. She has been dehumanized and demonized. Cf. 1278–80 and 1342–3.

1270   *s.d.*: with the exception of the suicide of Ajax in Sophocles' play of that name, violent action always takes place off stage in Greek tragedy.

1278–80   *stone | or iron*: the dehumanized Medea.

1284   *Ino*: Ino brought up Dionysus, the son of Zeus by her sister Semele. Hera, Zeus' wife, drove her mad out of jealousy and she jumped into the sea. In Euripides' version, she killed her two children and it was this that drove her to suicide.

1304   *it is my children's life that I have come to save*: see n. at 1062.

1316   *s.d.*: Medea swings into view, her dragon-drawn chariot supported by the crane which was generally used in Greek theatres for the occasional aerial appearance of gods. The demonic Medea has usurped their element.

1321–2   *the chariot that the Sun, father of my father, has given me*: far from intervening to stop the infanticide (see n. at 1251–2), Medea's grandfather the Sun has provided her with her getaway vehicle—as well as with the adornments that have destroyed Glauce (954–5).

1327–8   *can you look upon the sun and earth*: see nn. at 57, 1251–2, 1321–2, 1387–8. The elemental powers do nothing to prevent the murders.

1334   *after killing your brother by your hearth*: the usual story of the ship-board mutilation of Apsyrtus is varied to emphasize the impiety of Medea, who is here represented as killing her brother at the holiest part of the family home.

1335   *the Argo, that fair-prowed ship*: Jason looks back to the great days of his triumphant voyage. It has led him to this.

1342–3 *no woman but a lioness, more savage than Etruscan Scylla*: the dehumanization of Medea. Scylla was a monster who lived on the Italian coast on the Straits of Messina on the East side of the Etruscan sea. Female in form, she had six dogs' heads around the lower part of her body.

1361–77 *And you too feel pain . . . lament them*: stichomythia. It is striking that before this passage there have been only four lines of *stichomythia* between this confrontational pair (605–8). Euripides now uses it to stress their total alienation from each other.

1368   *a small hurt for a woman?* the theme of the sexually slighted woman. Note Jason's response (1369).

1381   *this land of Sisyphus*: Corinth. Cf. n. at 405.

1383   *this impious murder*: Medea admits the impiety of her act but hopes to lay the pollution to rest.

1386–7 *die a humiliating death . . . the Argo*: Medea usurps the role of the god who is likely to appear to foretell the future at the end of a Euripides play, and she correctly prophesies Jason's ignominious end. Either he was visiting Hera's temple where he had dedicated the stern of the Argo or he was sleeping underneath the ship. A timber fell off and killed him.

1389   *the Fury*: the Fury that Jason hopes will be roused against Medea from the Underworld by her shedding of her children's blood.

1392   *the treacherous host*: Jason had formerly been her male protector in Corinth (see n. at 255–8) but had abandoned her.

1395   *Wait till you grow old*: see n. at 1035.

1399–1400 *I long . . . poor wretch that I am*: Jason discovers how deeply he had loved his children.

1412   *hands*: the theme of hands finds its conclusion.

1415–19 *Zeus on Olympus . . . what has happened here*: though the first line is different, this is in effect the 'stock' ending of five of Euripides' plays.

HIPPOLYTUS

1   *s.d.*: Trozen is part of the territory of Theseus, king of Athens. It is on the southern side of the Saronic Gulf (see Map of the Greek World, p. xlvi). The statues of Aphrodite and Artemis, the

goddesses of love and chastity respectively, are a constant reminder of the two forces which control the action. And each goddess appears in person, Aphrodite at the start and Artemis near the end. Aphrodite is to give us information vital to our understanding of the play. While all the characters who speak the prologues in Euripides' plays do this, Aphrodite as a goddess tells us things which a human prologuist can only project as reactions or anxieties. Cf. the Nurse in *Medea*, 1–48. It is possible that, like Artemis at the end of the play (see n. at 1281 *s.d.*), she may appear above the house, i.e. in the air, the element of the gods. She may be standing on the roof of the stage building or suspended from the *mechane*, a kind of crane.

2   *Cypris*: in *Hippolytus* Aphrodite is usually referred to by this name, which means 'the Cyprian one'. (The exceptions are at 531, 539, and 765.) She was born from the sea and carried by the Zephyrs first to Cythera and then to Paphos in Cyprus.

3   *the bounds of Atlas*: i.e. the Straits of Gibraltar.

10–11   *Hippolytus . . . Pittheus*: Hippolytus is Theseus' illegitimate son by the warrior Amazon queen Hippolyta, whom he took captive and brought back to Athens to live with him. She died, and later Theseus married the Cretan princess Phaedra. Pittheus had formerly been king of Trozen, now ruled by Theseus, and is Hippolytus' great-grandfather (the father of Theseus' mother). He has brought up the illegitimate boy in Trozen away from the public eye of Athens.

17   *he spends all his time in the green woods with the virgin goddess*: Artemis is the goddess of hunting as well as of chastity.

26   *Pandion's land*: i.e. Athens, of which Pandion, Theseus' grandfather, had been an early king.

26   *the noble wife of his father*: the theme of Phaedra's nobility is here launched. Her almost obsessive concern with her nobility and her good name is to be irretrievably subverted by the shameful vindictiveness with which she tries to preserve them in her death by laying her charge against Hippolytus. Cf. n. at 47.

30   *the rock of Pallas*: i.e. the Acropolis of Athens, sacred to Pallas Athena, from which the land of Trozen can be seen.

34   *Cecrops*: the first king of Attica, the land of which Athens was the main city.

35   *in flight from the pollution of the blood of the sons of Pallas*: his cousins, the sons of Pallas, rebelled against Theseus, the legitimate king of Athens. He killed them and, since they were his relations, incurred blood-guilt. According to Euripides here, he went into exile for a year and is at present consulting an oracle (792).

40   *without a word*: the vital theme of silence is here launched. Cf.
          nn. at 273, 312, 394, 520, 706, 713–14, 911, and 1430.
          Bernard Knox (*Word and Action* (Baltimore, 1979), 207) has
          observed that the 'choice between speech and silence is the situ-
          ation which places the four principal characters in significant
          relationships . . . The poet has made the alternations and com-
          binations of speech so complicated—Phaedra chooses first
          silence then speech, the nurse speech then silence, then speech,
          then silence, Hippolytus speech then silence, the chorus silence,
          and Theseus speech—that the resultant pattern seems to repre-
          sent the exhaustion of the possibilities of the human will.'

42   *I shall reveal to Theseus what is happening*: in fact it is Artemis, not
          Aphrodite, who tells Theseus the truth of the situation (1287–9,
          1298–1312).

45   *Poseidon*: god of the sea, he was, according to Trozenian legend,
          Theseus' father. See n. at 887.

47   *with her honour safe*: the theme of Phaedra's good name is linked
          with that of her nobility (cf. n. at 26). In fact, the false informa-
          tion she levels against Hippolytus at her death severely compro-
          mises her honour. See 1310–12 and nn. at 728–31 and 773–4.

57   *the light of this day is the last that he will ever see*: as usual in Greek
          tragedy, though not always, the action takes place within a
          single day. This compression can lead to great dramatic inten-
          sity.

73–81   *My mistress Artemis . . . for base men to do so*: a passage of sur-
          passing beauty. We first see the chaste huntsman Hippolytus in
          an attractive light. The Greek word for bee was the name given
          to the priestesses of Artemis, and the insect is in many contexts
          association with virginity.

87   *I pray that I may finish the race of my life as I began it*: after
          Aphrodite's pronouncement that this is to be his final day (57),
          these words are deeply ironical, doubly so in that this huntsman
          is to be destroyed in a hideous race in which he is hunted down
          by the bull from the sea (1213–46).

87   *s.d.*: the Servant pleads with Hippolytus to show reverence to
          Aphrodite. His failure reveals the priggish and limited side to
          Hippolytus' nature.

90–105   *Certainly . . . common sense you need*: stichomythia, see
          Introduction, p. xxxii.

100   *Be careful*: reasonable hitherto, Hippolytus here shows an irra-
          tional sensitivity as he realizes that the Servant is treading on
          dangerous ground.

102   *Since I am pure, I greet her from a distance*: Hippolytus' priggish-
          ness comes out. Cf. 106.

107   *My boy*: the old Servant speaks to Hippolytus as to a rash son.

113   *As for your Cypris, I bid her a hearty farewell*: Hippolytus is
        superbly but insanely dismissive of a great goddess.

117–20 *You should forgive . . . wiser than mortals*: the rational and
        humane words of the old Servant show up the uncompromising
        ruthlessness which Aphrodite has revealed in her opening
        speech.

121   *the Ocean*: the fresh water stream which encircled the flat, plat-
        ter-shaped earth.

138   *Demeter's grain*: i.e. bread. Demeter was the goddess of corn (or
        grain).

141–4   *Are you wildly wandering . . . mountain mother*: the Chorus won-
        ders which divinity might have possessed Phaedra. Is it Pan, the
        goat-legged god, who like Hippolytus operates in the country-
        side, where the raving Phaedra wishes to be? (See n. at 208–11.)
        Is it Hecate, an Underworld goddess? Is it the Great Mother
        Cybele who governed the whole of nature? She was the moun-
        tain-mother since she was originally worshipped on Mount
        Cybele in Phrygia. Her votaries were called Corybantes and their
        rituals were frenzied in the extreme. All three gods could possess
        humans and cause fantasies such as Phaedra's.

145–6   *for a sin which concerns Dictynna*: Dictynna is a Cretan goddess.
        Is the Cretan princess Phaedra paying due rites to her in Greece
        where she was worshipped as Artemis? Artemis had a temple by
        the Saronic Lagoon, the Mere, near Trozen (148–50—see map,
        p. 190). This lagoon was separated from the sea by the narrow
        sandbar along which Hippolytus races his horses (228–31,
        234–5, 1126, 1134).

151   *Erechtheus*: an earth-born Athenian hero.

152   *the son of noble fathers*: the theme of nobility.

166–8   *the heavenly goddess who eases labour, | Artemis, lady of arrows*:
        the chaste huntress Artemis is paradoxically the goddess of
        childbirth. The mention of arrows reminds us that, while
        Artemis can ease childbirth, she can bring death through it as
        well.

196   *of what lies below the ground*: i.e. of what may or may not hap-
        pen in the Underworld.

208–11 *If only . . . lush meadow!* Cf. Hippolytus' virgin meadow (76–7).
        Phaedra here longs to break out of the indoor confines of a Greek
        woman's life and join in Hippolytus' outdoor life in the woods,
        relaxing, hunting (215–22), and racing (228–31).

214   *words that ride on madness*: the Nurse emphasizes the way in
        which Phaedra's wish challenges the female norm.

265   *moderation*: the praise of moderation is very Greek. The words 'Nothing in excess' were inscribed on Apollo's temple at Delphi.

273   *she keeps her silence*: the theme of silence. Cf. n. at 40.

281   *He is in fact out of this country*: Theseus has gone to consult an oracle (793). Cf. n. at 35.

285   *But I shall not let my efforts to reach the truth slacken even now*: the Nurse loves and feels genuine concern for her mistress. But her belief that there is no problem that cannot be solved leads to disaster.

312   *say no more*: the theme of silence. Cf. n. at 40.

320   *Has Theseus done you some wrong?* Theseus had had affairs with Hippolyta and Phaedra's sister Ariadne, whom he abandoned. Cf. 151–4 and n. at 10–11.

325–6   *clasping my hand . . . and your knees too*: to clasp the hand and knees of someone from whom you wanted something was a potent gesture, difficult to ignore. The process is known as supplication.

329   *to win glory*: the theme of Phaedra's good name (cf. 331–2). See n. at 47.

335   *I will give it . . . in your hand*: Phaedra yields to the Nurse. The latter's act of supplication has put her under great pressure, but the theme of silence has been established, and we, who know what Phaedra has to confess, will be longing for her to keep it to herself.

337   *O my poor mother, how terrible the love you conceived!* Poseidon caused Phaedra's mother Pasiphae to fall in love with a bull and the Minotaur, half-man, half-bull, was the result of her monstrous union. The family's amorous history is certainly a disastrous one.

339   *my wretched sister*: Phaedra's sister Ariadne was abandoned by Theseus but then rescued by the god Dionysus, who married her. See n. at 320.

369   *What awaits you . . .*: the audience, of course, know the answer to this. Aphrodite has told us.

374   *Pelops*: he was the legendary eponymous king of the Peloponnese, the vast three-pronged promontory which is southern Greece.

385–6   *a sense of shame . . . a burden upon the house*: a sense of shame can inhibit antisocial behaviour, but it can also lead to diffidence and indecisiveness. For a discussion of this difficult passage, see Michael Halleran, *Hippolytus* (Warminster, 1995).

394   *to stay quiet*: the theme of silence.

395   *For there's no trusting the tongue*: a key idea in this play.

403-4   *For I would not wish . . . witnesses*: Phaedra is obsessed with her good name. Cf. n. at 420-1.

409   *from noble houses*: the theme of nobility.

420-1   *never may I be found guilty . . . I have borne*: the theme of the good name (cf. n. at 403-4, and 423: 'May their mother's reputation allow theirs to stand high').

433-81   *My mistress . . . find them*: the Nurse's dangerous speech is full of corrosive, sophistical logic. It is magnificent because it is so convincing. She has a fatal arrogance which makes her believe that she can solve any problem through any means, however morally depraved.

447-50   *Cypris roams in the air . . . created*: the Nurse's tribute to Aphrodite's universal greatness is supremely memorable.

453-5   *Zeus once desired . . . all for love*: Zeus fell in love with the Theban princess Semele, and Dawn with the beautiful Athenian Cephalus.

467-8   *You would not . . . house*: it is worth remarking that the sculptures for the pediments of the Parthenon, which had been completed by the time *Hippolytus* was produced, were perfectly finished. The craftsmanship of the areas which it was thought would never be seen is in no way inferior to that of what was visible. The Nurse's corrupting moral relativism is exposed by a building only a stone's throw from the theatre of Dionysus.

478   *There are charms and words which cast a spell*: the Nurse speaks ambiguously here and later (cf. 517 and n. at 509). The charms and spells could be intended to cure Phaedra of her love. They could, on the other hand, be intended to make Hippolytus fall in love with her.

482   *what the nurse says is more expedient*: often in Greek tragedy the Chorus gives a pointer for audience reaction. Here it is repelled by the Nurse's speech, and no doubt we should be too.

509   *In the house I have a love charm*: again Phaedra is allowed to believe that the Nurse's intention is to cure her. But we may suspect that she plans to further a love affair between Phaedra and Hippolytus. The ambiguity mentioned in the n. at 478 continues to the end of the scene.

520   *do not mention any of this to the son of Theseus*: in this recurrence of the silence theme Euripides surely probes Phaedra's subconscious. Something in her knows that the Nurse is going to tell Hippolytus (cf. 524).

521   *I shall set this matter right*: these words have a sinister ring to them.

535-6   *by the river Alpheus | and in the Pythian dwelling of Phoebus*: Zeus was worshipped at Olympia in the West Peloponnese, by which the River Alpheus flows (see Map of the Greek World, p. xlvi).

The Pythian dwelling of Phoebus Apollo is at Delphi, where Apollo killed the Python—hence Pythian.

545-54   *The girl from Oechalia . . . your marriage*: Eurytus, king of Oechalia, promised his daughter Iole in marriage to whoever could beat him in archery. Heracles, son of Alcmena, did beat him and, on being denied Iole, came back to Oechalia, sacked it, and carried her off. Euripides cogently conveys the violence of Aphrodite. A Naiad is a water-nymph, here perhaps running from a lustful satyr, and a bacchant is an ecstatic female follower of Dionysus or Bacchus, the god of liberation and wine.

557   *Dirce*: the wife of a king of Thebes, metamorphosed into a river at that city.

558-62   *it was to the fire-girt thunder . . . blood*: Zeus had a love affair with the Theban princess Semele (cf. n. at 453-5). In her jealousy, Hera, Zeus' wife, persuaded Semele to demand that he appear to her in his full glory. When he did so, his fiery thunderbolt incinerated her. To preserve their child Dionysus from Hera's anger Zeus sewed him in his thigh, from which he was born anew (and thus twice-born).

565   *Quiet, women*: during the Choral passage Phaedra has been on stage by the door, listening to the Nurse as she tells Hippolytus of her love inside the house. She remains on stage throughout the scene between the Nurse and Hippolytus, who, if he does take in her presence, ignores her contemptuously.

601   *O mother earth and open sunlight*: as Hippolytus bursts out of the house, he calls upon the elemental earth and sun. He escapes the murky words of indoors which urge him to sleep with his stepmother.

605   *by this strong right arm*: supplication. Cf. knees two lines later, and see n. at 325-6.

611   *do not dishonour your oath*: Hippolytus must have sworn at the outset of their interview not to divulge anything the Nurse said.

612   *It was my tongue that swore. My mind took no oath*: a notoriously sophistical line, mocked by Aristophanes at *Frogs* 102, 1471. It must be remembered that Hippolytus does keep his oath and dies because of this. See 656-8.

618-24   *If you wanted . . . free from women*: there is surely an element of hysteria in Hippolytus' exposition of his system for producing children without the need for women. He loses contact with rational human discourse. Cf. *Medea* 573-4, for a saner though still repellent statement of the same idea. The note of hysteria may be felt throughout Hippolytus' speech.

651-2   *the partner of my father's inviolable bed*: Hippolytus is disgusted by the idea of sexual intercourse with a woman. But clearly the fact

that his father's wife is the proposed partner adds to his horror.
We are close to the taboo of incest.

653–4   *I shall wash my ears clean . . . running streams*: purifying water
(cf. 78) to add to the elemental earth and sun of 601.

672–3   *O earth and light! Wherever can I shun my fortune?* Like Hippolytus
at 601 (see n.), Phaedra calls upon the earth and sun. In her
case, it seems, they can afford her no refuge from her misfortune.

676   *victim of unjust deeds*: i.e. the Nurse's in telling Hippolytus of her
love, and perhaps Hippolytus' grossly unjust assessment of her.

678   *that hardest of all crossings*: Phaedra's thoughts are on death.

683   *Zeus my ancestor*: Zeus was the father of Phaedra's father Minos.
His weapon was the fiery thunderbolt. Cf. n. at 558–62.

689–92 *this man . . . shaming words*: Hippolytus has misjudged Phaedra,
but she misjudges him as spectacularly. Hippolytus keeps his
oath of silence. But she did overhear him speak the infamous line
612 (see n.).

706   *Stop—no more words*: a magnificent statement of the silence
theme. Now at long last Phaedra stops the Nurse's tongue.

709   *I shall set my own affairs to rights*: the self-possession of Phaedra's
words here looks back to the Nurse's previous manipulation of
her ('I shall set this matter right', 521).

713–14 *I swear by blessed Artemis . . . to the light of day*: at Phaedra's
request the Chorus, like Hippolytus, swears an oath of silence
which is to have disastrous consequences. Thus it condemns
itself to the role of the audience, which is forced to watch
Theseus' unjust treatment of his son in agonized passivity.

715   *But there is one further thing that I shall tell you*: the Greek translated here is the reading of W. S. Barrett (Oxford, 1964).

728–31 *But through my death . . . in virtue*: the magnificent resolution of
Phaedra as she goes off to kill herself is fundamentally flawed by
the vindictive motive that she reveals here. Aphrodite's statement that Phaedra will die 'with her honour safe' (47) is certainly problematic.

736   *the shore of Adria*: near Venice. The Chorus longs to escape.

737–41 *and the waters of Eridanus . . . Phaethon*: the Eridanus was a fabled
river in the west and a source of amber. The dead Phaethon fell
into it after his disastrous attempt to drive the chariot of his
father the Sun. His sisters mourned him on the banks of the
Eridanus. They were transformed into poplar trees and their
tears turned to amber.

742–51 *And I wish . . . of the gods*: The Hesperides (= the 'girls from the
West') are sweet-voiced nymphs who guarded golden apples in
their garden in north-west Africa. The lord of the sea's dark
waters is the sea-god Poseidon, who shut off the Mediterranean

at the Pillars of Atlas (the Straits of Gibraltar). Atlas was a giant transformed to a mountain which supported the sky. Zeus may have married Hera in the beautiful garden of the Hesperides.

760   *the shore of Mounichos*: a harbour at Athens.

773–4   *She will choose honourable repute*: but her allegations against Hippolytus make that repute short-lived. Cf. nn. at 47 and 720–31.

789   *s.d.*: Theseus arrives back from Apollo's oracle wearing garlands betokening happiness and optimism. Presumably Apollo has given him a cheering answer. We do not know why he visited the oracle; this was simply the means by which the dramatist got him out of the way for the first half of the tragedy, as was necessary.

798   *A young death*: is the youthful Phaedra about the same age as Hippolytus? But perhaps the Chorus is simply making a rhetorical contrast with old Pittheus (794).

804–5   *This is all we know . . . to your house*: the Chorus lie. They keep to the oath they have sworn at 713–14.

810   *s.d.*: when the doors were opened, a wheeled platform (*ekkyklema*) was rolled out from them. It displayed a *tableau* of what had happened inside the house, in this case the corpse of Phaedra.

816   *Who is it . . . life?* the Chorus maintains its pretence of ignorance.

850–1   *the light of the sun | and the starry radiance of the night*: elemental images.

855   *the thought of the woe that is to come*: the Chorus remembers the menace of Phaedra's final words (728–31).

856   *tablet*: two thin rectangular pieces of wood, hinged to each other, with a wax surface set on them—upon which a message has been scratched with a stylus (pen)—are folded against each other and tied together by threads. In this instance the threads are sealed with the imprint of Phaedra's signet ring (864) and tied to her hand (856–7).

885–6   *Hippolytus has dared . . . holy eye of Zeus*: Theseus unsurprisingly accepts the accusations of his dead wife. But the audience, who know the truth, will quail at the speed, violence, and highly public nature of his announcement. The holy eye of Zeus, the validator of justice on earth, will leave no crime unobserved.

887   *O father Poseidon*: at Athens Theseus was the son of Aegeus, at Trozen of Poseidon (45). In this play, he is only Poseidon's son in relation to the prayers. Elsewhere he is portrayed as the son of Aegeus.

892   *A time will come when you will see that you are wrong*: the Chorus can only plead. Its oath prevents it from supporting its plea with evidence (713–14).

911   *disaster is no time for silence*: in view of the appalling damage
          wrought by words, this recapitulation of the theme of silence is
          particularly poignant.

925–6   *Some clear test of their friends*: Euripides' characters constantly
          demand some external sign of inner virtue. The gap between
          appearance and reality is of considerable importance in this play.

928–31   *all humans should have two voices . . . deceived*: in this arresting
          passage Theseus encapsulates the tragic failure of words to con-
          vey the truth in this play.

952–4   *Well, now you can vaunt yourself . . . screeds*: his conviction that
          Hippolytus is a religious hypocrite leads Theseus to make crazy
          allegations against him. To think of the man whose hunting has
          emptied the land of wild animals (18) as posing as a follower of
          the doctrines laid down in the Orphic religion and thus espous-
          ing its tenet of vegetarianism is as absurd as to view the singu-
          larly priggish Hippolytus as a participant in ecstatic rituals.
          'Vacuous piffle' is Theseus' estimate of the poems of Orpheus and
          Musaeus which were the basis of the Orphic doctrine.

966–7   *will you claim that men can control their sexual urges while women
          cannot?* the male soothsayer Teiresias, who had been trans-
          formed into a woman for some years, claimed that women
          enjoyed love-making nine times as much as men. The goddess
          Hera blinded him for his plain-speaking.

976–80   *For if I suffer . . . harsh enemy to evil men*: on his youthful jour-
          ney from Trozen to Athens, Theseus destroyed a number of ter-
          rors which infested the route. Sinis, who lived on the Isthmus of
          Corinth, would bend down a pine and send his guests hurtling
          through the air to their death as the tree sprang up. Sciron
          would kick his guests over his cliff into the sea near Megara.
          Theseus is saying that the fame he won by his labours will be
          undermined if Hippolytus escapes unpunished. His reference to
          his labours shows Theseus not only as a force for civilization but
          also as a man well versed in violence.

993–4   *You see this light and earth*: Hippolytus seems to associate these
          elemental powers with his purity (601).

1009–10   *Did this woman surpass all others in physical beauty?* quite possibly
          Theseus considered that she did. Hippolytus' *bêtise* here is a nice
          touch, rather supporting his plea of innocence in sexual matters
          (1004–5).

1014–15   *This is certainly not true . . . are mad*: there are textual problems
          here and certainly the sentiment the translation assigns to
          Hippolytus is a strangely tactless one to put to a king. But then
          we have seen above that tact is not Hippolytus' strong point
          (1009–10).

1030–1   *when I am dead may neither the sea nor the land receive my body*:
the further element of the sea is now added. Cf. n. at 653–4. (For
'land', see also 1025.) Hippolytus' oath has enormous authority,
but it makes no impression on Theseus.

1033   *it is not right for me to speak further*: because of his oath (611).

1034–5   *She could not be virtuous . . . did not use it well*: by these riddling
words, as sophistical as the infamous 612 (see n.), Hippolytus
means that by her suicide the lustful Phaedra has preserved her
virtue—in fact it will prove that she does not succeed in doing
so—while his own virtuous reaction to what he thinks of as her
overtures was rash in that it drove Phaedra to kill herself.

1051–2   *Will you not let time give its evidence about me*: the action, con-
fined to a day (57), hurtles on.

1053   *the Black Sea and the places where Atlas dwells*: i.e. the limits of the
known world. For the Pillars of Atlas, see n. at 742–51.

1057–8   *As for the birds . . . I snap my fingers at them*: Theseus is rash, possibly blasphemous here. The flight of birds was one of the ways
by which the gods communicated with men.

1060–3   *O gods . . . all for nothing*: Hippolytus wonders out loud whether
to break his oath of silence. In a way, he could be said to be violating it by speaking these words, and one of his motives for
keeping his oath—that Theseus would not believe the truth if he
heard it—damages his integrity.

1078–9   *Alas . . . suffering*: Hippolytus' wish to stand outside himself for
the purpose of self-contemplation is disconcerting. There is something narcissistic about his sorrow.

1095   *Erechtheus*: an earth-born Athenian hero.

1102–50 *The care of the gods . . . away from this house*: the translation follows J. Diggle's Oxford Classical Text in dividing this ode between
a male and a female chorus, the huntsmen who serve Hippolytus
and the women of Trozen. If this is correct, such a divided chorus is unique in Greek tragedy.

1123   *Aphaia*: a goddess worshipped on Aegina, an island midway
between Athens and Trozen and, at the time of the play's writing, in the possession of the Athenians.

1130   *Dictynna*: the Cretan name for Artemis. See n. at 145–6.

1131   *the Mere*: see n. at 145–6.

1135–6   *And the music . . . in your father's house*: clearly the generous din-
ners in the palace (109–10) were accompanied by music in the
true Homeric style. Cf. Euripides, *Hecuba* 916 ff.

1138   *Leto's daughter*: Artemis.

1145   *I rage against the gods*: the Chorus voices its appalled sense of the
gods' injustice with a powerful simplicity.

1160   *I hope . . . the two neighbouring cities*: i.e. of Trozen and Athens.

We have here a glimpse of Theseus as the good king whose first instinct when bad news comes is to ask if it affects the citizens of his country.

1169–70 *Poseidon—truly then you are a father to me*: see n. at 887.

1189 *footstalls*: on the chariot floor to take the driver's feet.

1197 *the road which goes straight towards Argos and Epidaurus*: see map below. The headland is Cape Nísiza.

1206 *the rock of Asclepius*: presumably at or near Epidaurus, a cult centre of Asclepius, the god of medicine.

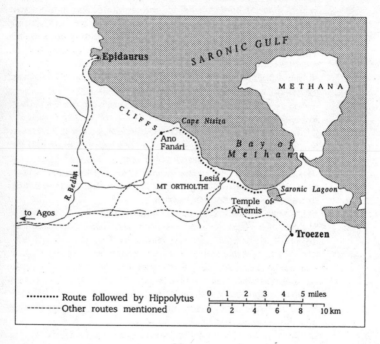

Map 2

1214 *the wave sent forth a bull*: from the elemental sea there bursts forth this monstrous creature. The bull is quintessentially Poseidon's animal manifestation and it is appropriate that the god should fulfil his pledge to Theseus in this way. Summing up recent approaches to characterization in Euripides, C. Collard

(*Euripides* (Oxford, 1981), 11) has suggested that this poet had 'a unique, precocious ability to project personality and its workings in ways which anticipate modern psychoanalysis'. The bull from the sea seems particularly Freudian in its significance, and its symbolic evocation of rampant male fertility suggests that Hippolytus is being destroyed by the very forces which he has so determinedly repressed. In this sense it can surely be viewed as something inside Hippolytus as well as an external force, what T. S. Eliot termed an objective correlative.

1219–22   *And our master . . . back on them*: Hippolytus, the expert horseman, does not panic.

1253–4   *if . . . someone filled . . . full of writing*: Mount Ida, a mountain range near Troy, was famous for its pine forests, and writing tablets could be made of split pine. The Messenger ends his speech not with the customary moralizing but with superbly dismissive contempt.

1260   *I feel neither pleasure nor distress*: the crudeness of Theseus' first reaction to the news of his son's imminent death (1164–5) here gives way to a measured dignity. Or is it self-protection against subsequent emotion?

1267   *I can convict him with my words and this god-sent disaster*: Theseus believes that Poseidon's prompt action confirms Hippolytus' guilt, but of course the sea-god was simply fulfilling his promise.

1269–70   *the bright-winged one . . . his arrows so swift*: the wings of Eros, the personification of love, symbolize the flightiness of love, his arrows its wound. Cf. n. at 525–42.

1281   *s.d.*: the goddess Artemis appears above the house, i.e. in the air, the element of the gods. She is either on the roof or suspended from the *mechane* (a kind of crane).

1290   *Tartarus*: a region far deeper even than the Underworld.

1328–30   *This is the way of the gods . . . we always stand off*: 'the way of the gods' thus leaves mortals utterly exposed to such divine vindictiveness as that of Aphrodite. Cf. n. at 1420–2.

1339–40   *The gods do not rejoice when pious men die*: but apparently they do nothing to save them.

1345   *Twofold is the sorrow*: the Chorus presumably refers to the tragedies of Phaedra and Hippolytus. But now Theseus too has become a tragic figure.

1366   *Hades*: i.e. the Underworld, where Hades was king.

1379–83   *Some blood-stained evil . . . has come against me*: like Phaedra (343) and Theseus (820, 831–2) before him, Hippolytus attributes his catastrophe to some inherited evil in the family. But he and his father are mistaken in doing so.

1395–6   *Do you see me, mistress . . . I see you*: It appears that Artemis is invisible to Hippolytus (and presumably to Theseus), while she can see them.

1396   *it is not proper for my eyes to shed a tear*: all gods avoid the pollution of mortality, but the point is also made that there are limitations to a god's sympathy.

1403–4 *One goddess . . . his wife*: Hippolytus realizes that his silent father has been destroyed by what has happened, and Artemis agrees that it is a threefold tragedy (cf. n. at 1345).

1407   *O you my father*: Hippolytus' compassion for his father is deeply moving. Euripides denied them *stichomythia* in their terrible scene of confrontation, reserving it for here (and 1446–56), where it emphasizes the intimacy and love which are now between them.

1415   *Alas, the gods! If only the race of mortal men could prove a curse to them!* the tremendous defiance of this line, spoken in a goddess's presence, looks back to the Chorus's rage against the gods (1146).

1420–2 *No, with this hand . . . no escape*: she is to kill Aphrodite's beloved Adonis. Artemis is as vindictive as her fellow-goddess. Cf. n. at 1328–30.

1425–6 *Unwed girls . . . before their marriage*: there was a cult of Hippolytus in the pre-marriage rites for girls in Trozen in Euripides' day. They would sing sorrowfully of Hippolytus and of Phaedra's love for him.

1430   *Phaedra's love for you will not slip into silence*: a final twist to the theme of silence. Phaedra's love is guaranteed not silence but eternal fame.

1437–8 *It is not proper . . . die*: the goddess distances herself from Hippolytus as his death is imminent. (Cf. n. at 1396.) Again the poet brings out the limitations of her love (cf. 1396).

1459   *Aphaia*: see n. at 1123. *Pallas*: Pallas Athena was the patron goddess of Athens.

1462   *for all the citizens to share*: the disasters which have befallen the royal family are a matter for civic concern.

ELECTRA

1   *s.d.*: Note the rustic setting. The plays on this subject by Aeschylus and Sophocles are located in front of Clytemnestra's palace. It is not a god or a hero who now appears before us but a humble farmer.

2–7   *King Agamemnon once set out for war . . . barbarian spoils*: the Trojan prince Paris had seized Helen, the beautiful wife of the Greek Menelaus, king of Sparta, and run off with her to Troy.

(Helen is viewed as morally culpable (212, 1037).) Menelaus' elder brother Agamemnon, king of the most powerful Greek state of Argos, then led a huge expedition against the Trojans to win her back. After a ten years' war, the Greeks sacked Troy and returned home with Helen.

4–5   *Ilion . . . Dardanus*: Ilion is another name for Troy, derived from Ilos, the founder of the city. Dardanus was his son.

9   *through the tricks of his wife Clytemnestra*: trickery is to prove an important theme in the play: both Aegisthus and Clytemnestra die through it.

10–11   *Tantalus . . . his own*: Tantalus was the founder of the ill-fated dynasty which now rules in Argos. His two grandsons were Atreus, father of Agamemnon, and Thyestes, father of Aegisthus. The 'daughter of Tyndareus' is Clytemnestra, who married first Agamemnon and then his cousin Aegisthus.

18   *to the land of the Phocians . . . to bring up*: Strophius, ruler of Phocis (see Map of the Greek World, p. xlvi) and father of Pylades (see n. at 82), was Agamemnon's brother-in-law.

30   *She had a pretext for her husband's death*: Clytemnestra explains what this pretext is in 1018–34: Agamemnon had killed their daughter Iphigenia, luring her to her death under false pretences, to enable the Greek fleet to sail to Troy. But Electra believes that it was Clytemnestra's adulterous liaison with Aegisthus that motivated her (164–6).

35   *Mycenaean*: Mycenae and Argos are treated as geographically indistinguishable.

36–8   *no fault can be found . . . nobility*: these lines are highly characteristic of this play. We are constantly invited to assess how we can measure the true worth of men (cf. 52–3, and see especially 368–90).

43   *Aphrodite*: the goddess of love is invoked to be the witness of the Farmer's abstinence.

47   *I sigh for my so-called brother-in-law*: is there irony here as the Farmer expresses sympathy with Orestes over the apparent degradation of his family? After all, given the Farmer's natural nobility (380–2), Orestes should be delighted to have him as a relation.

57–60   *It is not necessity . . . treats me*: Electra makes it clear that some of her misery is self-inflicted. Cf. 72–8. A princess, she insists on performing menial tasks.

74–5   *It is my task to see to everything inside the house*: these words are picked up in 355–9, 404–5, 413–14, and 422–3. They help to establish an atmosphere of homely simplicity as Electra performs the duties of the humblest peasant woman or even a slave.

82   *Pylades*: Orestes' close friend. He is the son of the king of Phocis,

where Orestes was brought up in exile (cf. n. at 18). He remains silent throughout the play, perhaps with a mocking glance at *Libation Bearers*, where Aeschylus keeps his Pylades totally mute save for three momentous lines in which he tells Orestes not to disobey Apollo's instructions to kill his mother.

87–9   *Without anyone knowing . . . murderers*: Orestes is giving this information not to Pylades—who already knows it—but to the audience. Understandably Pylades does not respond, and the fact that he keeps quiet here may make his later silences easier for us to accept. Apollo's oracle at Delphi has urged Orestes to kill Aegisthus and Clytemnestra. Orestes has returned to his country with a cautious timidity and secrecy. This is a motif common to the treatments of the story by all three dramatists, but, by causing Orestes to skulk so far from the city (94–7), Euripides gives it the greatest emphasis. The point should be made, however, that he has come to the area where his father's tomb can be found, a honourable motivation.

90–1   *offered him a lock of my hair and slaughtered a sheep*: the gift of a lock of hair and the sacrifice of a sheep were customary tributes at the tomb of a hero. Since the head and the hair signified strength and life, the cutting of the latter—which began the sacrifice—symbolized submissive grief. And the cut human hair replicated safely the shorn hair offered from the animal about to be killed. The blood of the sacrificial victim was thought to seep through to the dead hero.

102   *dawn now lifts her bright white eye*: Greek plays were performed in the open air in daylight. The dramatist tells us that it is night and then dawn through his words (cf. 54, 78, and 90).

108   *her close-cropped head*: this suggests both mourning and the status of a slave.

111   *s.d.*: Orestes and Pylades—and their attendants (360, 394)—hide behind the altar of Apollo near the house.

126   *the pleasure that comes with many tears*: to what extent does Electra enjoy her misery?

130–4   *what city . . . halls*: Orestes is, of course, present, though hidden. This vein of irony is to be richly mined.

137   *Zeus*: the king of the gods, who should promote vengeance for Agamemnon because he is the god of kings.

144   *Hades*: the god who rules the Underworld, the home of the dead.

146–7   *as I claw my own throat . . . my close-cropped head*: scratching one's cheeks and beating one's head with one's hands were clichés of poetic grief. Because they led to self-mutilation, they were aspects of mourning discouraged at Athens by Solon (Plutarch, *Solon* 21).

151-6   *as a tuneful swan . . . wretched man*: the tradition that swans sing in mourning (*Hercules Furens* 110 (Moschus), 3. 14-18), at times lamenting their own imminent death (Aeschylus, *Agamemnon* 1444-5; Plato, *Phaedo* 84e3 ff.), adds pathos here. And, just as the swan lies trapped in 'the tricky snares of the net', so Agamemnon was caught up in the robe thrown over him in his bath by Clytemnestra to put him at her mercy before she killed him with the axe.

157-8   *your flesh washed . . . repose*: women washed a corpse before laying it out. This gives a sinister overtone to the bath Clytemnestra gave Agamemnon on his return from Troy—the prelude to his death.

164-5   *she made you the victim . . . two-edged sword*: Aegisthus may have mutilated the corpse with his sword after Clytemnestra had killed him with the axe.

166   *s.d.*: The Chorus consists of young country women sympathetic to Electra.

168   *not wine but milk*: milk from his own goats was the upland herdsman's drink.

169   *he brings news . . . to Hera's temple*: the festival is probably the Heraia, the main annual festival of Hera, goddess of marriage, held at the Heraion between Argos and Mycenae. After a procession had escorted Hera's priestess there from Argos as she rode in a chariot drawn by cows (animals associated with her cult), the girls of marriageable age presented a robe to her. The virgin wife Electra will hear of this festival with disturbed emotions.

190-2   *Come, let me lend you . . . robes*: Electra has no need to be looking so unglamorous (cf. 184-5). Presumably Euripides has given the country women gold ornaments which in real life they would surely not have possessed in order to underscore this point. She wishes to show Aegisthus' brutal impiety to the gods (59), perhaps in a bid to force their hand to action. She is also clinging defensively to her misery.

220-89   *Stop, you poor woman . . . out of the house*: stichomythia; see Introduction, p. xxxii.

221   *O Phoebus Apollo*: the altar near the house is Apollo's. The god was thought to protect house entrances. It may be that his statue stands by the altar.

256   *some vow of chastity*: sexual abstinence could promote purity and reverence. Cf. *Hippolytus* 78-81.

259   *He considers that the man who gave me in marriage had no right to do so*: in Euripides' Athens the head of the family had complete authority over an unmarried woman who was a member of that

family. Who is the head of Electra's family? Many would have said that it was her mother's husband Aegisthus. But the Farmer clearly believes that it is her brother Orestes.

261–2   *But he also has integrity . . . speaking of*: both Electra and Orestes speak of the basic goodness of the Farmer.

265   *Women love men*: Electra views her mother as regarding sex as her priority.

279   *Yes, with the same axe*: Electra's violent certainty contrasts with the diffident, explorative approach of Orestes.

282–3   *If only Orestes were nearby . . . I wouldn't recognize him*: here the irony reaches its climax.

289   *he was cast out of the house*: in fact both Orestes (90–3) and Electra (323–31) know well that Agamemnon was given a tomb.

307   *I myself labour at my own clothes with the shuttle*: this was customarily work for slaves, except in the case of ceremonial robes.

309–10   *I myself carry water from the river. I have no place at festivals*: as we have seen (66, 175–80), these two complaints at least are self-inflicted.

312   *Castor*: Castor and Polydeuces, the Dioscouri (see 1238 ff.), were the brothers of Helen and Clytemnestra and thus Electra's uncles. They had become gods and a constellation in the sky. The idea that Castor wooed Electra seems to have been Euripides'. In the Athens of his day an uncle was permitted to marry a niece.

314   *of Phrygia*: Trojan, here with contemptuous overtones.

317–18:   *their robes from Ida's land fastened with golden brooches*: Ida = Troy. (The Ida mountain range is near Troy.) In marked contrast with Electra, the slave girls are beautifully adorned.

324–5   *has never yet received libations or a shoot of myrtle*: libations are offerings of honey, milk, wine, etc., which are poured upon the ground. The Old Man is to offer myrtle, a customary ornament for tombs, at that of Agamenon (512).

344   *It is a shameful thing . . . for a woman to stand around with young men*: the conventional attitude in Athens.

355   *You, I suppose, have told them the others*: perhaps an element of humour here? The Farmer knows Electra well.

360   *Attendants*: so Orestes and Pylades have some servants with them (cf. 394)—or are these the Farmer's slaves?

373–9   *So how can a man . . . alone*: the editor of the Oxford Classical Text, considers this passage and a later one in this speech (386–90: *It is men like this . . . nature and courage*) inauthentic, but I see no problem in regarding it all as Euripidean. Orestes concludes that there is no touchstone to identify a good man. Appearances are deceptive and a man is what he is.

387   *empty-headed hunks*: this reference to brainless sportsmen launches the metaphors concerning athletics in the play. Cf. 614, 763, 824–5, 854, 862–3, 870–4, 883, and 956. Like the concepts of ennobling action and aristocratic values, that of sporting prowess is for ever being questioned and usually found wanting.

399–400   *the oracles of Apollo do not fail*: but see 1245–6—Euripides is, as ever, supremely questioning of the role of the gods. However, the point that Orestes is questionably making is that, while Apollo speaks the truth, humans may misinterpret—intentionally or otherwise—such communications from the gods as the flight of birds, entrails, etc. Perhaps even Apollo's own priests might distort his utterance.

410   *Tanaus*: this river is about 35 km away from the Peasant's home, if the latter is on the river Inachus.

431   *s.d.*: the Farmer, the one unequivocally virtuous character in the play, leaves the stage never to reappear, before a third of the action has passed.

432–86   *Famous ships . . . by the sword*: looking back to the terrible war that was the prelude to the story of Electra, the Chorus sings of the voyage to Troy and of the dreadful horror of the bloodshed there. The ecstatic picture of the first two stanzas is eclipsed by the nastiness of the fighting so powerfully conveyed in the rest of the ode. The play as a whole may reflect such a transformation of heroic vision into brutal bloodbath.

434   *Nereids*: sea goddesses, the fifty or so daughters of Nereus, the old man of the sea. Thetis, the mother of Achilles (438, 449), was one of them.

435   *the dolphin which loves the pipe*: the dolphin was legendary for its attraction to music and to ships (see e.g. the story of Arion (Herodotus, 1. 24)).

439   *light-footed Achilles*: Homer's swift-footed (athletic) Achilles, though technically subordinate to his commander-in-chief Agamemnon, was the greatest of the Greek warriors.

442–4   *The Nereids . . . Hephaestus' anvil*: going against the mainstream versions of the Trojan story, Euripides makes Achilles receive his armour from Hephaestus, the god of fire, before the start of the Trojan War, rather than in its tenth year after the original set had been stripped by the Trojans from the corpse of his friend Patroclus. The Nereids take the armour from Euboea (an island in north Greece which was possibly a legendary site for

Hephaestus' forge and/or the home of the Nereids) to Achilles up in the nearby mountains (see next n.).

445–9   *up along Pelion . . . the sea-nymph Thetis*: another variation upon the traditional story. Here Achilles leaves for Troy from the cave in the mountains of north-east Greece (Mount Pelion and Mount Ossa), where the civilized centaur Cheiron (*the horseman father*, 448) has been educating him—as opposed to his father's home at Phthia or alternatively Scyros, where his mother has hidden him disguised as a girl to prevent him from going to Troy.

453   *Nauplia*: the harbour at Argos.

454   *your famous shield*: cf. Homer, *Iliad* 18. 478–608.

459   *Perseus*: under the guidance of Athena and Hermes (who lent him his winged sandals), he flew to the dwelling of the Gorgon Medusa and decapitated her. Her gaze turned all who looked upon it to stone.

462   *the rustic son of Maia*: Hermes was god of livestock, among other things.

464–77   *And on the middle . . . around their backs*: for Euripides' grisly choice of images on the shield, see J. Morwood, 'The Pattern of the Euripides *Electra*', *American Journal of Philology*, 102 (1981), 362–70.

468–9   *which turned away the eyes of Hector*: the Trojan prince and general Hector, who had killed Achilles' friend Patroclus, fled before the dazzling armour of Achilles (Homer, *Iliad* 22. 131–7).

472   *Sphinxes*: deadly monsters, part women, part lion, with a bird's wings.

474–5   *the fire-breathing Chimaera . . . colt of Peirene*: Bellerophon on his winged horse Pegasus killed Chimaera, a fire-breathing lioness with a goat's torso, a goat's head on the middle of its back, and a snake as its tail. Peirene was a spring at Corinth created by a blow from Pegasus' hoof. It was also said that he was tamed here by Bellerophon with Athena's assistance. Pegasus had sprung from the freshly slain Gorgon (cf. 459).

480   *daughter of Tyndareus*: Clytemnestra, but perhaps with a glance at Helen.

487   *Where, where*: the Old Man's repetition here is no doubt due to breathlessness. He is well advanced in years (490–2).

497   *Dionysus*: the god of wine.

499   *a weaker drink*: the Greeks watered down their wine.

500   *someone*: an attendant of the Farmer's.

507   *reared to prove no benefit to yourself*: had he lived, Agamemnon would have looked after his old tutor.

513–15   *on the altar itself . . . golden hair*: see n. on 91–2.

520 ff.   *Put this lock . . .*: in Aeschylus' *Choephori*, 168–80, the tokens by which Electra recognizes Orestes are a lock of hair, footprints, and a woven cloth. Euripides' heroine scornfully rejects all of these, only to accept the clichéd evidence of a childhood scar, a reach-me-down version of the scar by which his old nurse recognizes Odysseus in the *Odyssey* (see n. on 573–4). Euripides eagerly drains the myth of any potential nobility.

528   *one has been grown by a noble man in the wrestling schools*: coarse, therefore, because uncombed, ground in the dust, and possibly bleached by the sun owing to the athlete's open-air exercise (as opposed to a woman's largely indoor existence).

538   *and visited the tomb*: the text is incomplete and I have filled it out with these words.

550–1   *Well, they are noble . . . base*: the theme of the possible gap between appearance and reality. Cf. n. at 373–9. There is a certain irony in the fact that it is the old man who revives it: he is about to propose an ignoble scheme.

558–9   *the bright stamp on a silver coin*: forged coins are likely to look new.

560–76   *You are Orestes' friend . . . your dearest friend in the world*: stichomythia, broken by a continuous two-line speech for the imparting of the crucial information. There is an increase in intensity after the freer dialogue of 547–59.

573–4   *A scar . . . he fell*: cf. Homer, *Odyssey* 21. 217–19, where Odysseus is recognized through a scar. But, while Odysseus got his scar in a violent encounter on a boar hunt, Orestes was hurt chasing a harmless animal, presumably a pet, at home with his sister.

587   *beacon*: Electra replies to the Chorus's image here at 694.

612–84   *Then what do . . . time to go*: stichomythia; see Introduction, p. xxxii.

614   *crown*: the metaphor refers to the athlete's crown of victory. Cf. 854.

625   *a festival for the Nymphs*: this is described in 800 ff. The Nymphs, countryside gods of trees, mountains, springs, and rivers, brought health and prosperity.

637   *invite you to share in the feast*: the Old Man correctly assumes that Aegisthus will observe the conventions of hospitality.

638   *cruel fellow-diner*: Orestes is indifferent to the obligations involved in accepting hospitality.

647   *I shall arrange the killing of my mother*: after sixty-two lines of silence, Electra breaks into the *stichomythia* with this chilling line.

654   *Nine days since*: the 'tenth-day sacrifice' (note the inclusive Greek

counting) brought to an end the period of defilement of a woman who has just given birth. It was thought that the blood of childbirth led to this defilement.

657–8   *Do you think she cares about you . . . low birth*: Electra rightly believes that her mother will feel concern for her in such circumstances (1130 ff.), but she is wrong in thinking that Clytemnestra will weep over her supposed grandchild's low birth. Clytemnestra in fact proves to be a sympathetic character.

671–83   *O Zeus . . . impious polluters*: a powerful passage in which the three characters pray for vengeance.

674   *Hera*: see n. on 173–4.

678   *Queen Earth*: she must release Agamemnon's ghost if he is to come to fight alongside them. Electra beats on the ground to attract her attention.

699–746   *A story is told . . . of famous brothers*: the Chorus sings of an unhappy episode from the grim family saga of the house of Tantalus. Whichever of his grandsons, Atreus and Thyestes, possesses the golden lamb is entitled to be king of Mycenae. Atreus has it first, since Pan brought it to him. However, Thyestes seduces Atreus' wife and with her assistance carries off the lamb and lays claim to the kingdom. In response to this impious behaviour, Zeus reversed the course of the sun.

700–1   *Pan, guardian of the fields . . . reed pipes*: Pan was the god of the countryside and protector of flocks and herds. He played on the pan pipes, i.e. multiple pipes, his own invention.

716   *the Muses*: the nine goddesses who inspired the arts.

731–6   *he torments . . . Zeus*: the Chorus describes the dislocation of climatic conditions caused by Zeus' reversal of the sun's course.

734   *where Ammon dwells*: Ammon's oracle was at Siwa in Libya.

737–46   *This is what they say . . . brothers*: the Chorus does not believe that Zeus would have intervened in the workings of the sun in order to punish injustice on earth. Even so, it feels that stories such as this one are useful in that they implant fear of the gods. It would have been well, it thinks, if Clytemnestra had heeded its advice and not killed her husband. The movement of this ode is from harmony to dislocation.

757–9   *Your words mean death . . . messengers would have come*: Electra displays extraordinary defeatism. Her emotions can veer wildly.

763   *lies on the ground*: a metaphor from wresting (athletics).

777   *the well-watered gardens*: an attractively fresh setting for the terrible events to come.

778   *picking sprigs of delicate myrtle for his head*: a sinister note in view of the funereal associations of myrtle evoked earlier (324, 512), though it is in fact a proper sacred adornment for the living.

779   *Welcome, strangers*: here and later the hospitality of Aegisthus is
        made very clear.

781   *Thessalians . . . Alpheus*: from Thessaly in north-east Greece.
        Achilles had come from here. How like the greatest of the Greek
        heroes will Orestes prove himself? The Alpheus is one of the
        rivers at Olympia in south-west Greece.

793   *'We have just purified ourselves . . .'*: Orestes wishes to avoid
        putting himself under a religious obligation to Aegisthus.
        Alternatively he may have actually done this in preparation for
        a different 'sacrifice'.

800–2   *baskets . . . cauldrons*: the baskets contained the barley grain and
        knife, the cauldrons the holy water.

803   *barley meal*: the worshippers threw this at the victim and the
        altar in a ritual of aggression to 'justify' the killing.

811–12 *cut some hair from the calf . . . holy fire*: an offering which is a pre-
        lude to the sacrifice. Cf. n. on 90–1.

824–5   *quicker than a runner . . . hippodrome*: one of the most notable of
        the athletic images in the play.

827–9   *And in the intestines . . . looked*: the portal vein and gall bladder
        are visible, though they would normally be concealed by the lobe
        of the liver. The absence of the lobe as well as unspecified defects
        in the portal vein and gall-bladder are bad omens.

838   *Aegisthus, taking the innards*: Orestes blasphemously kills
        Aegisthus while he is performing a religious ritual.

862–3   *he has won the garland . . . Alpheus*: more athletic imagery.
        Alpheus (cf. 781) is one of the rivers of Olympia and the Chorus
        is referring to the Olympic games. Cf. nn. at 387 and 781.

866–7   *O light . . . O Night*: Electra calls upon the Sun, the Earth, and
        the Night. These are the witnesses conventionally invoked at
        such moments. (See e.g. Euripides, *Hecuba*, 68.)

870–1   *let us bring out . . . in the house*: the theme of Electra's self-imposed
        misery. Even from her own cache of ornaments she could have
        made herself more attractive than she chose to. But, now that
        Aegisthus is dead, she can perhaps be more open about her pos-
        sessions. The 'ornaments for the hair' are the victory crown for
        the triumphant Orestes. Cf. 854, 872, and nn. at 387, 614, and
        862–3.

883   *a futile furlong in the stadium*: this refers to a race of just under
        200 metres, which was the shortest and most prestigious of the
        races. Athletic imagery. Cf. nn. at 387 and 824–5.

886   *the most dutiful of men*: Strophius, king of the Phocians (cf. n. at
        18).

890   *hold the gods the authors of this good fortune*: this will avoid divine
        resentment.

896–8   *fling him out for the wild beasts . . . air*: even though the pious Nestor
expressed the view in the *Odyssey* (3. 309–10) that Aegisthus
should have been left as a prey for the dogs and birds, such treatment of a corpse risks divine resentment (cf. Sophocles, *Antigone*).

900   *I feel ashamed*: she thinks it may be wrong to speak ill of the dead
in case it arouses divine resentment (cf. 902).

907–56   *Well then . . . last lap of life*: this speech is a reversal of a normal
encomium.

919   *would prove faithful*: there is no evidence at all to suggest that
Clytemnestra was unfaithful to Aegisthus.

931   *'he's the woman's man—she's not the man's woman'*: a devastating
insult for a Greek male. Since Aeschylus' *Agamemnon*, Aegisthus
had been so typecast, with Clytemnestra as the virago.

941   *It's one's nature that one can trust in, not wealth*: the theme of
appearance and reality. Cf. nn. at 373–9 and 550–1.

956   *on the last lap of life*: athletic imagery.

965   *net*: does this look back to the net in which Clytemnestra entangled Agamemnon before killing him in Aeschylus' *Agamemnon*?

967 ff.   *What are we to do?* In this and his following lines Orestes' resolve
weakens at the prospect of the impious act of matricide. The
vengeful Electra, who feels no such qualms, uses her stronger
will to force him through with it. His faith in Apollo, who has
told him to kill his mother, is shattered (971). Was it a fiend, he
asks, who gave him this unnatural command (979)? Such fiends
'are supernatural powers, sometimes incarnate, associated with
calamity, usually punitive and effecting the downfall of a House
. . .' (C. Willink (ed.), *Orestes* (Oxford, 1986), 337).

975–8   *Now I shall stand trial . . . vengeance for your father*: these lines
make clear the impossible dilemma in which Orestes is placed.
For the trial of Orestes, see 1264–7.

980   *sitting on the holy tripod*: Apollo's priestess, the Pythia, the
human medium through whom he made his prophecies, sat on
the god's tripod, a three-legged seat, at Delphi to deliver her
oracular utterances.

990   *the good sons of Zeus*: Castor and Polydeuces, the Dioscouri, the
two major stars in the constellation of the Twins.

994   *I reverence you as much as the blessed gods*: the glittering
Clytemnestra with her glittering equipage (966, 1001–3) is a
god-like figure, but she is soon to suffer a dreadful fall.

1002   *the daughter I lost*: Iphigenia.

1020–3   *he lured my daughter . . . Iphigenia*: the seer Calchas prescribed
that Agamemnon, who had committed some offence against
Artemis, should sacrifice his daughter Iphigenia to appease the
goddess and calm the winds which were holding the Greek fleet

at Aulis, the port in north-east Greece where the Greeks had assembled, and preventing it from sailing to Troy. Agamemnon lured Iphigenia to Aulis with the pretence that she was to marry Achilles. Euripides dealt with this subject in his *Iphigenia at Aulis*.

1021   *went off taking her from home*: had Agamemnon returned from Aulis to Mycenae to collect his daughter?

1032–4   *with his girlfriend, a mad prophetess . . . house*: Agamemnon brought back Cassandra, the daughter of Priam and Apollo's priestess, to Mycenae as his mistress. While norms of Greek behaviour allowed a king to have a concubine, he would have been violating what was acceptable by attempting to install her in the house he shared with his wife.

1035   *Women are flighty creatures*: Euripides' sympathetic Clytemnestra does not insist that she is completely in the right.

1037–8   *a woman likes to imitate the man*: but Clytemnestra's affair with Aegisthus began before Agamemnon returned from Troy.

1042   *ought I to have killed Orestes*: there are many moments of irony in this scene. Orestes is in the cottage waiting to kill his mother.

1045   *death*: a hint at the possible meaning of a line probably lost after 1045.

1049   *argue . . . with complete freedom*: Clytemnestra grants her daughter the privilege of free speech which every Athenian citizen had (cf. *Hippolytus*, 422).

1082   *Greece chose to be its general*: in Euripides' Athens, generals were elected by vote while all other state officials were elected by lot. This election process enhanced the prestige of the generalship. Agamemnon too had been actually chosen to lead the Greeks (though by the kings, not the ordinary people).

1105–6   *I'm not so very pleased, my child, at what I've done*: sympathetically human, Clytemnestra is free from Electra's moral absolutism.

1120   *he dwells in my house*: irony, for Clytemnestra will assume that Electra refers to the royal palace at Mycenae, while in fact Aegisthus' corpse is at present in Electra's cottage.

1140   *that the soot-stained house does not blacken your clothes*: it is Clytemnestra's own blood that will stain her garments.

1142–4   *The basket is prepared . . . you are struck*: the lines recall the preparations for Aegisthus' sacrifice and death (799 ff.).

1143   *the bull*: Aegisthus.

1158   *the heaven-high walls | upreared by the Cyclopes*: the size of the stones which make up the walls at Mycenae was so vast that only giants, the one-eyed Cyclopes, could have built them. In the surviving ruins, the gateposts of the famous Lion Gate are 3.2 metres high; on top of these is a massive lintel, 4.5 metres long, 1.9 metres thick, and, at its centre, 0.9 metres high.

1163–4   *Like a mountain lioness . . . the water meadows*: just before
         Clytemnestra is killed, a simile very much in the Homeric vein
         evokes the brutality and grandeur of epic to convey the horror
         of her killing of Agamemnon.

1171   *s.d. ekkyklema*: a wheeled platform which was rolled out from the
         doors of the stage building. It was used to display a *tableau* of
         what had happened in the house, in this case consisting of the
         blood-stained corpses of Clytemnestra and Aegisthus. Electra and
         Orestes may also be standing on the platform. If so, they soon
         step down.

1177   *O Earth and Zeus*: cf. n. at 866.

1184   *who bore me, her daughter*: Electra lays stress on the fact that it is
         her *mother* whom she hated so violently—and unnaturally.

1190–1   *O Phoebus . . . fulfilment*: i.e. it was not obvious how just the ora-
         cle was, but the painful reality of its consequences is only too
         clear.

1197–9   *dance . . . marriage*: Electra feels that the normal course of a
         young woman's life is irretrievably lost to her. In folk-etymology
         the name Electra means 'unwedded'.

1214–15 *she put her hand to my chin*: supplication.

1221   *I threw my cloak before my eyes*: as Agamemnon had done when
         sacrificing his daughter (Euripides, *Iphigenia at Aulis* 1547–50).

1230–1   *we who loved you . . . put this cloak around you*: the now dutiful
         children lay out their mother's corpse for burial.

1232   *s.d.*: the gods Castor and Polydeuces appear either on the roof of
         the stage building or suspended from a *mechane*, a kind of crane
         which was used in flying scenes. The sky is the element of the
         gods. It is not uncommon in Greek tragedy for a god to appear
         at the end to foretell the future and to bring the action to a con-
         clusion.

1241   *stilled the sea's swell*: the Dioscouri look after men at sea.

1246   *He is wise but what he proclaimed to you was not*: the theme of the
         justice or otherwise of Apollo. Cf. 971 and 1301–2. If there is a
         statue of Apollo on the stage (see n. at 221), Castor's condem-
         nation of him gains in dramatic effectiveness.

1249   *Give Electra to Pylades*: now that Aegisthus is dead, Orestes is cer-
         tainly the head of the family and as such has authority over
         Electra (cf. 259).

1252   *Furies*: the dog-like, snake-wielding Furies could be roused from
         the Underworld to punish deeds of blood within the family.

1254–7   *Pallas*: Pallas Athena, the patron goddess of Athens. At the
         centre of her shield (or aegis, a kind of breastplate made of
         goatskin) the head of the gorgon Medusa was portrayed.

1258-63 *There is a hill of Ares . . . steadfastly*: in Euripides' day, the Areopagus court on the hill of that name (close to the Acropolis) was responsible for homicide trials. According to this play, the first trial there was that of the god Ares, who had killed Halirrhothius, son of Poseidon, for raping his daughter Alcippe.

1271 *chasm by the hill itself*: still to be seen in the north-east corner of the Areopagus.

1273-4 *an Arcadian city . . . near the Lycaean shrine*: the city is Orestheion, abut 20 km east of the sanctuary of Zeus Lykaios on Mount Lykaion.

1280-3 *she did not go to Troy . . . to Ilium*: the basis of Euripides' *Helen*. Zeus either wanted to solve the problems of the population explosion or to destroy the race of men so that the gods could lead their happy life without disturbance. This bland statement of the malignancy of the king of the gods in causing a devastating war over a phantom leaves us with a shockingly bleak view of the human condition.

1288 *the Isthmian land*: Corinth.

1289 *Cecrops*: the mythical first king of Athens.

1301-2 *Fate and necessity . . . must be*: cf. n. at 1246.

1306-7 *the single doom of your fathers*: the curse on the family went back to Tantalus, who served up his son Pelops at a feast for the gods. It has come down through the generations to Electra and Orestes.

1344 *with snakes as hands*: either their hands taper into snakes instead of fingers or they grasp snakes coiled round their arms near their projecting heads.

1347 *the Sicilian Sea*: the sea between southern Greece and Sicily.

HELEN

There are so many Greek names in this play which have not been Latinized or Anglicized that it has seemed best to keep to the Greek spelling, though Greek 'k' has been transliterated as 'c' and Helene becomes Helen.

1 *s.d.*: Helen, who has taken refuge at the tomb of Proteus, the previous king of Egypt, is to explain the situation in a Prologue.

1 *These are the streams of the Nile, the river of fair virgin nymphs*: she gestures, conjuring up the reality of the Nile for the audience. Every river has its nymph (or water-sprite). The great river Nile has many.

3 *with melting white snow*: the sources of the Nile are indeed in the mountains.

7   *when she had renounced her husband Aiacos*: Psamathe (= Sandy),
            a Nereid (or sea-deity), tried to avoid marrying Aiacos by assum-
            ing different shapes, but to no avail. Later she abandoned him and
            married Proteus.

9   *Theoclymenos*: this character is an invention of Euripides. His
            name means 'famous because of a god'.

13   *Theonoe*: the name, as 13–14 make clear, means 'she who knows
            about things divine'.

15   *Nereus*: an Old Man of the Sea who had knowledge of things hid-
            den from men.

17–21   *my father is Tyndareos . . . if this tale is true*: Helen playfully tells
            us of her dual paternity. In fact, throughout the rest of the play
            it is assumed that she is the daughter of Zeus. The latter's sup-
            posed pretence to Leda, the wife of Tyndareos, that he was a
            swan seeking refuge from an eagle is particularly absurd in view
            of the fact that the eagle is Zeus' bird.

24   *Alexandros*: a Trojan prince, also known as Paris, who tended his
            herds on Ida, the mountain range above Troy. He was the son
            of King Priam (35).

25   *Hera . . . Zeus*: Hera is the wife of Zeus, goddess of marriage;
            Cypris is Aphrodite, goddess of love (see n. at *Hippolytus* 2): 'the
            maiden born from Zeus' is Athena, who sprang fully armed from
            the head of Zeus.

38–41   *For he brought war . . . the strongest man of Greece*: after Paris had
            supposedly run off back to Troy with Helen, her husband
            Menelaos, the king of Sparta, and his brother Agamemnon led a
            vast expedition to Troy to get her back (49–51). For Zeus' moti-
            vation in causing the Trojan War, see n. at *Electra* 1280–3.
            Achilleus is the strongest man of Greece.

51   *Ilion*: another name for Troy.

52   *Scamander*: a river of Troy.

67   *s.d.*: Teucros was the half-brother of Aias. He explains his pres-
            ence in Egypt in the course of this scene. There is a splendid dra-
            matic panache to the initial entry of each major character.
            Helen, who launches the play, must be manifestly the most
            beatiful woman in the world. Now Teucros, the leading Greek
            archer in the *Iliad*, comes on with his bow and arrows. Cf. nn.
            at 385 *s.d.*, 859–60, 1164 *s.d.*, 1185 *s.d.*, 1282–3, 1389 *s.d.*,
            and 1642 *s.d.*

79   *that woman's misfortunes*: Helen conceals her identity.

87–8   *Telamon*: the king of the island of Salamis near Athens, and
            father of Aias and Teucros.

89–141   *stichomythia*: see Introduction, p. xxxii.

99   *He once came as a suitor of Helen—as I hear*: many Greeks paid court to the beautiful Helen. Euripides makes Achilleus one of their number. It is a delightful touch to have Helen almost give away her identity but then save herself with 'as I hear'.

102   *Another*: to Aias' rage. Odysseus was awarded Achilleus' arms by Agamemnon and Menelaos. After a fit of madness, Aias committed suicide.

118   *I saw her just as clearly as my eyes see you now*: a fine irony.

124   *he is not in Argos at least, nor on the banks of the river Eurotas*: Menelaos would be aiming to return to Sparta on the banks of the river Eurotas, but he might well have wished to land at Nauplia in Argos to visit his brother Agamemnon at nearby Mycenai. (He would have discovered that Agamemnon had been murdered by Clytaimnestra, his wife and Helen's sister.)

137   *the sons of Tyndareos*: Castor and Polydeuces, Helen's twin brothers and like her possibly fathered by Zeus. In 140 Teucros refers to the belief that they became a constellation (Gemini = the Twins), one of particular assistance to sailors because of its visibility.

154   *hunting, slaughtering the wild beasts with the help of his dogs*: Theoclymenos' enthusiasm for hunting is repeatedly stressed (cf. 545, 981, 1169, 1175); this gives a sinister ring to the fact that he is also 'hunting' Helen as his bride (63 and cf. n. at 314).

156   *the reason for this*: presumably Theoclymenos wants to keep very tight security on Helen. He thinks that Menelaos will come to Egypt (890–1).

162   *Eurotas*: the river of Sparta. Cf. 124.

169   *Sirens*: usually seen as sea demons who would lure sailors to shipwreck on their rocky coast with the beauty of their music and then devour them, these mythical creatures, half-woman and half-bird, are here viewed as chthonic deities connected with funeral monuments and the grave.

175   *Persephone*: the goddess of the Underworld and wife of its king, Hades.

178   *paean*: usually a paean is a song of triumph; the word is here used ironically.

179–90   *By the dark-blue water*: this washing scene recalls that described by the female Chorus in *Hippolytus* on its entry (121–30).

190   *cries out against her union with Pan*: Pan, god of shepherds and flocks, was depicted on vases as half-man, half-goat, frequently in lustful pursuit of a nymph.

192   *barbarian*: i.e. non-Greek.

194   *Achaean*: i.e. Greek.

205   *Castor and his brother*: see n. at 137. Like Helen they are from
       Sparta but they no longer engage in the athletic pursuits of
       young Spartan men (208–11).

214–16 *when Zeus . . . begot you upon your mother*: the Chorus is in no
       doubt that Zeus is Helen's father. Cf. n. at 17–21.

224   *to a barbarian*: i.e. to the Trojan Paris.

227   *your father's halls*: Tyndareos, Helen's mortal 'father' (but see nn.
       at 17–21 and 214–16), had been king of Sparta but had
       bequeathed his kingdom to Menelaos.

228   *Athena, the goddess with the house of bronze*: a reference to the
       famous bronze-plated temple of Athena at Sparta.

243–4 *Hermes . . . the swift-footed son of Maia*: Hermes, the son of Maia
       by Zeus, was born on a mountain in Arcadia and was the god
       of travel. He wore winged shoes.

250   *Simois*: a river of Troy.

257–9 *For no woman . . . bore me to Zeus*: the usual tradition is that, after
       mating with Zeus in the guise of a swan, Leda gave birth to two
       eggs. Out of one of them were hatched Polydeuces and
       Clytaimnestra, out of the other Helen and Castor. Cf. n. at 17–21.

273–4 *the gods have removed me from my fatherland and exposed me to a
       barbarian civilization*: a heavy fate for a Greek.

282–3 *the girl . . . in her virginity*: Teucros had in fact made no mention
       of Helen's daughter Hermione. Helen is determined to run the
       gamut of possible woes.

290–1 *If my husband were alive . . . us alone*: she means that Menelaos
       would know through private tokens that she, and not the phan-
       tom, was the real Helen and would convince their fellow-
       Spartans of this.

308   *he stated clearly that my husband has died*: not true. Teucros has
       informed her that people *say* that he is dead (132).

314   *the one who hunts me for his wife*: the theme of Theoclymenos the
       hunter. Cf. n. at 154.

315   *You must leave the tomb where you are sitting*: it would be blas-
       phemous to drag Helen away from the tomb while she is in con-
       tact with it. Thus she feels safe there and is alarmed at the
       thought of leaving it.

357–9 *a sacrifice to the trio of goddesses . . . ox-stalls*: disaster began with
       the Judgement of Paris on Mount Ida (cf. 23–30).

375   *Callisto*: Zeus fell in love with this virgin companion of Artemis
       and raped her. According to the usual tradition, Artemis trans-
       formed her into a she-bear. (Thus 'the wild-eyed lioness' of 379
       is a puzzle.) Artemis then killed her—which presumably is what
       is meant by her laying-down of her burden of grief (380). This

story is a surprising one for Helen to choose in her search for a woman whose involvement with the divine proved to have a happier outcome than her own.

382   *daughter of Merops*: we know no more of this daughter of Merops than we are told here, save that she may have been taken down alive to the underworld by Proserpina.

385   *s.d.*: Menelaos' costume is a bizarre conglomeration of remnants from his wrecked ship (422). Another striking entry (cf. n. at 67).

386–9   *O Pelops . . . gods*: possibly because there was a famine in his kingdom, Pelops' father Tantalos had killed him and served him up as a meal for the gods, who, horrified at the father's actions, brought the son back to life. Later Pelops won his wife, the daughter of Oinomaos, king of Pisa in south-east Greece, by dastardly cheating in a chariot race. Menelaos thus refers to two particularly vile episodes from his family history.

395   *I was no despot*: the relative freedom of the Greeks contrasts with Theoclymenos' apparently tyrannical rule (cf. 276 and nn. at 449, 480, 542, and 1624).

436   *s.d.*: the Old Woman is vividly characterized. Beneath her fierce exterior there beats a heart of gold (481–2).

445–75   *Ah, don't wave your fist . . . hid in the cave*: stichomythia; see Introduction, p. xxxii.

449   *a shipwrecked stranger—such men are guaranteed protection*: in the Greek world, yes, for there Zeus, the most powerful of the gods, ensures that the rules of hospitality, which would have guaranteed a welcome and a meal for Menelaos, are observed. These rules do not seem to be honoured in Egypt.

474   *Lacedaimon*: another name for Sparta.

480   *your gift from your host will be death*: a grim perversion of the Greek rules of hospitality (see n. at 449), by which gifts were exchanged between host and guest.

519   *Erebos*: the Underworld.

538   *She said that he was somewhere near this land*: Theonoe is not up to date with her information here, for Menelaos is, of course, present on stage. Euripides extracts maximum value from dramatic irony.

541   *Ah, who is this?*: the moment of recognition—a key and no doubt eagerly awaited ingredient of Greek tragedy—looks as if it has arrived, but Euripides, to splendid effect, succeeds in delaying it until 622.

542   *Proteus' impious son*: we have a growing sense of Theoclymenos as a brutish tyrant. See n. at 395.

543   *bacchant*: a female worshipper of Dionysos, the god of liberation
        and wine, whose cult was ecstatic and frenzied.

545   *his huntsman's hands*: in Helen's eyes Menelaos is now the hunts-
        man.

553-93 *I am no thief . . . convinces me, not you*: stichomythia; see
        Introduction, p. xxxii.

556   *I have laid my hands on this tomb*: she has re-established contact
        with the tomb and feels safe. See n. at 315.

569   *Hecate*: Hecate, goddess of the crossroads (570), presided over
        magic. She might appear with a torch in both hands and was
        associated with the world of the shades.

592   *I found my husband but shall not keep him*: it looks as if the recog-
        nition scene is to be aborted. Cf. n. at 541.

607   *the sacred cave*: sacred either because it was the shrine of, say,
        the local nymphs, evidence of whose cult the Servant must have
        seen, or because it had sheltered the phantom Helen.

613   *the sky my father*: i.e. the air out of which I was made (33-4).

619-20 *I shall not allow you to make fools of us like this again*: presumably
        the Servant advances to manhandle Helen, but steps back when
        she and Menelaos embrace at last in mutual recognition.

639-40 *whom my brothers . . . procession*: Helen's brothers Castor and
        Polydeuces are often seen as horsemen, and they rode on white
        horses in the torchlight procession at her wedding with
        Menelaos.

643   *god*: probably not Hermes, but the divine power that oversees
        events.

653   *the goddess*: i.e. Hera.

670   *the son of Zeus and Maia*: i.e. Hermes. See n. at 243-4.

679   *Why did Hera harbour such rancour against you over the contest?*
        despite Hera's offer to make Paris ruler of all Asia if he gave her
        the prize for beauty, a golden apple, Paris awarded it to
        Aphrodite (Cypris), whose bait was the most beautiful woman in
        the world, Helen of Sparta. Hera was enraged. (Athena, the third
        competitor, promised him wisdom and victory in all his fights.)
        Cf. Euripides, *Trojan Women*, 924 ff.

689-90 *Unmarried and childless . . . marriage*: see n. at 282-3.

707   *Were all our toils in vain then, all for a cloud?* the Servant's
        appalled realization, representing the feelings of the ordinary sol-
        dier, gives way in his speech (711-33) to such vacuous word-
        spinning that the Oxford editor has pronounced most of it
        inauthentic. But Euripides may be making a serious point here.
        Stunned by the horror of the pointless tragedy of the Trojan
        War, he takes refuge in meaningless clichés.

722–4   *Now I bring back your wedding to mind . . . the team of four*: a strik-
         ing touch. The Servant has vivid memories of Helen's wedding
         (cf. 639–41).

749–51   *Calchas . . . Helenos*: Calchas was the prophet on the Greek side
         in the Trojan War, Helenos the prophet on the Trojan side. The
         Servant vents his rage on the prophets who failed to point out
         the reality of the situation.

766–9   *the shipwrecks . . . Perseus*: a reference to the shipwrecks of his
         fellow Greeks as they tried to return across the Aegean from
         Troy to Greece; Nauplios, the father of Palamedes, a Greek
         treacherously murdered at Troy, lit misleading beacons on the
         island of Euboea to lure Greek ships to destruction; 'the look-out
         place of Perseus' is at the western extremity of the Nile delta,
         where Perseus saved Andromeda from a sea-monster.

782–841 *What have I done . . . win glory by our deaths*: stichomythia; see
         Introduction, p. xxxii.

807   *my marriage*: there is ambiguity here. Theoclymenos will try to
         kill him both because Menelaos is Helen's husband and because
         he wants to marry her himself.

822   *The name is certainly oracular*: see n. at 13.

825   *we both supplicated her*: to make a request of someone and at the
         same time to touch them, preferably on the chin or knees or
         both, is known as supplication. In the Greek world the person to
         whom the request was made would be under considerable pres-
         sure to agree to it. Cf. *Medea*, n. at 65.

847–8   *Thetis . . . Neleus' son*: Thetis is a Nereid (a sea-goddess), the
         mother by Peleus, a mortal, of the Greek hero Achilleus who was
         killed at Troy; Aias is the brother of Teucros and son of Telamon
         (see 92–102 and n. at 87–8), called Telamonian to distinguish
         him from another, inferior Greek warrior of the same name;
         Neleus' son is Nestor, the oldest of the Greeks at Troy, who lost
         his own son Antilochos there. Thetis, Telamon, and Nestor are
         three parents who would have great cause to reproach Menelaos
         if he now showed cowardice in trying to win Helen, the cause
         in which their children had died.

854   *a ridge of hard rock*: i.e. with no soil to be sprinkled over the
         corpse to provide even a token burial and thus allow the dead
         man to reach the Underworld.

856   *the house of Tantalos*: for two episodes from the disastrous history
         of this family, see n. at 386–9.

859–60   *The building echoes with the noise of bolts shot back*: this 'stage
         direction' with its demand for great thudding sounds ensures a
         fine sonic build-up for Theonoe's entrance, which should then

make a splendid visual impression with its pyrotechnic ritual (865–72). Cf. nn. at 67 *s.d.* and 385 *s.d.*

866–7   *fumigate the heaven's air . . . purity*: the censing is a cleansing ritual.

894   *suppliant*: see n. at 825.

901   *your own piety*: a pious sister, an impious brother.

917–18   *You should not defer more to your wrong-headed brother than to your good father*: a pious father, an impious brother.

928   *Phrygians*: i.e. Trojans.

940–1   *follow your just father's nature*: pious father, pious daughter.

948–9   *If I became a coward, I should bring the greatest disgrace upon Troy*: because it would be shameful for Troy to have been sacked by a man who could slip into cowardice.

961   *falling at the tomb of your father*: this act of Menelaos' adds great authority to his subsequent words. Is Helen already back at the tomb herself (980)?

967   *a man formerly supreme in his reputation for piety*: compare Zeus' estimate of Proteus at 47.

969   *Hades*: king of the Underworld. It was to regain Helen that Menelaos had sent so many corpses to Hades' realm. If he cannot get her back, he feels that Hades is in honour bound to restore those dead men to life.

981   *tries to starve us*: the Greek literally means 'hunts us with starvation'—Theoclymenos as huntsman. Since it would be impious to drag Menelaos and Helen from the tomb, the only way to kill them would be to wait till they starved to death.

993   *you will not be killing people of low repute*: i.e. your victims will be the famous Menelaos and Helen.

1003   *Nereus*: Theonoe's grandfather. See n. at 15.

1013–16 *Yes, all men . . . immortal air*: an enigmatic passage. It is tempting to accept A. M. Dale's estimate of it as 'a piece of high-toned but vague mysticism appropriate to Theone' (Euripides, *Helen*, ed. A. M. Dale (Oxford, 1976), 1013–16 n.). A. Pippin Burnett describes Theonoe's office as 'so markedly Egyptian and exotic' (*Catastrophe Survived* (Oxford, 1971), 93). Another view is that of C. Segal, who writes that Theonoe is associated 'with a supra-human cosmic wisdom and with a pure, spiritual conception of the gods which contrasts with the delusions of the other characters . . .' (*Euripides and the Poetics of Sorrow* (Durham, NC, 1993). Whether one finds something absurd in Theonoe's vatic portentousness will depend on one's reading of the play as a whole. We have recently (e.g. in 842–50) found Menelaos, the one-time hero of the Trojan War, indulging in a war hero's absurd braggadocio.

1020–1   *I am doing him a favour . . . piety*: a hint that the brutal and impious huntsman may yet see the light.

1034–5   *The next step is for the two of us to put our heads together*: a delightful episode ensues. Helen suggests that they plan their get-away jointly, but Menelaos offers futile proposals. The way is thus paved for Helen, with fine self-deprecation ('if a woman can make a good suggestion', 1049), to take over the planning of the operation. The rhodomontade of so much of his utterances since 840 cannot disguise the fact that Menelaos is not very clever. Thus Helen's intelligence is thrown into relief.

1051   *The words are ill-omened*: for a Greek, to allow oneself to be spoken of as dead might seem ominous, as if it were inviting that fate.

1054   *with shorn hair . . . before the impious king*: women cut their hair short in mourning. Helen feels that any fraudulent exploitation of funeral rituals is justified by Theoclymenos' impiety.

1056   *This is not the most original of ideas*: Menelaos underestimates the complexity and subtlety of Helen's scheme.

1073   *You must make all the decisions*: once on board the ship, Menelaos can come into his own as a man of action (1072). But it is Helen who set up the scheme (see n. at 1034–5).

1079   *these wrappings round my body*: it must be remembered that Menelaos, dressed as he is in flotsam and jetsam (cf. n. at 385 s.d.), looks absurd until his final appearance. See n. at 1389.

1082   *What then appeared simple wretchedness may perhaps be crowned with success*: reversal is a fundamental feature of Greek tragedy, and in this line there is a broad hint that the miseries of the play's opening may lead to joy.

1087–9   *I shall go . . . bloody*: the most beautiful woman in the world will disfigure herself in order to escape with her husband.

1098   *Dione*: one of the first generation of gods, she was, according to one tradition, the mother of Cypris, as here.

1102–6   *Why is your appetite for evil . . . deny it*: Helen's rage against Aphrodite bursts forth explosively in a powerful passage. But then, after the futile plea for moderation, comes the coda acknowledging the goddess's delicious enchantment. These are lines of great psychological insight.

1110   *O sorrowing nightingale*: the Thracian Tereus married Procne but then raped her sister Philomela and cut out her tongue so that she could not betray him. However, she made what had happened known to Procne by telling the story through her embroidery. Procne took a terrible revenge by killing her son by Tereus and serving him up to his father as a stew. The sisters fled and, as the vengeful Tereus pursued them, begged the gods to save them. In pity, the gods transformed Philomela to a swallow, Tereus to a hoopoe, and Procne to a nightingale. In some versions of the myth, the roles of the sisters are reversed, but in either case the nightingale has much to sorrow over.

1128   *Nauplios*: see n. at 766-9. The Capherean rocks were a headland of South Euboea. In later times, such beacons have warned sailors to steer clear, but for the Greeks they meant a harbour.

1159-60   *when words could have settled the quarrel*: after the Trojan War had started, Menelaos and Odysseus went on a diplomatic mission to Troy but it failed (*Iliad* 3. 205 ff.).

1164   *s.d.*: the huntsman Theoclymenos can be immediately identified by his hounds and his hunting gear (1169). Cf. n. at 67 *s.d.*

1165   *Hail, tomb of my father*: the reportedly impious Theoclymenos makes a good impression with this dutiful address to his pious father's tomb.

1178-9   *the daughter of Tyndareos . . . at the tomb*: he does not notice Menelaos, who is crouching there (1203).

1185   *s.d.*: an arresting change of costume for Helen (1186-8). See nn. at 67 and 1389 *s.d.*

1193   *O my master*: Helen begins to hint that it is now possible for her to agree to marry Theoclymenos.

1199-1277   *She has, and one who was present . . . of their due*: stichomythia; see Introduction, p. xxxii.

1226   *It is natural that you should weep for this sad fortune*: J. Diggle believes that something has fallen out of the text here. Certainly Helen's next line is a misfit as things stand. Perhaps in the missing line(s) Theoclymenos asks, 'How am I to know that this man's tale is true?' (Euripides, *Helen*, ed. Dale, 1226 n.).

1238   *What is it that you seek . . . in supplication to me?*: So Theoclymenos does understand the Greek custom of supplication. The Greek word for 'seek' literally means 'hunt'. Helen is now the hunter playing on Theoclymenos' piety.

1242   *Pelops' house is wise in such matters*: i.e. a royal Spartan will know all about Greek customs.

1246   *I have no knowledge of Greek customs*: the Greek literally means 'I am left behind by Greek customs'—which adds a further ironical touch to the duping of Theoclymenos.

1263   *Arms of bronze*: Menelaos is ensuring that he will be well armed.

1272   *A swift-sailing Phoenician ship*: Phoenician ships had a high reputation. In the Persian navy they were the élite.

1282-3   *I shall give you fine clothing in place of these rags*: another spectacularly contrasting change of costume (cf. 1297 and n. at 1185).

1302   *the Mother of the Gods*: Demeter, the Mother of the Gods (specifically of Persephone and Wealth (Hesiod, *Theogone* 912–13, 969)) and the Mother Goddess of the Earth, who presided over agriculture and fertility, searched sorrowfully for her daughter Persephone, whom Hades had dragged down to the Underworld.

1307   *her daughter with the name that must not be spoken*: Demeter and her daughter Persephone were the goddesses of the Eleusinian Mysteries. As it was unlucky to speak their names, they were known simply as the twin goddesses. Persephone was called Kore (the Girl).

1308–11   *And the noisy cymbals . . . to her chariot*: Demeter here is assimilated to Cybele, the Mother of the Gods, whose rituals were ecstatic and who rode in a chariot drawn by lions.

1314–19   *and there followed . . . fate to fulfilment*: these lines seem to refer to a tradition that the goddesses Artemis and Athena were playing with Persephone when she was seized by Hades. They threatened the ravisher with their characteristic weapons, but Zeus prevented the fighting by sending down a thunderbolt, for the abduction had taken place with his complicity.

1327–8   *To mortals she brought no fruitfulness*: Demeter decided to abandon her role as goddess of fertility until her daughter was restored to her, and the earth became sterile.

1346–52   *Then first of all . . . loud clamour*: we must assume that it is implicit in this delightful scene, in which the musical instruments of her cult are restored to Demeter, that Persephone too is given back to her mother. Here we look forward to the play's happy ending. Persephone, like Helen, has been snatched off to a potentially fearsome place. Demeter, like Menelaos, has travelled far (cf. 1676) and caused terrible devastation and destruction, and, again like him, she has got her loved one back. But, while Euripides focuses on Demeter's smile and the thrilling music, the story of Persephone has its element of sadness. Because she had eaten a pomegranate seed in the Underworld, she had to spend part of the year (the winter when the earth is infertile) down there with Hades. Demeter may laugh as the instruments of her cult are given back to her (1349) but tragedy is not far to seek, since her daughter cannot be fully restored. So perhaps the play will not end so very happily after all.

1353–68   *You Helen . . . only in beauty*: the text of this stanza is particularly corrupt, but the Chorus, it appears, feels that Helen has neglected Demeter's cult and that this has been the cause of her sufferings. In 1358–65, the ecstatic rituals of Dionysos, god of liberation and wine, are assimilated to those of Demeter. The

bullroarer was an instrument whirled round on the end of a
string in the worship of Dionysos.

1382–3   *dressed him in fine clothes*: see n. at 1282–3.

1389   *s.d.*: Menelaos is splendidly dressed, wears a complete suit of
armour (1379), and carries a shield and spear (1376–7). In contrast to his bizarre appearance so far in the play, he now looks
like the hero who conquered Troy. Within two hundred lines of
each other, Helen and Menelaos make two of the most spectacular—and underappreciated—costume changes of Greek drama.
The former (see 1185 *s.d.*) eclipses her beauty in the black
clothes and cropped hair of mourning, while the latter casts
aside his ludicrous concatenation of rags and enters in glorious
robes and full armour. Appearances are enormously important
in this play. The underlying question is what is appearance and
what reality.

1413   *Sidonia*: Sidon is in Phoenicia. See n. at 1272.

1414–17 *Shall not the man . . . if you wish*: this is a crucial exchange.

1428   *Do not be a slave to your slaves*: with quick intelligence, Helen
plays upon the fact that Theoclymenos is a barbarian despot (cf.
276).

1430   *the Pelopid line*: Pelops was Menelaos' grandfather.

1436   *stranger*: the Greek word for 'stranger' also means 'guest' and
'host'. In fact Theoclymenos is proving the perfect host. In
responding to supplication (1237–8) and showing Menelaos true
hospitality, he has espoused Greek values, and Helen and her
husband's exploitation of these to dupe him is far from sympathetic.

1465   *the land which Perseus founded*: Perseus (see n. at 766–9) founded
Mycenai near the harbour of Nauplia where Menelaos plans to
land (1586).

1465–74 *the surging river . . . holy ritual*: the Eurotas, the river of Sparta;
the temple of Pallas is Athena's bronze-plated temple at Sparta
(cf. n. at 228); the daughters of Leucippos are the wives of Castor
and Polydeuces (cf. nn. at 17–21 and 257–9); Hyacinthos is a
beautiful youth, loved by the god Apollo. While they were com-
peting with the discus, Apollo's accidentally hit and killed
Hyacinthos. In his memory, the Spartans used to hold the
Hyacinthia, primarily a fertility festival, here described.

1494   *Dardanos*: the founder of Troy.

1497   *you sons of Tyndareos*: Castor and Polydeuces, now a constellation of particular helpfulness to sailors. The Chorus hopes that it
can assist Helen's getaway over the sea and, if necessary, hinder
Theoclymenos' pursuit (cf. n. at 137.)

1508   *the strife on Ida*: i.e. the Judgement of Paris.

1511   *Apollo's towers*: with Poseidon, Apollo built the walls of Troy.

1540   *handsome men they were*: a somewhat surprising tribute from the Egyptian Messenger.

1555-9   *The bull . . . from handling it*: the plan is working out beautifully, but these vivid lines focus our attention on what could be a major hitch.

1595   *why hesitate to butcher the barbarians*: butchering barbarians has of course been Menelaos' occupation at Troy, but the slaughter of innocent Egyptian sailors remains disconcerting. The nobly garbed Menelaos reverts to grisly thuggery as he slaughters unsuspecting Egyptians.

1619-20   *I still don't believe . . . he was*: the Chorus blithely feigns ignorance.

1622-3   *if the ship could be pursued | and taken*: cf. 1268-9.

1624   *I shall take vengeance on my sister who has betrayed me*: will Theoclymenos revert to a brutal despot? Will he commit the terrible impiety of killing his sister?

1627   *O, you there, my master*: the Servant shows enormous courage in standing up to the barbarian king. There is a parallel to this wonderful episode in the Servant's attempt to reason with Hippolytus (*Hippolytus*, 88-120), but the more arresting comparison is with the end of III. vii of Shakespeare's *King Lear*, when a servant, appalled by Cornwall's abuse of Gloucester, draws his sword on him and is killed for his kindness.

1638   *I am a subject then . . . not wrong*: a fine split line. Theoclymenos' despotic absolutism is set against the Servant's brave insistence that power should go hand in hand with justice.

1642   *s.d.*: Castor and Polydeuces either appear on the roof of the stage building or are swung in above it (perhaps riding on dummy horses (cf. 639 and 1665)) on a crane. See nn. at 67 *s.d.*, and *Electra* 1232.

1673   *I am speaking of the long low island which guards Acte*: Makronnisi (= Long Island) off Cape Sounion in Acte (old form of Attica).

1674   *Helene*: the Greek spelling of Helen.

1676-7   *Menelaos . . . the island of the blessed*: just as Helen will become a goddess (1667), so Menelaos will not die in Sparta but will go to the island of the blessed, for he is Helen's husband and thus the son-in-law of Zeus (cf. *Odyssey* 4. 563-9). *Menelaos the wanderer*: the summation of a significant theme (cf. n. at 1346-52). At times the play has the quality of a travelogue.

1680   *to please you both . . . over your sister*: Theoclymenos happily accepts the will of the gods. He embraces the value of piety, and thus one conspicuous aspect of the drama is the schooling of a barbarian to Greek virtue.

1684–7 *You can rest assured . . . equal in this*: a handsome and generous-spirited tribute to Helen from Theoclymenos.

1688–92 *The divine will . . . happened here*: the 'stock' ending of four or, with a variation in the first line, five of Euripides' plays.

*The
Oxford
World's
Classics
Website*

www.worldsclassics.co.uk

- Information about new titles
- Explore the full range of Oxford World's Classics
- Links to other literary sites and the main OUP webpage
- Imaginative competitions, with bookish prizes
- Peruse the Oxford World's Classics Magazine
- Articles by editors
- Extracts from Introductions
- A forum for discussion and feedback on the series
- Special information for teachers and lecturers

www.worldsclassics.co.uk

American Literature

British and Irish Literature

Children's Literature

Classics and Ancient Literature

Colonial Literature

Eastern Literature

European Literature

History

Medieval Literature

Oxford English Drama

Poetry

Philosophy

Politics

Religion

The Oxford Shakespeare

A complete list of Oxford Paperbacks, including Oxford World's Classics, Oxford Shakespeare, Oxford Drama, and Oxford Paperback Reference, is available in the UK from the Academic Division Publicity Department, Oxford University Press, Great Clarendon Street, Oxford OX2 6DP.

In the USA, complete lists are available from the Paperbacks Marketing Manager, Oxford University Press, 198 Madison Avenue, New York, NY 10016.

Oxford Paperbacks are available from all good bookshops. In case of difficulty, customers in the UK can order direct from Oxford University Press Bookshop, Freepost, 116 High Street, Oxford OX1 4BR, enclosing full payment. Please add 10 per cent of published price for postage and packing.